PRAISE FOR SHOPTALK

"Dennis Brown is a superb interviewer. He cares, he does his homework and, most of all, he listens. And in addition to all that he's a terrific writer. The end result is *Shoptalk*, an important collection of fascinating stories about an important collection of American writers and theater people."
—Jim Lehrer
of "The MacNeil/Lehrer NewsHour"

"A standout...The famous names are not always the obvious ones, and neither are the questions or answers. In *Shoptalk*, you can eavesdrop on Edward Albee, Richard Wilbur, Mary Mercier, and both Tennessee Williams and his mother—not to mention that rarest of interviewees, David Merrick."
—Frank Rich, *The New York Times*

"Brown is a smart, well-prepared interviewer who prompts his subjects to say some fascinating things about their work and careers."
—*School Library Journal*

"A must read for anyone who enjoys the performing arts. *Shoptalk* offers fascinating and revealing insights into the hearts and souls of some our most distinguished playwrights and authors...I was mesmerized."
—Stacy Keach

"*Shoptalk* is bound to please people who write, people who admire people who write, and avid movie and theater fans, too....All the talk is about theater and film, and Brown, unlike some interviewers, does ask the right questions. Perhaps more important, Brown allows his interviewees to meander around, to digress and go off on tangents, all of which makes for a more entertaining portrait of each person."
—*St. Louis Post-Dispatch*

"Brown captures a basic truth about the American theater."
—*San Francisco Chronicle*

"*Shoptalk* should be required reading...I think the more we learn about others who have chosen the theater for a life, the more we can forgive ourselves for having done the same."
—George Grizzard

"The most fascinating, clear-eyed interviews of these often interviewed people I have ever read." —Mary Beth Hurt

"You may buy *Shoptalk* for the names on its dust jacket—among them Tennessee Williams and Edward Albee—but you'll remember it for its intimate, melancholy portraits of well-known but uncelebrated writers like Jason Miller and Frank D. Gilroy....Brown has succeeded admirably. The book is an honest presentation of writing dramas as a serious business....As a series of portraits, *Shoptalk* reminds us that writing for the American theater is still a vocation in the oldest sense of the word."
—*The News and Observer*, Raleigh, NC

"*Shoptalk* is probably the best book of interviews I've ever read. Dennis Brown is a superb interviewer: perceptive, sensitive, articulate, and compassionate. He has been able to elicit from a disparate group of people, extremely candid and memorable interviews, far removed from the usual puffery and claptrap."
— Howard Siegman
Professor Emeritus of Dramatic Literature
Hofstra University

"Fascinating." —Liz Smith

SHOPTALK

Conversations about Theater and Film with Twelve Writers, One Producer— and Tennessee Williams' Mother

DENNIS BROWN

FOREWORD BY KEVIN KLINE

Newmarket Press
New York

FOR FLORENCE,
FINALLY...

This book published simultaneously in
the United States of America and in Canada.

93 94 95 10 9 8 7 6 5 4 3 2 1

Library of Congress Cataloging-in-Publication Data

Brown, Dennis, 1945–
Shoptalk : conversations about theater and film with twelve
writers, one producer—and Tennessee Williams' mother / Dennis Brown;
foreword by Kevin Kline.
p. cm.
Includes index.
ISBN 1-55704-170-9
1. American drama—20th century—History and criticism.
2. Dramatists, American—20th century—Interviews.
3. Screenwriters—United States—Interviews. 4. Motion pictures—
United States. 5. Theater—United States. I. Title.
PS352.B76 1992
812'.509—dc20 92-2975
CIP

QUANTITY PURCHASES
Companies, professional groups, clubs, and other organizations may
qualify for special terms when ordering quantities of this title.
For information, write Special Sales, Newmarket Press,
18 East 48th Street, New York, N.Y. 10017, or call (212) 832-3575.

Book design by M.J. DiMassi

Manufactured in the United States of America

First Edition

CONTENTS

ACKNOWLEDGMENTS vii
FOREWORD BY KEVIN KLINE ix
INTRODUCTION 3
1. MAN FROM MISSOURI: Lanford Wilson 7
2. SEASON IN THE SUN: Jason Miller 23
3. RULEBUSTER: Frank D. Gilroy 45
4. WINNERS AND LOSERS: William Goldman and Mary Mercier 59
A PORTFOLIO OF PHOTOGRAPHS 93
5. MOTHER AND SON: Tennessee Williams and Edwina Dakin Williams 101
6. A CERTAIN AMOUNT OF SPLEEN: Edward Albee 121
7. SOLITARY MAN: David Merrick 135
8. WORDSMITHS: Alan Jay Lerner and Richard Wilbur 151
9. INCIDENTAL GIFTS: William Inge 171
10. QUIET WARRIOR FROM WHARTON: Horton Foote 183
11. HAPPY ENDING: John Patrick 195
FOR FURTHER READING 201
INDEX 205

ACKNOWLEDGMENTS

This is the page most readers skip. "Let's get on with it," you might be saying. "Why do I need to read a lot of names of people I don't know?"

As a reader, I've breezed past many an acknowledgments page myself.

But now that I'm a writer, I perceive the acknowledgments as maybe the most cherished page in the book. If you're not interested, move right on to the Foreword. But please allow me my one and only public opportunity to credit a few of those to whom I owe so much.

To begin at the beginning . . .

Some of these profiles have appeared, in altered and highly abbreviated form, in the *Los Angeles Times*, the *Kansas City Star*, the Cleveland *Plain Dealer*, the *St. Louisan* magazine, and, most frequently, the *St. Louis Post-Dispatch*.

Clarence Olson was my book editor at the *Post-Dispatch* for twenty-one years. It was under his aegis that many of these interviews were initiated. For twenty-one years we spoke on an almost-weekly basis, and never a cross word. How many associations can make that claim? The literary world lost a gentle, devoted, sensitive editor when he retired in 1991.

Irv Letofsky, former Sunday Calendar editor for the *Los Angeles Times*, understood the precarious nature of the free-lance writer, who is so callously buffeted about by bureaucrats and other Blue Cross–paid-up members of the establishment. Irv's terse letters (one response to a lengthy, detailed story inquiry read, in its entirety, "Dennis, Yes, Irv") were a source of constant encouragement and support to a young writer, on the other side of the continent, whom he didn't even know.

James Sutorius and Sharon Spelman were my benevolent landlords during those annual forays to New York City in the 1970s. Many of the meetings recounted in this volume would not, could not, have occurred had they not provided me with lodging.

Through the years, a few folks have read this material as it sought its shape. I am especially grateful to Mark Fitzgibbons, Philip Giberson, William Glover, Harriet Hall, Mary Beth Hurt, Roberta Maxwell, and Marian Seldes for their enthusiasm, and to the much, much missed José Ferrer for his constructive criticism.

Edmund Lyndeck's perusal of the finished manuscript was invaluable. This is the only page of the book he hasn't read (which means this is probably the only page with a grammatical error).

Finally, Esther Margolis at Newmarket Press uttered those six magic words every first-time author dreams of hearing: "We want to acquire your book."

To all, my heartfelt thanks.

FOREWORD

In chapter four of this volume, William Goldman remarks, "People who are interviewed a lot—not like myself, but people who really are—they're desperate, *desperate*, to be put down accurately on paper. . . .And no one gets them down. It's because most interviewers don't take the time to do any homework. But basically, I think, most of us will open up if anybody takes us seriously."

Taking his subjects seriously is exactly what Dennis Brown has done, and the result makes for stimulating reading for anyone interested in the mysteries, ironies, and vagaries of the creative process—especially for those who want to hear how it's really done from the horse's mouth, or, in one case, the horse's mother's mouth. We readers are treated to candid, thoughtful, and, at times, painfully revelatory conversations with a diverse group of America's foremost playwrights and screenwriters.

I share Mr. Goldman's disenchantment with interviews. By now I think the world has been interviewed to death. We are bombarded constantly with endless information about people, most of it useless. Whether it's a literary figure, political luminary, celebrity, or even the mother of six watching her house burn down and being asked the ultimate inanity, "How are you feeling at this moment?," the form is most often a dreary exercise for both reader and subject.

How refreshing to read a collection such as this, that renders portraits of its subjects rather than caricatures, that favors discourse over sound bites and insight over gossip.

Dennis Brown is blessed with the gift of letting others gab. I say this from experience, having more than once been interviewed by him myself. He inspires one's trust immediately. His homework is apparent, as is his intelligence and genuine enthusiasm. But above all is his love of the art itself and his respect for those who created it. In his introduction, he describes the ideal interview as one in which the subject "feels free to think in front of you." It sounds so simple, and yet it is rare.

Here, his subjects speak candidly of their work, and of their inspirations, frustrations, triumphs, torments, and lasting scars. As disparate as their geographical and emotional backgrounds are, common themes emerge. "Write what you know" is one of them. Another is a notion of home as that which one knows best.

If these writers are refreshingly unreticent about sharing the secrets of their work process, they are equally forthright in discussing the pain of failure, the panic to succeed, the pitfalls of success, and the struggle to reconcile all three.

Obviously, the theater and cinema, by their very nature, require an audience to complete the creative act; thus, the preoccupation with public success and failure is both natural and appropriate. Unlike the novelist, poet, or essayist, who may hope to be appreciated at least posthumously, if not now, by a more enlightened readership, playwrights and screenwriters are cursed with the imperative to succeed *now*, today, in public. Again from Goldman: "We live in a pop culture, fast turnover, and I don't know how people in the public eye cope with it. But one way is to keep striving."

Taken together, these interviews conjure an unsettling image of an America as yet unable to accord more than fleeting value to the artists who shape its dramatic heritage. Until such time, we can thank Dennis Brown for letting us hear their voices so clearly. They have much to say.

Kevin Kline
New York, New York
March 1992

SHOPTALK

INTRODUCTION

And then what happened?

What are your most vivid memories of . . . ?

Why did you . . . ?

When . . . ?

I asked a lot of people a lot of questions in the 1970s, back when I was young and inquiring, and not so concerned with trying to hold my own with the interviewee.

I especially remember a Sunday afternoon in Cleveland, Ohio, in October 1972. I had grown up on José Ferrer's movie portrayal of Cyrano de Bergerac. At college my roommate and I played the recording of the film's dialogue excerpts till the mellifluous speeches were embedded in our minds. ("When I think/I tremble, and the bell swings and rings—*Roxane!* . . .")

Now Ferrer was directing a play at the Cleveland theater where I worked. He graciously gave me an afternoon to ask away about his career. About *The Shrike* and *Othello* and *Cyrano de Bergerac*.

Our interviews weren't *for* anything. They were simply for me. Because I wanted to know.

After several hours of tape-recorded conversations, we adjourned to a local restaurant. During dinner, Ferrer spontaneously penned an ink drawing on his white linen napkin. The cartoon features a man, nose Cyrano-bulbous, sprawled out on a couch trying to sleep. Above his head appears the word-sound "Z-Z-Z-Z."

A second person, a youth, sporting beard and spectacles, recognizable only to those who know me, thrusts a microphone into Ferrer's face while asking, "And then what happened?"

Little did I know when he drew the cartoon that it would portend my future, that those four words would come to serve as a precis for my life.

And then what happened?

Why did you . . . ?

When . . . ?

A question, you must understand, is not something to be taken for granted. But when you truly care about the other person, and when the two of you are able to establish a chemistry of confidentiality and trust, then that person feels free to think in front of you, and you become a part of each other's experience.

For me, that process begins with enthusiasm. I wanted to be with all the people in this book. Primarily, they're writers. (I have yet to meet a writer who didn't have something worth saying.) I sought them out because I knew they had answers to my questions. I knew they had stories and reminiscences I wanted to share at first hand. They had lessons to teach, and I was an eager and receptive pupil.

After I moved to New York in 1979 and went to work at CBS Entertainment, I pretty much stopped initiating interviews. For a decade, this mass of 1970s material sat hidden away on a closet shelf. Occasionally someone would ask, "Why don't you do something with it?"

"No," I'd respond, "it's all old stuff."

And yet . . .

For a decade these writers had been my personal tutors. Now, as I began to write plays and screenplays myself, their hard-learned comments no longer were merely "good quotes." Now their words haunted my conscience.

Then I realized the obvious:

That these interviews were not growing older and more dated with the passing years. . . .

That an insightful remark made by a playwright in the 1970s can be as timeless as a truth told by a philosopher in ancient Greece. . . .

That what was instructive about these interviews in 1971 or 1979 will still be valuable a decade later or a century later. . . .

That a sentence worth remembering is always a blessing. . . .

That in addition to the legacy of their plays and films, from which we all benefit, these writers had given me an added legacy: their words, their thoughts. And it was downright selfish of me to keep that legacy cooped up on a closet shelf. . . .

INTRODUCTION

So I took the transcripts out of the closet and looked at them anew.

With the perspective of a decade's distance, I was amazed to discover that they share one central unifying thread: An inordinate number of these people talk about disappointment, unhappiness, frustration. Balanced though their careers have been by eleven Pulitzer Prizes, eight Academy Awards, and more than a score of Tony, Obie, and Drama Critics Awards, nevertheless an almost palpable pain threads its way through their thoughts until finally it emerges as a haunting leitmotif.

I've attempted to prune the interviews down to the point where they no longer read like dusty conversation pieces from the 1970s, but rather like a distilled "good parts" version, bounding from insightful observation to illuminating anecdote to timeless truth. (I also added an interview from the late 1980s, someone else I tracked down in order to hear a few stories.)

Are my questions unique? Wholly original? I hope not. The point is, I wanted to ask them myself. The interviews have slept long enough in my dark closet; may they now inhabit the brightly lit bookshelves of others.

Dennis Brown
Los Angeles, California
March 1992

CHAPTER ONE

MAN FROM MISSOURI

"I don't think it's going to ruin any of us to make some money on our work."
—LANFORD WILSON

Back in 1970, while driving through the soft Ozark Mountain foothills that roll across south-central Missouri, I veered from my route long enough to visit the tiny rural town of Lebanon. There was nothing much there in 1970, though the local pharmacy (complete with ice cream counter) was a congenial place to while away a half hour. Not surprisingly, I was the only person who didn't know every other person in the store.

Although my brief visit occurred nearly a decade before Lebanon attained some slight asteriskal celebrity as the locale of the Talley trilogy, including the Pulitzer Prize-winning *Talley's Folly*, I paid brief homage to that inconsequential little hamlet for only one reason: because Lebanon was the birthplace of Lanford Eugene Wilson. Missouri hasn't produced all that many notable playwrights, and even fewer who appreciate their heritage. Wilson's plays indicate that he does, so I wanted to get a feel for his roots.

Like so many other college students in the late 1960s, I came to Lanford Wilson early, back when he was being produced Off-Off-Broadway, and at colleges and in workshops. When we first met, three years after my lazy pilgrimage to Lebanon, Wilson was on the cusp of success. *THE HOT L BALTIMORE* had recently won an

Obie Award and the Drama Critics Award as Best American Play.

We met at his literary agent's office. The slender, willowy thirty-six-year-old writer arrived from lunch with his producers, who had given him a page proof of the *BALTIMORE* ad that would appear in the following Sunday's *New York Times*.

The ad boasted about the recent prizes.

The agent carped that the ad was too small.

But nothing could dim Wilson's garrulous high spirits, which continued throughout our time together in a private conference room.

How much influence, I asked, had his Missouri background had on his writing?

"It's going to get stronger and stronger," he replied, diving into the interview with disarming abandon. "I am so thankful that I had the background that I did. When I was five years old in Lebanon, I had a grandmother with Indian blood who would go around picking wild greens in the fields. And I could still—I don't, but I could—pick a mess of greens. But from her, I learned the trees and the birds. I didn't know until I came to New York that there were people who didn't know the names of the trees.

"Still, the seasons just drive me out of my mind. People want fresh strawberries in the middle of winter and I say, 'No!' It's such great fun to have seasons. And that all started back there in Missouri. When I came to this city, of course I forgot all that immediately, for there was all of this new—excuse the word—input. It was very exciting, and a lot of my plays, like *Balm in Gilead*, reflect that first awareness of the entire social scene that I had no idea about before. *HOT L* is a combination of the two. The play I'm working on now goes further, is more strongly rooted in the land."

He was referring to *The Mound Builders*, which would be produced by the Circle Repertory Company two years later.

When he was five, Wilson's family left Lebanon and moved fifty miles west to Springfield. Five years later, they moved to nearby Ozark, where Wilson lived for eight years. At age eighteen, he moved from Missouri to California, an experience he chronicled in *Lemon Sky*.

After he left California, Wilson moved to Chicago.

"I wrote my first play at an advertising agency in Chicago during lunch hours around 1957," he said. "Actually, when I went to Chicago I thought I'd be a commercial artist . . . until I saw what commercial art was. Then I decided I'd be a painter. I did about ten paintings. They were terrible.

"At the same time, I kept writing stories. Not realizing I was a writer, but writing stories. Everyone said, 'Your dialogue is very good, but your description is horrible.' And one story would have been better as a play, so I wrote it as a play. I'd always had this interest in theater. 'Long about this time I decided that I didn't want to be a terrible painter. Writing was fulfilling me more. So I started working on plays."

In 1963, at age twenty-six, he gravitated to New York, where he took such hang-on jobs as dishwasher, reservation clerk, riveter, waiter.

Did he intend to write for Off-Off-Broadway? I asked.

"No. New York theater to me was a culmination of Broadway, *Newsweek* and *Time* magazine reviews, *Theatre Arts* magazine—which I loved dearly and had a subscription to—the John Gassner series of *Twenty Best Plays* and the Fireside Theater Book Club. I expected all those great American plays, or comparable ones, to be on. I was wildly disappointed. The first time I really felt involved in a theater experience was down at the Café Cino six months after I got to New York."

Wilson became involved with Off-Off-Broadway when it was nurturing a young generation of writers.

"The greatest thing about the early days was that it was like a five-year apprenticeship for all of us," he said. "I don't know any place, even today, other than Off-Off-Broadway that offers people what we had. Working on one-act plays with live audiences that we had to get ourselves. It was dragging them in off the streets."

Talent has a way of clustering, and it clustered in Greenwich Village in the mid-sixties. These starving writers were filled with ambition and confidence.

"We knew," Wilson enthused. "We knew. When Sam Shepard's first play was done, there was a general cheer all across the Village. Everyone knew that someone else was added to the list. We would sit talking about theater all night long in some café, and before we would leave every time someone would say, 'Does this remind you of Van Gogh and Gauguin sitting together?' We always knew! Someone would come over and start talking about plays. And suddenly there would be Michael Smith and Terrence McNally and Paul Foster and Sam Shepard and Joyce Aaron, whom he was going with at the time. She helped Sam enormously. She says six words in a row and makes you want to write, just the way she talks. Rochelle Owens and Megan Terry would be there. And Irene Fornas, who has always been a main force in the group. We would all be sitting around talking, and some stranger would come over and say, 'I was working on a play,' and we'd cut off immediately. Boom. It was like, 'This person is going nowhere.'

"I suppose that sounds as if we were a clique, but it was a clique of forty-five people, plus all the directors and actors. It's not so much that we were elite. We just had a very sure sense of talent."

Wilson's plays began to criss-cross Greenwich Village: *Home Free!*, *The Madness of Lady Bright*, *The Rimers of Eldritch*, *Balm in Gilead*.

In 1969 Wilson came to Broadway. *The Gingham Dog* closed after five performances.

"I still think the play itself is very powerful and says something completely different from the way it was perceived by the critics, who all bombed it. But now I realize it was directed to say what they got. Nevertheless, the second act of *Gingham Dog* is one of the best pieces of writing I've ever done. I just love it."

In the first act, I reminded the playwright, one of the characters explains that he moved from Kentucky to New York because he thought people in Manhattan were open and responsive, with scope. The character, Vincent (portrayed by George Grizzard), says, "I wasn't sick of small Southern towns, I was sick of small people—ambitions—hopes—small hopelessness, even." Is that Lanford Wilson speaking?

"There are always two sides to these things," the playwright replied, "and that's one side. That's the side that makes me want to shake rural people and say, 'My God, there's something outside of this alfalfa field.' There's something outside of people dragging around saying, 'Well, I don't know, it looked like it was gonna rain yesterday, but it doesn't look like it's gonna rain today.' I just want to shake them!

"And the other side, of course, is that the only thing that's important is that alfalfa field, and it's desperately important whether it rains or not. And if that's happening, it's certainly more important than what's happening on Capitol Hill.

"You know, I could never write a didactic play if I had to. The closest I come to didacticism is 'Our cities are dying,' which drives me crazy and drives me up the wall. We've got to get back to the garden. That is a theme that is in every play of mine, and I believe it sincerely. We've got to get back to the ground. Plow up some of these streets and plant trees. We've got to. This is just no way to live."

In 1970, the autobiographical *Lemon Sky* was produced at the Buffalo Studio Arena. The production, which featured Charles Durning and Christopher Walken as father and son, moved to Off-Broadway. It garnered excellent reviews but little public interest and closed after sixteen performances.

Three years later Wilson enjoyed his first commercial success with *THE HOT L BALTIMORE.*

How did the play evolve?

"I had a crisis about two years ago after I wrote—this will eventually answer your question—after I wrote *Serenading Louie*, the blackest play I've ever written. *Louie* is really the very best writing, line by line, that I've ever done. And it's not a good play. The play itself is a mess. It's very long speeches, is what it is, and the long speeches are better than I've ever written.

"But it's also the most depressing play I've ever seen. It's just dump, dump, dump on the audience all night long. We did it down at the Washington Theater Club in Washington, D.C., and after the show there was a line of people taking tranquilizers at the water fountain. Honestly, there was.

"So I said, 'I want to write a comedy. I want to find something positive.' Well, I wrote six pages of a comedy and it sounded like everyone's comedy, or anyone's comedy. It was very funny, and I said 'I don't want to do that. If all there is is material to make you laugh for two hours, what a silly reason to go to the theater.' At least, I felt that way then.

"So I started another play. I wrote thirty pages. Then I stopped and spent five months on a TV movie. This is when I bought a house out in Sag Harbor and said, 'I could finish the whole restoration of that house with the money I get from this.' A big fifteen thousand dollars. I had turned down other things that would have paid the same amount. But this was working along with Tennessee Williams. I thought we might actually get something worthwhile. It's called *The Migrants*, and it's about the migrant workers who go up and down Florida. I thought, 'I'd hate to see anyone else handle that.'

"It was strange working with Tennessee Williams. He finds it difficult to talk to people, and I find it difficult to talk to him. We get along fine, but at the beginning he was difficult to get to know. After we got past that, it was a wonderful experience. We heard that the migrant workers were all winos, so one day we took a big jug of wine and went to meet them. Tennessee and I got bombed out of our minds. They didn't have a drink.

"When I finished my five months on the movie I'd been away from playwriting long enough where I said, 'I've got to really get to work. I've got to write a play.' And not just any play. It was that sense of 'I've got to write an important play. I've got to write a major play.' And that's just not the way to work.

"I reread that first thirty pages I'd written before the TV movie, and they were terrible. Of course, the first thirty pages are always terrible until the characters start to be interesting enough where I can begin to see them in the round, see what their situation is. Then the first thirty pages always go.

"But thirty pages was as far as I'd gotten, and of course it was terrible. Well, I lost interest in that idea, and all of this accumulated. The result was one mammoth writer's block. So I decided what was wrong was I had been away for too long from theater participation. When I was writing well and writing a lot, I was completely involved in the theater. Where you go to rehearsals, and you help paint the set, and you say, 'I can't stand that light,' instead of sitting there and being nice like I had been for the last three plays, professional productions where you whisper something to the director and the director says, 'Well, I have great trouble discussing that.' With Marshall Mason at the Circle I can say, 'That's horrible.' I feel perfectly free. Someone asks Marshall a question and he says, 'I haven't got a clue. Ask Lance.' And we work well.

"So about the time I developed the writer's block, the Circle decided to do my play *The Great Nebula in Orion*. But we were only using four actors. So I wrote a quick fifteen-minute play called *The Family Continues*, mainly so the other people in the company would feel like they were doing something too.

"Writing that, and working on the set and going to rehearsals, got me back into the theater. People came to review it, and they said, 'Gosh, this is very nice, but when are you going to have a full-length play?' So I forgot all about writing a 'major' play or a comedy and all of that, and *HOT L* came very logically out of the need to work on a full-length play for the company.

"What this company needed was scene study and character work, so I became involved in giving them juicy, wonderful characters. Because of *Serenading Louie* and the dumping on people, I *will not* allow a character to go down into the depths of despair. What the characters in *Serenading Louie* said over and over again was, 'I don't know, I don't know, I don't know.' I didn't want any of that in this play. I had a big note to myself that read, 'Please love this time.

Let's don't talk to the audience!' My characters had talked to the audience in the other plays, and it looked as if that's what I did.

"Instead, I knew that every character in *HOT L* would have it figured out. I wanted every character to have a strong drive, so they would all have an answer. 'This is what life is all about.' Not necessarily philosophizing, but many of them would have a strong commitment. And all of those various commitments clashing was where the final statement, if there was one, was going to be."

I told Wilson that I don't know the people who populate his plays. Then I asked if he is as loving and sympathetic to these bedraggled folk in real life as he is in print.

The usually garrulous Wilson took a long pause before answering.

"No," he finally replied. "One day I give the bum fifty cents, and the next day I say, 'Oh, please, I just can't take it. I cannot deal with it today.' "

He paused again, then continued: "I'm aware of anguish and pain, and it's certainly not just in the down-and-outers. That's why I pick the down-and-outers, because it's so obvious there. But it's in anyone. I'm always aware of it, and I try to deal with it as best I can. But I'm not that strong."

It's one thing to understand a downtrodden character while you're viewing a play, I suggested, but another matter entirely to confront that same character on the street outside the theater. Had I seen some of the *HOT L* characters on the street, I'd have wanted to move to the other curb.

"But you see," their creator implored, "the characters in this play don't want a thing from you. And the people on the streets, except for the bums, generally are not asking for anything. You feel guilty because you think they are. My characters wouldn't come up to you on the street, not one of them. They all have their own lives, their own answers. They all have their own ways of getting ahead. I've talked to these people on trains. I've talked to them in coffee shops. And generally speaking, they're really not asking for anything."

Are you the kind of person who can just go up and start talking to strangers?

"No. I'm the kind of person that people come up and start talking to me."

Why do you think that is?

"I can't figure it out. But it happens all the time. I get all the crazies. It's just incredible. They'll pick me out of a crowd from half a block away. 'There's someone who can't say no.' "

And can you?

"Sometimes. It depends on if I happen to have any money or if I happen to have any time. You sometimes do feel like an incredible fraud when some public disaster of a person asks you for sympathy or help and you say, 'I just haven't the time.' But I think and I hope I'm responsible to my friends.

"It's strange. You're not alone in viewing my characters as you do. But when I was writing *HOT L* I did not think of these people—I never have, never have—I did not think of them as losers or down-and-outers. That's an interpretation that has been imposed on the play. You see, it's not a play about a dying America. It's a play about refusing to die in America. So I didn't think of my characters as the bottom of the barrel. I was trying to find the people that I thought were strong and positive and had something to say."

And yet, they've had to retreat to their own world, haven't they? We only see them in the insular society of that hotel lobby.

"I see what you mean. I don't think of them as the prototypes of success, yet I also don't think of the hotel as a refuge. No, of course I do. I think of any structure as a refuge."

Just as the Circle Theatre proved to be a refuge for you.

"Absolutely. Still is. Will become more and more. You know, at the Circle we try to avoid thinking about critics and critical fame and critical pressure. We just try to succeed as much as you can in the middle of New York City.

"Yet the critics are always there, lying in wait outside that refuge. Critics scare me to death. As a playwright, you can't allow yourself to think about the fantasy of reward. You have to concentrate on your work or you're dead. But all of that peripheral fantasy of rewards and recognition and a play being done across the country depends on the critics' reactions. So they scare me to death.

"If all we playwrights had to worry about were writing terrific roles for terrific actors and telling the audience a story that pertains somehow to the society they live in so they can recognize it, if that's all we had to worry about—and hopefully that's all we *will* worry about—we could write so much better. It's wildly important that the critics don't *expect* something. I hope I remember to say that to them when I get their award next week."

The awards are beginning to come. Attention is being focused on you. Is it time for you to move into the center ring?

"No. I've got to keep working this way, because it's the right way to work. At least it's right for me."

What do you say when you write your next play and some producer offers you a check for twenty thousand dollars?

"But he won't see it. I don't write plays for producers to read to do on Broadway. None of the Off-Off-Broadway people do. You know, when *Gingham Dog* was done on Broadway, the lighting people would be playing poker and not even looking at the light board when they got their cues. And some of the actors would be trying to get their agents on the phone during intermission. That's just not the sort of people that we work with and write for."

But eventually the works of Van Gogh and Gauguin were purchased by the establishment. Your work is being discovered by the establishment right now. Isn't it possible that the pressure is going to become even stronger than you imagine? Already *HOT L BALTIMORE* has come from Off-Off-Broadway to Off-Broadway. Now the cry is out, "Take it to Broadway." Maybe it will become a movie.

"People are always saying, 'Now of course you want to protect the movie.' I don't give a shit about the movie. I don't want to protect the play as a movie. I'm not into movies. I have no interest in film at all.

"Just remember: Even if it *is* sold to the movies, the play is still there. That's the fortunate thing. The play is still there. The movie of *The Glass Menagerie* was a piece of trash, but no one thinks about it. The movie of *The Night of the Iguana* I hated desperately, but the play is still this magnificent work of art. So it doesn't matter what happens to *HOT L* now. We did it at the Circle, and you cannot corrupt that performance. If we're selling out in September, expect it to move to Broadway. And it really won't bother me a bit, though it would be awful if we made a fool of ourselves and closed immediately.

"But you see, it's not there that a work is corrupted. It's when you're writing it, when you're rehearsing the original production, that you must make no compromises. This is when you must not say, 'Oh, it would go better *if* . . . people would like it better *if* . . . at the same time, it may not say as much about the character *if* . . .' But those things would never have occurred to us while we were working on this play."

Lanford Wilson was as good as his word.

When we spoke in 1973, Wilson was a writer on the rise, yet he assured me that commercial success would not lure him away from the Circle Theatre Company, which he and three others had founded in 1969.

He was not lured away.

In 1975, *THE HOT L BALTIMORE* spurred a flop television series.

That same year *The Mound Builders* (set in southern Illinois) ran for twenty-nine performances at the Circle (whose name had been changed to the Circle Repertory Company).

In 1978, *5th of July* (set in his home town of Lebanon, Missouri) also was produced at the Circle. It ran for 168 performances.

In 1979, *Talley's Folly* (again, Lebanon) enjoyed a triumphant engagement at the Circle and then moved to Broadway, where it ran for eight months and won the Pulitzer Prize.

In June 1979, between the closing of the original Circle production and the Broadway reopening, Wilson and I met again, this time at the Circle Rep administrative offices. The forty-two-year-old writer seemed unchanged. He was still outgoing, ebullient, and forthcoming, and he looked not a day older.

I reminded him that the first question I'd asked six years before had concerned the influence of his Missouri background on his writing.

"I always knew I'd get to it," Wilson said, as he stretched out across a broken-down couch. "I remember opening night of the original production of *HOT L* at Circle Rep, which wasn't all that long before we first talked. John Lahr was very, very excited and kept saying, 'This could move, this is incredible.'

"And I said, 'I don't want to talk about that. Let me tell you about this idea I have for a play called *The Mound Builders*. It will take place in Missouri and use all of that Missouri background that I know so well. There will be Eastern people visiting the place, and I'll be able to combine the two, this dichotomy that I live in.' That's what I wanted to talk about, this mysterious, weird play that would be so different from *HOT L*."

Eventually, the locale of *The Mound Builders* was moved from southern Missouri to southern Illinois.

"It had to be," Wilson explained, "simply because the Indian-mound excavations are there. The plot changed, too, from what I told John Lahr, but the themes did not. I have a great fondness for *The Mound Builders*. That's my favorite play. I think *Mound Builders* is going to be what I'm known for."

Yet when it opened at Circle Rep in 1975 it ran five weeks and closed. Is it luck that one play hits big and another doesn't?

"Yes, it's luck," the playwright answered. "*HOT L BALTIMORE* is no better than *Lemon Sky* or *Rimers of Eldritch.* It just happens to be that impossible thing: commercial, whatever that is. That doesn't mean it's any better."

The Mound Builders is not commercial?

"Apparently not. It is, however, the best play I've ever written, one of the best plays that's been written in years. Yet no one dreamed of doing it on Broadway. We tried to find someone to move it when it was time to move from the Circle, and no producer would touch it."

Perhaps *Mound Builders* is a play whose time has not come.

"I think that's true. It's also true of *5th of July*. Its time will come. I think people are a bit taken aback by the homosexuality in the play and really cannot get to what the play is talking about apart from that. After fifteen other plays are written where the people are homosexual and that has nothing to do with the theme, then they'll be able to look at *5th of July* and see something quite different."

5th of July, which is set in Lebanon in 1977, eventually impelled Wilson to write *Talley's Folly*, which is set in Lebanon in 1944.

How did *5th of July* evolve?

"*5th of July* started out going to be set on maybe Long Island," Wilson said, habitually wiping his falling hair from his eyes for the umpteenth time. "I started with the idea of the garden that was being built. Eventually I realized that it just did not work for me in the East at all, that I wanted it in the Midwest. Then the aging protesters, the sixties children, came in thematically, and it moved to Missouri.

"I wanted a very wealthy house, so I moved it to the outskirts of some town. I wanted a name like Egypt or Lebanon, some biblical connection. I finally said, 'To hell with it, I'll use Lebanon, Missouri.' Not because I'm from there, but because the name worked.

"Then, in order to be able to write about the house and the property and this family in 1977, I had to plot out the entire history of both the house and the family: 'The house was built in 1861 by slaves working for so-and-so.' I did the entire history, but especially over the last twenty, thirty, forty years.

"As I plotted out the history, I realized how many interesting times this country has gone through just before, during, or just after wars. I felt that the economic history of the country could be charted by picking up this family at mid-war, roughly thirty-three years apart, all the way back to 1860. So that's what I'm doing. It'll probably be five plays. And I *hope* to get through them very quickly so I can go on to something else."

In relating the evolution of *5th of July,* Wilson also had begun to explain the genesis of *Talley's Folly,* since it evolved from the former play:

"In *5th of July,* Sally returns to the house with the ashes of her dead husband, Matt. I created Sally's history all the way back to her childhood in the 1920s. Doing that made Matt develop as an important character, both to her and to me. And I thought to myself, 'What a great part that would be for Judd Hirsch.'

"I could see Matt as this young character, Judd's age, when they were engaged in the 1940s. And I realized that time during World War II when Matt came down to propose could make a wonderful one-act, two-character love story, a coda to the other four plays in the cycle. For a long time I said, 'Oh, who would be interested?' And I finally said, 'I would. I would just love to see that story. I don't care if it's romantic and sweet and soft-bellied. I want to do it.'

"I started last May, and it took till January. It came fairly easily. In fact, it was great fun to have hit so well on what I intended to write. I already knew everything about Matt and Sally, of course. If was just getting them down on paper—though sometimes it's difficult to get characters down on paper when you already know them, because you're not figuring them out."

If you already knew everything about Matt and Sally, did you make many changes in their characters as you wrote?

"In that first draft Matt drove down from St. Louis to Lebanon ready to propose, already knowing that Sally couldn't have children. His only object was to get her to say that. He had it all worked out in his head.

"But Marshall Mason kept saying, 'I don't know. It's not a waltz, it's a lullaby. What's at stake? Nothing.'

" 'I beg your pardon,' I indignantly replied. 'It's absolutely perfect.' I had just finished the play and was very defensive.

"He said, 'Well, let's hear it.' So we heard it. We had a reading of it here at the office. Terrific, fabulous response from everyone . . . I thought. Then a month later I listened to the recording of what people had actually said:

" 'It's real nice, but I wasn't too . . . It's just very sweet.'

" 'It's marvelous. I just love the idea. I drifted away a couple of times, but I . . .'

"You get the idea. But there's so much there, they were saying. Anyway, they were nicer than Marshall. He said, 'No way, no way. There is just no grit. There is no suspense. Matt has nothing at stake. We'll talk.'

"I came to that meeting with Marshall and Milan Stitt, our dramaturge, with a real chip on my shoulder. I knew it was the best first draft I'd ever done. Well, either Marshall was more tactful than I've ever known him to be, or else he had planned a very careful strategy, or else he just felt passionately about it, because in nothing flat I was listening to the two of them and writing notes. And in that day we changed the script so that Matt comes down there ignorant of Sally's problem and lays himself on the line, so he has a great deal at stake.

"Then Marshall and I, in the office, read the new draft. He did a very clever thing. He said, 'I'll read Matt and you read Sally.' With me reading Sally, I said, 'I don't like my part.' I thought to myself, 'He's doing all the talking.' So we finished reading it and I said, 'No, no, no, that's not it yet.' And within five minutes I realized that when Matt tells Sally his life story, to her it probably looks like a setup. So that if she then were to respond to his story by getting angry, it would give a whole new infusion in the middle of the play. So I went into one of the typewriters here and rewrote her entire part from the middle to the end. From that day the play clicked.

"Now that it's written and produced, I think it's the most perfect thing I've done. Perfect in that its scope is small, like a short story. You only talk about one thing. We don't have fifteen other things going on like in the other plays. *Talley's Folly* is a gem. It really is."

Wilson created the role of Matt Friedman specifically for Judd Hirsch. How does a playwright do that?

"Judd informed the entire play. I was thinking of him a lot even in the conceptualization of the play. I knew Matt looked like Judd. I knew physically what size Matt was. All of that. Then, Judd is one of those actors who can do anything. I mean, he has a great mimic talent."

Stop right there. In the play, Matt does a Humphrey Bogart imitation. Is that sequence included simply because Judd Hirsch could do it?

"Absolutely. The Bogart imitations came directly from the fact that I knew Judd could do that and I wanted him to be able to show it, *and* I wanted it to be right in character. In addition, Judd can also be as deep as a well. In quiet, retrospective moments he can be astonishingly deep. So with Judd you're working for an instrument that has such an incredible range that you want to take advantage of it and have him show it all."

So you act like a tailor and cut the material to his size.

"I don't think of it as being a tailor," Wilson clarified. "I'm not fitting that instrument. I'm challenging that instrument: Can you do an imitation and one line later go deep into the center of the earth and come back and answer it in an imitation? If the actor can, it makes for incredible twists and turns. What I'm doing is taking utter, merciless advantage of everything the actor can do, then throwing down a gauntlet, saying, 'And now do this.' "

I commented on the lack of profanity in *Talley's Folly*.

"It's the first time in years that I've written a play where there is no swearing at all," Wilson pridefully said. "There is not a 'durn' in the play, let alone all those other words, like in *5th of July*, where they have mouths filthier than the Missouri River."

The line "You do not have the perception that God gave lettuce": Is that something you heard when you were growing up in the Ozarks?

"Right. It's a line I've had for twenty years. I've used it a couple of times in conversation. There are so many lines like that.

"My mother still lives in Missouri. Last year when I went down to my stepfather's funeral my uncle met the plane.

"I said, 'How's Mom?'

"And he said, 'Oh, your mother's got more guts than an Army mule.' First line out of his mouth. I've tried to avoid using those lines, but I'm not going to be able to stand it much longer. I'm really going to have to write a character who talks like that, and every line out of his mouth is going to be one of those wonderful Missouri-isms."

You really haven't changed much in the past six years, have you?

"No, not a bit."

You haven't changed in your personality, in your themes—

"And yet everyone says, 'Every play is so different.' I don't see that. I think the plays are dangerously the same."

Tell me about the public Lanford Wilson. You're becoming one of the best-known American playwrights.

"I don't *feel* that," he insisted, as cigarette ashes cascaded onto his chest. "I don't *see* that. I have survived—and I'm talking about within myself, and it's a tenuous survival, believe me, I mean, it's hanging on—I have survived by being able to concentrate on my work. And most of the other crap—the newspaper and television interviews and such—has nothing to do with my work at all."

With *Talley's Folly,* I suggested, overnight he was on top again. It was the biggest thing that had happened to him since *THE HOT L BALTIMORE* six years before.

"Oh yeah," he confirmed. "Bigger, probably. It will be if we all now manage the show correctly."

Do you prepare for that? Or if you do prepare for it and it doesn't happen—

"I never prepare for it," he interrupted. "I'll tell you the truth. It swept us utterly off our feet that *Talley's Folly* was so well received . . . for about a week. Then you get your footing again and you say, 'Okay, now wait a minute. Where are we and what are we gonna do?' It's an interesting process, throughout which you have to remember that the reason we did the play was not for all this hullaballoo. It was because we wanted to tell this wonderful story. Nothing will happen to us that's good if we do not concentrate on the play.

"So you listen to the proposals, and you know when to say, 'No, that's going to get out of hand, we're not going to be able to control that.' And 'No, we don't want to use Dustin Hoffman and move it to Broadway,' and Dustin, don't kid yourself, would not do it. A number of producers who want to do it on Broadway have not even seen the play. They just read the reviews.

"So we *try* not to get swept away in this PR show biz. But we have to be very good at business and show biz in order to survive. In this business, you're one-half sincere writer and one-half show-biz manipulator. The work comes first, but we're also prepared to take utter advantage. I don't think it's going to ruin any of us to make some money on our work."

The success of the Pulitzer Prize–winning *Talley's Folly* sparked a Broadway production of the original play in the Talley cycle. *5th of July* opened on Broadway in November 1980, less than a month after *Talley's Folly* closed. Its time had come, even sooner than Wilson could have imagined, and *5th of July* ran for 511 performances.

In 1981, a third play in the cycle, *A Tale Told,* was produced at the Circle. The play concerns the goings-on in the Talley front parlor while Matt and Sally are becoming engaged a few hundred yards away at the old boathouse.

A Tale Told became problematic when one of the characters spoke at length to the audience. (Perhaps Wilson had forgotten his old note "Let's don't talk to the audience!"). Though he revised the play under a new title, neither version enjoyed a continued life. No additional plays in the originally conceived five-play cycle have appeared.

Wilson's next play, *Angels Fall*, was set in New Mexico; his next after that, *Burn This*, in New York City.

His stature and reputation continue to grow.

But there are those who think his writing has never been as understanding as when it was rooted to home.

CHAPTER TWO

SEASON IN THE SUN

"The work is the refuge."
—JASON MILLER

Ask Lanford Wilson a question and you'll get an answer, more often than not a long one.

Ask Jason Miller a question and you'll get a pause, more often than not. . . .

Lanford Wilson thinks while he talks.

Jason Miller thinks and then talks.

If Lanford Wilson spoke with the open delight of an Ozark mountain breeze, Jason Miller's words were as wary, weighed, and measured as mercury.

If Lanford Wilson conveyed an aura of accessibility, Miller's demeanor was intense, guarded.

Bums would think twice before hitting on him.

Miller was no less friendly than Wilson; he was, however, considerably more reserved. You always sensed a cauldron inside Jason Miller. The flame was on low, but someday it was going to boil over.

He was born April 22, 1939, and grew up among the coal mines of Scranton, Pennsylvania. After being graduated from the University of Scranton he attended graduate school at Catholic University. There he met and married a classmate, Linda Gleason, who also aspired to act. Miller's roguish manner apparently offended his father-in-law, Jackie Gleason, and the star did not assist the struggling couple.

For eight lean years, Miller's career never surpassed the survival level. Twice he returned to Catholic University to act, once with Helen Hayes in *Long Day's Journey into Night,* then with Geraldine Fitzgerald in *Juno and the Paycock*. But roles were sporadic, and he was forced to take such jobs as welfare investigator, waiter, truck driver, messenger.

Miller had written some one-act plays as a college student. While he was doorman for the original production of *Man of La Mancha* he wrote his first full-length play, *Nobody Hears a Broken Drum*. Set in the coal regions of Pennsylvania during and after the Civil War, it was produced Off-Broadway in March 1970 and closed after six performances.

By late 1971, with his family living on unemployment insurance in a cramped apartment in Flushing, New York, Miller seriously considered abandoning the theater.

Then *That Championship Season* happened.

He wrote this, his second play, on a three-hour-per-day writing schedule while he was in Dallas acting a supporting role in a dinner-theater production of *The Odd Couple*.

When the drama was produced at New York's Public Theater in May 1972, success struck the thirty-three-year-old actor-playwright with lightning speed. Miller was showered with superlatives, buried under an avalanche of adjectives. As if to prove that lightning can indeed strike twice, two months later it was announced that Jason Miller would make his motion-picture debut in the leading role of the film version of the best-selling novel *The Exorcist*.

Michael McGuire, a mutual friend of Miller's and mine and a member of the original cast of *That Championship Season,* offered to intercede with my request for an interview. Miller consented. But, new to the game, he asked that I spend a day with him and his family so that we could get to know each other before we turned on the tape recorder.

In July 1972, with *That Championship Season* selling out at the Public Theater and with *The Exorcist* in preproduction, I traveled to Neponsit, New York, where the Millers had rented a spacious home near the Atlantic Ocean.

When I arrived, a babysitter informed me that Miller was at the beach.

So were two thousand other people.

I had never seen a photo of him, but Michael McGuire had told me about Miller's blazing laser-beam eyes. For twenty minutes I threaded my way through a mass of sunbathers and swimmers in search of a stranger with fierce eyes.

An impossible task, I kept telling myself. . . .

Until I saw them.

Miller was sprawled out on the sand, soaking in the scorching sun. I introduced myself, and he greeted me like a long-lost friend. I was instantly included in his world.

We wandered back and forth between the beach and the house several times, talking all the while as if we were college roommates holding a reunion. Still, it didn't take long to realize that Miller is an acutely shy man who thrives on private conversation but who would die a dozen deaths in a public forum.

Nor did it take long to appreciate why Miller spent as much time as possible outdoors. Inside, he was a virtual prisoner of the telephone.

Three months ago, this man could not get his telephone to ring.

Three months ago, Jason Miller was Anonymity personified.

Now, each new call arrived like the burst of a tommy gun. Sun and surf provided a welcome respite.

In the late afternoon, while Jason was out in the garage lifting weights, I returned with Linda and the kids to the beach. She talked about the lean years, when restaurant meals were out of the question, and when being able to scrape together enough money to buy a bottle of wine was the only triumph in sight.

That night, Jason, Linda, and I enjoyed a lazy dinner at a nearby seafood restaurant, then sat in the front yard watching for shooting stars and looking to the future. *That Championship Season* hadn't even moved to Broadway yet, but already he had begun to write a film adaptation. Eventually I went to bed and read myself to sleep with the screenplay for *The Exorcist.*

Next morning after breakfast Jason and I stretched out on the living-room floor. Miller was a man with a lot on his mind. He was almost ravaged by ideas. And cutting through those thoughts were his piercing, penetrating eyes, which added a sense of purpose and passion to everything he said.

After the failure of his first play, I asked, how difficult was it to write this second one?

"I waited about two months," he said. "I spent the first month letting it all settle in my head. Then I put it behind me. After that month of self-indulgence, I realized that the important thing now was to get back to work. That's where the salvation is—in the work. I knew I had to write again. Fortunately, what came out of me was a story that intrigued me, and I never thought about failure for it. I thought about the story for a month before I went to the paper."

Once he went to the paper, he felt the confidence that other actor-playwrights have experienced. "Playwrights who have been actors know what a word feels like in your mouth," he explained, "what a speech feels like, how a relationship is played. They understand that, not academically or theoretically; they understand it practically, viscerally, in their guts. And I think it gets into their work. If you act for five or six years, structure, mood, pace, tempo get into your blood. It becomes a reflex action; it no longer has to be thought about."

Miller's play concerns the twentieth reunion of a state-champion high-school basketball team at the home of their former coach. Four of the original five players gather to relive their moment of truimph; as the evening progresses the men are revealed as sad, empty people clinging desperately to that one brief victory. Filled with prejudice and fear, they speak for the broad swath of American losers. Each character was born out of Miller's frustrations. A successful playwright could not have written this drama.

"It seems to me that all good writing—at least writing that I respond to—is autobiographical in some sense," he said. "Either you've observed it or you've experienced it. I've observed more than I've experienced in *Championship Season*. Actually, in the first draft the guys were only about thirty-three, thirty-four years old. Close to my own age. I put them at thirty-nine in the third draft. I wanted to get near the end of a decade. That must do something in your head, to come to the end. Especially hitting forty, which is, like one of the characters say, 'halftime.'

"There's still half a life to be lived, but these guys unfortunately haven't the strength or the courage or the honesty, and they're hurting. They have too many injuries. They simply are too damaged at this point. Damaged by life, and by what they are, and by what they have not become. Damaged by what now they know they will never become."

The most bigoted of the bunch is the Coach.

"I'll tell you," said Miller, who then hesitated, as if debating how much he did want to tell. That decision made, he continued. "I'll say it now. I agree with a lot of things the Coach says. I agree with a *lot,* and I think a lot of people *also* agree. It's just a question of how far you're willing to admit it. Because the Coach is mouthing the bigoted thoughts we all hold secretly in our own minds. Prejudice is very important in this play. The Coach says things that most people don't say aloud, but they think it. Or at least they're confused by it."

Having conceded his own prejudice, Miller freed himself to embark upon a dissertation of his play's intentions.

"Let me tell you what I obliquely tried to do. I tried to catch the religious element in sports. At this stage of our development, it seems to me that religion is no longer a motivating force. Remember *La Dolce Vita,* when Fellini brings the Christ statue in by helicopter? It's brilliant. The people are sunbathing, and they pay indifference to it. In one image Fellini says what theologians are writing books about.

"This Christian symbology no longer moves people. We've lost our root contact with it. So that today when I look around, our athletes have become comparable to the Parthenon gods and the Catholic Church. Athletes are emulated, and they're quoted. They've become symbols of transcendence.

"You walk into bars and you see all the pictures of the softball teams and the old trophies. These guys come in and sit there and look at themselves. They look at what they were like twenty years ago. And then the football game comes on, and you watch middle-aged men totally identifying with youth. *Total* identification. Down to their souls. They come out of themselves. They're in the game. They're playing the game, they're being hit.

"So there is a religious significance in *Championship* when Phil says, 'I went so far nothing on earth could touch me.' Trying to catch that youth.

"I know what Phil's talking about. The *whole being* experiences athletic success. When I was a middle linebacker in high school, I intercepted a pass and ran for a touchdown. I can still remember catching it on the forty-yard line and cutting through four or five guys and watching the blockers form and then suddenly seeing, like Lombardi says, 'daylight.' Suddenly there was nobody in front of me but all this green, and I felt like nothing was ever gonna catch me. 'Now I'm free. I'm going.' It was a feeling like I could run forever. Now I'm about at the seventy-yard line. I look over, and my father's running alongside of me. Honest to God. Running alongside of me.

"I wrote Phil's car speech parallel to this moment. When Phil says, 'I'm just speed,' the image in my mind was that intercepted pass. That feeling came back to me. As soon as I went into that speech, I saw what my mind had done. Had changed the interception to a Porsche.

"There are other religious symbols in the play. There's a stained-glass window in the Coach's home, which from the very first I wanted. Just a little stained glass.

"Then, the trophy, which is in form very close to the Catholic chalice, and it's always in an exalted position. That was conscious."

By sheer coincidence, the rented Neponsit home was owned by a high-school basketball coach. As Miller spoke, we had a clear view of a den whose shelves were crowded with gaudy golden trophies.

"Remember in the play when they put their hands together and pray for Martin, the one member of the team who doesn't attend the reunion? What they're doing there is commemorating their youth in their own church, with the stained-glass windows and the chalice. They're talking about their gospel—the gospel according to James and George and the Coach. They're immortalizing themselves.

"Winning that trophy was really a sacred moment in their lives which they will go to any length to maintain as holy and untainted and pure. That's why they won't accept the revelations at the end that the Coach forced Martin to break an opposing player's ribs. It was immortality even at the risk of unethical behavior. That drive superseding everything: I *will* break's somebody's ribs to have this cup.

"Tom says, 'We're myths,' and he quotes the Greeks. But for those five men, the Greeks' principles have been perverted and twisted so that the sense of excellence is no longer enough. You *must* dominate; you *must* triumph. It's as if victory, not excellence, is religious now.

"It makes you stop and ask yourself, what is sports all about? What does it mean to the players, and what does it mean to those guys sitting there watching and getting involved? I mean, if you took sports away from this country, Christ, the homicide rate would probably quadruple. Really. Football Friday night, Saturday afternoon, Saturday night, Sunday afternoon. Now Monday night. It's satisfying some need, you know, that maybe we haven't really explored. What is it doing to the consciousness of the country? Why has it become so *absolutely* necessary? Why is it front-page news when Joe Namath reports to camp? You are tempted to say it's diversion and escape.

Well, it's more than mere diversion. It goes deeper into the culture. And I wanted that in the play too.

"With athletes the whole being is involved. The mind and the body are mutually dependent. But make it five minds and five bodies working in rhythmic teamwork with overtones of ballet and orchestration, and you say to yourself, it's a beautiful and almost religiously ritualistic thing that you're seeing.

"What is 'team'? What is the feeling of belonging to a winning team? What was the visceral blood feeling to triumph with four other people in the middle of the arena, with forty thousand pairs of eyes staring down at you? What did that do to them? Was this experience something they had too quickly and too early? Was it in some way evil?"

Evil was much on Miller's mind these days, for he was about to portray a Jesuit priest.

"When I went to see Bill Friedkin about Father Karras in *The Exorcist,* it was one of the few times I ever went up for a play or movie where there wasn't pressure to get it," he said. "Pressure forces you into a lot of false reactions. Not only in reading for a film, but also in meeting the people who are going to make it. Fortunately, at this point I had a successful play, so I could go in with the attitude that while I'd love to do this film, my whole life didn't hang in the balance."

What was it about this profoundly troubled priest, I asked, that he most related to?

He paused for half a minute. The silence was broken only by a ringing telephone in a far room. Miller waited it out, then answered, "The certainty of being mortal, yet always in contention with an instinct that demands some kind of immortality. Karras is deeply introspective and painstakingly methodical. He doesn't want to go back into that medieval darkness. He believes that science is a means to truth. In the beginning he is defending his philosophy of life, which says that possession cannot exist, which says that everything can be measured. Finally he realizes that he is being confronted with the immeasurable, which is God. But it's the reverse: Satan."

This wary Catholic paused again, then plunged on. "The Church has become a corporation," he accused. "But despite some of the terrible things that have gone on in that corporation, if you examine underneath the Church, you realize it's not all authoritarian. It has a tremendous freedom. Some of the concepts of the Church are truly beautiful. But the humanism which has come down through the ages is being swallowed up by institutionalization. So the Church seems to be losing its character a little.

"I found that to be true when I lived in a monastery. When I acted in *Long Day's Journey into Night* at Catholic University I lived in a monastery for eight weeks. I was made to feel like an outsider in many ways. By certain members there I was considered alien. And I saw a very unpleasant thing happen down there, a very sad experience.

"There was a guy who was rooming next to me. He was going for a master's degree, and he was sent there by the New York State Rehabilitation Board. He had been a crane operator who had had some kind of disease and had gone temporarily blind. Because it could recur, they told him he could never do that kind of work again. He was about forty years old with five children, and he was going back to college. An average mind, going back and taking psychology. I don't know who advised him. But New York was paying for him to live there. The monastery was letting out rooms, because they didn't have the priests and the brotherhood like they once did, so they had the rooms to spare.

"And I met him in a bar on the campus one night. He was a big, heavy man, bearish, and always kind of awkward. It was strange at the bar. He started to cry, and I said, 'What's the matter?'

"He said, 'They're not gonna take me back next year.'

"I said, 'Take you back where?'

"And then he explained the whole story about the blindness and how this was ideal for him because he couldn't find an apartment and this was cheap and he could send some of the money home to his five kids.

"I said, 'Why won't they take you back?'

"And he said, 'They voted me out. They had a meeting and they said that they no longer wanted to accept guests.'

"And I said, 'But that's the whole concept of monastery. They used to take travelers in off the road and feed them. At least you're paying. I don't understand that.'

"And he said, 'You know, I used to believe in priests.' And then he started telling me how he would have to sit alone in the monastery because no one would talk to him. And how he was never invited into the rec room, and things like that.

"I didn't know any of this, and I thought, 'Well, there's the death of charity. It's gone.'

"I talked to a couple priests, and I said, 'How could you guys do that?'

"They said, 'It's our sense of community. The sense of community life is being imperiled.'

"I said, 'You don't have any community here. The community is gone. Your obligation was to take this man in. He wasn't even here on charity, and you had rooms all over the place. I don't understand that kind of thinking. How can you reconcile that and still maintain Christian principles? The man is by no means cured. You've put an added expense on him. He has a tough enough time studying. Have you thought about those human considerations at all?'

"It infuriated me! I got so pissed off at the whole thing. We're talking about the insensitivity of it. I said, 'Fuck, you guys haven't changed. You can grow long hair and not wear your cassocks; you're still a bunch of fucking medieval monks afraid to let anybody in.' I said, 'Medieval monks were better. They went out on the streets and brought the beggars in. How the hell do you reconcile that?'

"The man cried! He actually cried. He wasn't even drunk. He was so fucking hurt. So hurt. I said to a priest, 'Don't you understand what you've done to the man?'

"And when he left—I was there when he left, because his school year ended before our play did—he cleared out his whole room. They gave him one of those big plastic bags to put all his stuff in, and he just left it in the middle of the floor. Left the whole bag full of books and things. And he left without saying good-bye to anyone. He probably never will go back to school. I mean, this was incalculable harm they've done to another human being.

"But it was corporation. It was almost like a corporate decision. They all sat around their little table and said no to the guy. They said 'sense of community.' And interestingly enough, the next year I returned to Washington, D.C., and I wasn't invited back there. And they had even more rooms open. I had made three or four good friends there. One of them told me, 'I don't know why you weren't invited back.'

"I said, 'I know why.' "

But Miller also was looking past Father Karras. He had more plays in mind. A question: The next time he sat down to write, where in his head would the critics be?

"If they're in the foreground," Miller said, "I probably won't write again. If, now, one of my primary motivations for writing becomes to elicit unqualified praise from a group of men who for the most part are anonymous to me, I think I'm in a lot of trouble. I'll get into mannerisms and make the fatal mistake of trying to repeat an earlier success. Let's face it. *Championship* has reached a point of appreciation that borders on your fantasies. Some of those reviews I wouldn't have dared to write in my fantasies. But the whole myth in this country is how success destroys. I know there's no way I'm gonna top *Championship Season*."

So the next time you write, you put all those rave reviews into your desk drawer?

"Yes, I have to. Because you're always starting new. Today is today; it's not yesterday. You can draw a certain amount of strength from having a success, but then you have to go out and take a step that is a challenge. You have to come near the abyss in a certain way, come near the danger of doing something radically different or new. It's almost like an act of faith. The next play I write has to be something that is not supported by anything but me and the act of writing. The work is the refuge."

Two months later, *That Championship Season* made a smooth transfer from the Public Theater to Broadway. The play was Broadway's "hot ticket" when I returned to New York in February 1973. Miller was immersed in filming *The Exorcist,* which at the time was long over schedule, with no end in sight. The day I visited him at the Hell's Kitchen studio, he was filming what came to be known as the pea-soup sequence. He would leave his dressing room in costume, return forty-five minutes later covered with what appeared to be green slime, change into a duplicate outfit, then depart to get splattered anew. At least half a dozen costumes hung on a rack. We chatted during his frequent changes.

I inquired about a comment I'd read in an admiring John Simon essay. The critic had suggested that in *That Championship Season* Miller pointedly had named the school Fillmore High School as a symbol of America's pervading mediocrity. As Simon observed, Fillmore is "a school named for a President whose face could at best be carved in a molehill."

Had this, I asked, been Miller's purpose in using Fillmore's name?

"No," he replied. "I chose it because I went to Fillmore Grade School. In addition, I grew up—and my parents still live—on Fillmore Avenue."

So much for symbolism.

* * *

I didn't see Miller for two and a half years, but during those thirty months he was subjected to more success, turbulence, and confusion than some people encounter in a lifetime.

That Championship Season ran for 844 performances and established itself as the longest-running Broadway drama since *A Streetcar Named Desire* a quarter-century before. During the eleven months between April 1972 and February 1973, Miller won the Pulitzer Prize and the Tony Award. *The Exorcist* created a sensation upon its Christmas 1973 release. In early 1974 Miller was nominated for an Academy Award as Best Supporting Actor. (He would lose to John Houseman for *The Paper Chase.*)

But all the glory was more than offset by personal and professional setbacks. A divorce from Linda was pending. His writing was not forthcoming. His first film after *The Exorcist,* the Robert Mulligan–directed *The Nickel Ride,* a gritty character study of an underworld hustler, had been all but shelved by its distributor.

Miller and I met again in September 1975 in Los Angeles. He had just returned from Costa Rica, where, while filming a fishing sequence for ABC's *American Sportsman,* he contracted a painful but undetectable leg injury. Rather than travel to his own home north of Malibu, he checked into the Beverly Wilshire Hotel, which served as his base for a series of doctor's appointments. (In several weeks it would be discovered that two tapeworms had penetrated Miller's leg and were dining on his bone marrow.) He also needed to buy a suit (he didn't own one) to wear to a press conclave two days hence on behalf of the CBS special *A Home of Our Own,* in which he starred as Father William Wasson (yet another priest), who runs an orphanage in Mexico.

On this sunny September afternoon, without a penny in his pocket ("No problem, they know me here") and casually garbed in an old sport shirt and khaki jeans, he sat in the hotel's El Padreno Room, surrounded by celebrities like Warren Beatty, Roman Polanski, and Tony Randall, and spoke with me again. Miller had always been intense; now he seemed like a man possessed. There was an anger in him that could be traced to something more than tapeworms.

"I should know pretty soon whether or not *Championship* is going to be filmed," he uttered in a furtive hush that implied spies at the neighboring table. "They're worried about there being no possibilities for foreign distribution. I said, 'Is that your thinking? Look. It ran in Mexico for six months and got the Best Foreign Play Award.

It ran in Canada for a year, three different touring companies, and two of them in French. A forty-city tour in Scandinavia, and it's still running in Norway. Opening in Spain next month. Opened in Berlin. Opening in Heidelberg. Opening in Dusseldorf. Opened in Dublin, Rio de Janeiro, and Portugal.' I said, 'You're telling me there's no fucking distribution?!' The only country it went down in was England."

What happened there?

"We wouldn't let them use an English cast," Miller rationalized. "We used an American cast, not the original ensemble. But I'll tell you. On opening night, and it wasn't a papered house, they got something like sixteen curtain calls. And English critics hacked it. I never saw such viciousness in my life. Then this John Barbour, one of their better critics, wrote me about a month after it closed. He started out, 'Well, we have made a mistake once more.' He quoted reviews of *The Glass Menagerie,* which they murdered, *Death of a Salesman,* which they murdered. And he said, 'Now we've done it to *Championship Season.*' "

I suggested that despite all Miller's public attention and awards in the past three years, his private life hadn't gone so well.

"In a certain way," he said, "to get a Pulitzer Prize at age thirty-two can be a bit of an albatross around the neck. I had to go through that period, make some mistakes, start on a play, throw it away, and deal with all the attendant benefits of winning a Pulitzer. There are distractions, and I got caught up in some of the distractions—plus my own personal life. The last eighteen months have been a bit Kafkaesque.

"But things have leveled off. The relationship with Linda is as amicable as it can be when coming out of a kind of shocking, traumatic thing like a divorce. That kind of trauma reverberates for a long time in your head, in your soul, wherever it reverberates.

"My children were just here for three weeks. Jennifer, Jason, and Jordan. They're extraordinary children. Extraordinary because all through the lean years they never complained. I've seen kids who were whiners and complainers. They never were. They knew I was about my work and trying to do something important. And I know those lean years were hard for them to take in a lot of ways. And then success is just as hard for them to take, because the uprooting it did to Linda and to me it certainly did to them."

The first thing Miller did when he attained success in New York was to move his family from a tiny apartment to a spacious house within two blocks of the Atlantic Ocean. Then when he came to Los Angeles, on his own, he promptly moved to the beach at Malibu. What, I asked, was his affinity with the beach and the ocean?

He considered for a moment, then answered, "I think it's one of the ways I try to get close to my father. My father was a merchant marine when he was fourteen years old. When I was a child, he told me a great deal of sea lore. Then he became an electrician and got involved with maintenance at this plant that builds bathtubs. He would be a bundle of anxiety and short-temperedness from working this horrendous job.

"But every August he would get his two weeks' vacation. Then he and my mother and I would drive to Rhode Island, where he was born. He'd make that pilgrimage to his parents' graves, and then we would go to the coast right off Block Island. And he would totally change. He was at peace, at rest and relaxation. And so, consequently, was I. We'd have fun on the beaches, and he'd tell me sea stories about 'the old men.' You always called a ship captain 'the old man.' And he taught me how to swim in the ocean. He'd take me out on his back. It would be very cold water, and then I'd get off his back. We were like two porpoises in the waves and the surf.

"So when I'm around the ocean, I do feel a kind of serenity. It's like a big tit, or something that cradles you. And it's always changing. I like to just sit and watch the changes of the colors, and the changes of the light. The change in the composition of the beach in the morning. Then you get up the next day, and part of the beach is gone. And it's always bringing something new up. New wood. New shells. I suppose it's the universal metaphor for the unconscious. And it's where we've all come from. So I'm attracted to the mystery of it, and the unpredictability."

Caught in the web of his own reverie, Miller harkened back to the halcyon days of his recent past. "Remember when you visited us at Neponsit?" he suddenly asked. "That summer was the happiest time of my life. That was my Camelot. And like every Camelot . . ." His reverie trailed off, only to be re-anointed with enthusiasm. "But to be able to take my family to a home! Listen. Before *Championship* we lived next to a railroad in three and a half rooms. The three children were jammed into this Wheaties box in Flushing. The windowsills used to be their drawers where they'd keep their little things. So being able to give them rooms was a prize memory I'll never forget. One of the most thrilling things about success was that each of my children could have a private room."

I recalled an incident I'd not mentioned before. During the Neponsit visit, Miller's daughter approached me late one afternoon to ask, "Do you know where my daddy is?" When I said he was upstairs, Jennifer asked, "Is he crying?" Her concern made me wonder if there had been times when his despondency had grown so strong in that tiny Flushing apartment that she'd seen him in tears.

"The night after *Nobody Hears a Broken Drum* opened," Miller recalled, "she came out at five o'clock in the morning. I was just sitting there looking out the window. She got out of bed and came out and put her arms around me. She knew. I never told her it hadn't gone as well as I'd hoped for. But the reviews had come out, and I was just sitting there. I'll never forget the way she put her arms around my neck."

He paused to savor the memory of that precious moment, then continued, "I sold away the rights to that play for a thousand dollars. Well, I was young then. I *had* to get something on. But the real problem was that Jordan was in the hospital for an operation when the time came to sign the option. I needed the money. It may seem like a mistake now. Then, it was necessary."

He recently had portrayed the title role in a yet-to-be-aired TV movie, *F. Scott Fitzgerald in Hollywood.* Though the two men don't look alike, Miller could appreciate Fitzgerald's sense of desperation.

"There's a great deal of desperation to play in that character," the actor agreed. "Fitzgerald's a man whose whole career was walking a tightrope—and one day he looked down and there was no net. When he tried to get into films, he never felt he belonged. He never fucking belonged out here! He began to feel the fire was starting to go. He had monetary problems, a smashed marriage, a sick wife. All this, plus an ebbing talent. And the guilt. Didn't tend his own garden. A lot of weeds got in there.

"Curiously enough, as much as he wrote about the rich, I really believe he hated them. I believe he despised them in some other level of his being. His decline really started with the Wall Street crash in 1929. You can time it. The world was no longer interested in the rich as escapists. The rich put this country goddamn near the brink of destruction. The rich were jumping out of windows. They no longer were the myths that fascinated people. We were beginning to question those people, and we weren't liking what we found. But this was his milieu. And when that world collapsed, his talent collapsed. He couldn't find other fertile ground to lay his seed in. He was trapped within his fatal attraction to the rich, not only in their life-style, but in their literary value to him. He mined that vein, and when that vein went, he went.

"The beautiful thing about it was that he made a desperate lunge here in Hollywood, a tragically sad attempt to change his life. He endured incredible humiliations to try to get back on top. The man who had been the center of the fucking world was slipping into anonymity and obscurity.

"He had that kind of romantic fatalism where women became myths and goddesses to him, and then they became all too human. There was no balance. Fitzgerald was a total extremist. He was one of the last of the true romantics. His skull should have cracked open on a pyre in Malibu. He and Zelda flew too near the sun, the both of them. They flew too fucking near the sun, and whoosh!"

The longer he talked, the more apparent it became that Miller was drawing on his own life and past in order to paint this word-portrait of Fitzgerald.

"I suppose so," he conceded. "But I certainly understand what Hollywood did to a temperament like Fitzgerald's, because you're dealing with fantasy. This is the fantasy capital of the world. And out of these fantasies, enormous monies are made. Reputations are created and destroyed. The best business out here is real estate, because there's always an empty house. Some poor bastard came out here and made it for two years, was a passing Hollywood fancy. . . ." Miller paused, then bitterly acknowledged, "Someone said that to me once out here: 'You're a passing Hollywood fancy.' "

As he chewed over the phrase in silence, I asked, What if it were true? How important would it be?

He took a long time before answering. Then: "I don't like to be a passing fancy in anything. There's a sense of being manipulated."

I suggested that when we'd spoken by telephone just prior to the Academy Awards ceremony, Miller had conveyed an inordinate interest in winning that Oscar.

He responded with a question of his own. "What does the Coach say? The Coach says, 'It's in silver, boys. It'll last forever. I carved your names in silver.' That's in me. It's that dangerously competitive strain which sometimes throws my perspective off. I mean, otherwise I couldn't have written the Coach.

"Things like that are important to me. I recall one day I'm trotting down the street at Century Plaza. As I pass the Shubert Theater I see a big poster for the touring company of my play. It says FORREST TUCKER IN 'THAT CHAMPIONSHIP SEASON.' And I can't find my name. I'm not talking about equal size. I can't find my fucking *name.*

"So I go into the theater. There's no play running now, and an usherette opens the door, and I said, 'I'd like to see the manager.'

"She says, 'You can't see the manager.'

"I said, 'It's very personal, and I want to see the manager *now.*'

"So they bring this guy out, and I said, 'Do you see that sign? You've got about an hour to get my name on it.'

"He said, 'Who are you?'

"I said, 'I'm Jason Miller, and where the fuck is my name?' I said, 'Forget that. I not only want my name on it. You have a marquee out there? I also want my name on the marquee with the play. Otherwise the fucking show doesn't go on.'

"The next day they sent me a PR guy. I said, 'Don't give me any shit. Just get the name on.' And they did."

An incident like that suggests the strain you've been under during the past three years. Haven't you found the fusion of being an actor and a writer more to cope with than you thought it would be?

"Dead right. It has become very, very difficult. But there must be a way, and I think it comes down to a Spartan sense of discipline which I have not yet developed. I must cultivate that. I must. Curiously enough, I think I have it when I'm working.

"I remember, when we made *Home of Our Own* down in Mexico, the writer kept running around telling everyone, 'You're gonna win an Emmy, this is gonna win an Emmy, we're all gonna win Emmys.' And I wanted to say, 'That's not how you win Emmys.' You have to keep your mind focused on the work, and nothing else. The awards, if they come at all, come later and have nothing to do with the creative process. Consequently, we don't have a particularly special film.

"Yet I'm glad I made it, glad I spent that time in Mexico. It's an amazing country. The farmers down there are digging in the fields, in the mud, and they come up with broken images from pre-Columbian and Aztec pottery. The past resurfaces. It takes a long time, but then all of a sudden those objects return to ground level, where they are found.

"Well, memory is like that too. As I get older, my own past constantly resurfaces. Suddenly images come back into your mind. You think about people you haven't thought about for twenty years.

A face appears, and the sound of a voice appears. I'm beginning to realize those are the faces and voices that motivate me to write. It's interesting, when your past becomes a mystery to you. When you ask yourself, 'Who was I when I did that? Why did I do that?' "

Miller gazed around the El Padreno Room, and he suddenly seemed ill at ease, out of place, more comfortable talking to the Mexican waiter than to the celebrities who occasionally stopped at the table. I asked if he'd established roots in California.

"No," he quickly replied. "I don't have established roots anywhere. I'm constantly on the move. In the last eighteen months I've been in five countries and all over the United States. I don't know where I belong. I certainly don't belong in Scranton, Pennsylvania, anymore. Nor do I belong in New York. But a man needs roots. A man has to settle somewhere."

Perhaps, I suggested, the problem had to do with identity. In New York you were a playwright. Out here you're perceived as something quite different, a movie actor.

"There's a funny thing about making movies," he said. "When I made *The Exorcist* in New York I went home to my family every night. But we made *Nickel Ride* out here. I'd never been in California before, and I was here for three months. The marriage started to go when Linda came out to visit while I was making *The Nickel Ride*.

"When you make a movie, you're the center of attention. There's a small community of about a hundred people around you, and you're constantly getting attention. Getting attention, and giving it back. You make friends. You make acquaintances. You get to know their style of work, and for five or six weeks you create a little civilization.

"And then one day it's gone. Gone. You don't even see that civilization decline. One day it's the end of the picture, and they go. And you're left suspended between what you've been playing and who you are. But who I was was associated with the East, with Linda and family and with *Championship Season*. Now I'm on the edge of the continent. I had to stay here two weeks to do some looping, and I'd wake up in the morning with lines in my head that I'd already done. You get up at 5:30 A.M. for six weeks, and then one day you wake up at 5:30 A.M. and there ain't nobody picking you up. But you get up at 5:30.

"So one night I was walking around, and I went into the Avco Movie Theater. There's a bar down there. I had a couple drinks, and I look out the back and I see these trees. I see this water spray going. So I said to the bartender, 'What's that?'

"He said, 'That's a cemetery.'

"A cemetery behind a movie theater? That's strange. So, given my good Irish Catholic instincts, if there's a cemetery in the area I'll go down and take a look. So I go back there, and it's about eleven o'clock at night. Now I'd finished the film about four days earlier, and I was in limbo. The familiar was gone. The thing that I'd worked on with my head and my brain and my balls and my mind was gone. So there was a sense of buoyancy and fragmentation, isolation and exhaustion.

"Anyway, I left the bar and followed this path till I reached the cemetery. I'm looking around, and then I realize that the stillness is being disturbed by the people coming out of the movies. I can see them and I can hear their chatter. I'm next to the mausoleum, and suddenly I notice a rose. That's strange, right? A rose. Two roses. So I walk over. The stone says MARILYN MONROE."

A cemetery stillness hovered over Miller's story. The patrons chatting at the bar across the room might have been those moviegoers heading for their cars.

"Marilyn Monroe. Behind the Avco Movie Theater on Wilshire Boulevard. I just stood there."

In the quiet, I reminded Miller that three years ago he had described Father Karras in *The Exorcist* as a man whose world was crumbling. I asked the actor-author if he was in control of his own life right now.

"During the past eighteen months I was not," he said. "I was preoccupied by personal problems. I had to be operated on twice. Then there was the accumulation of the Pulitzer and the Academy Award nomination and the general rush of attention. The national tour and the opening in England ran simultaneous with that. So I was dismembered a bit. Fragmented a bit. I was dealing with things I never had to deal with before. My dealings with money became terribly distracting. I just don't have a good money head. I needed advice, yet I didn't know how to go and ask for advice. And then, when I did seek advice, I unfortunately took the wrong advice. So the alertness which one needs to maintain a career has, by and large, been missing from my life during the past eighteen months.

"And yet during those eighteen months I made two movies and finished the screenplay for *Championship Season*. So there was work. But I've had the disappointments of the marriage breaking up, of *The Nickel Ride* not being treated with the respect I felt it deserved, of the delay in filming *Championship Season*. I allowed these things to become barriers.

"Rejection is stunning. I mean, it can stun the mind. And there's a cruel law in nature: Either you grow or you die. I've been growing, but not at the rate I would like. But I think I've pretty well got things under control now. I've hopefully broken some of the bad habits, especially—like Fitzgerald—a morose preoccupation with my failures.

"Now, this can all become very self-indulgent. But when one is experiencing it, one doesn't realize that it's self-indulgent. It always seems necessary and right. Perspective gets distorted, and I made mistakes that normally I don't think I would have made, mistakes out of desperation and a little bit of panic.

"You know, a lot of my life, for both better and worse, has been very impulsive. In the last eighteen months I have been dangerously bankrupt in my use of time. I've overdrawn and squandered. Now I'm beginning to think a little bit more before I leap. I'm trying to weigh factors and protect myself. I'm coming into a critical area of survival—survival with an amount of integrity and personal dignity. Because time's winged chariot is going by. And that is the precious commodity."

As we prepared to leave the bar, word was spreading through the room: Patty Hearst had been captured by federal agents. It had been more than nineteen months since her kidnapping.

I left Jason Miller standing in the inner courtyard at the Beverly Wilshire Hotel, not a penny in his pocket, waiting to be picked up by "Dandy" Don Meredith to go to dinner with Dinah Shore.

It took Miller another seven years to get *That Championship Season* filmed. But he tenaciously stuck to it, and ended up directing the picture. In July 1982 I visited location filming in Scranton, his hometown. It wasn't easy gaining admittance onto the set. One of the eager young production assistants (who turned out to be Jason, Jr.) did his best to keep me out. After I was identified, I was allowed in.

Miller was a dynamo on the set. He sprang from setup to setup like a sprinter. But the next day, when he and the cast had to appear at a City Hall reception, he was as nervous and shy as he'd been when I'd first met him a decade earlier in Neponsit. Midway through the reception, he slipped outside and took solace in the admiring company of a group of nuns.

As the years passed (and we both moved from coast to coast) I heard from him infrequently and took to keeping track of him through his performances. I think he's always good. (Am I too subjective, or did he not give the most moving performance in Paul Shrader's *Light of Day?*) But more and more those performances were supporting roles, character work.

He still writes. His TV-movie biography about Mary Thomas was lean, tough, and funny. The dialogue crackled with vitality, and the film brought an Emmy Award nomination to Alfre Woodard, who played the title role. Not much attention to Jason Miller, though.

When he came to Los Angeles in early 1990 to film a featured role in *The Exorcist III* we spoke on the phone. "New York is no longer the capital of my imagination," he said. (How can you not love a man who coins phrases like that in everyday conversation?) We joked about how his son, that young kid who had tried to keep me off the movie set, was now a budding film star named Jason Patric.

Miller did his two weeks' work and then went home to Scranton, where he now lives and works with the community theater. A magazine article reported that he had an office in an abandoned coal shaft.

But I find it hard to imagine him enveloped by the darkness.

I'll always remember him best in the brightness—especially on a piercingly sunny afternoon in October 1975, three weeks after our session at the Beverly Wilshire Hotel. I visited Miller at his rented beach house, which sat on a bluff north of Malibu. A peeling wooden stairway led down to the secluded beach, which was blocked off by huge, crusty boulders corroding ankle-deep in the sea. But the most spectacular view was from the sun deck high on the bluff. That's where we were sitting when, for no special reason, I asked him how his mother had come to name him Jason.

"She didn't," he replied. "She named me Jack. I chose Jason for myself."

Why?

"I always liked that story in mythology," was his simple explanation.

I was tempted to remind him that while Jason did succeed in capturing the Golden Fleece, in Thomas Bulfinch's *The Age of Fable* the tale concludes, "What became of the fleece afterwards we do not know, but perhaps it was found after all, like many other golden prizes, not worth the trouble it had cost to procure it."

I was tempted to say something of the sort. Instead I sat silently in the brilliant sun and sipped my lemonade, while Jason Miller stared out across the blue Pacific at argosies on the horizon that only he could see.

CHAPTER THREE

RULEBUSTER

"I've busted every rule, so no matter what
I do it doesn't surprise anybody."
—FRANK D. GILROY

The odds are better than even that you haven't read Frank D. Gilroy's fable of the old West. Not many people have.

From Noon Till Three, subtitled *The Possibly True and Certainly Tragic Story of an Outlaw and a Lady Whose Love Knew No Bounds*, is a delight. This sliver of a novel might not be easy to locate, but if you do locate it, the reading will go down smooth and easy.

It cleverly employs the *Rashomon* concept to narrate the same tale from two points of view. The reader is left to determine which version is true.

I first read the novel when it was published in 1973. During the next two years I read it again—and again. In October 1975, during a visit to Los Angeles, I learned that Gilroy was wrapping up post-production work on his novel's film adaptation, which he had written and directed, and which stars Charles Bronson and Jill Ireland. My repeated requests to the United Artists publicity department to meet with Gilroy elicited a keen lack of interest. Finally I tried calling him directly at the postproduction facilities at Columbia Pictures in Burbank. Within seconds he was on the line.

"Sure, I'll be glad to talk to you," the Pulitzer Prize–winning playwright turned film director said. "Come on over tomorrow."

No time to go to the library.

No time for research.

None of my own books to fall back on.

When that happens, you rely instead on curiosity and eye contact. With the right person, spirited conversation can be more fluid than a list of predetermined questions.

Frank Gilroy was the right person.

The next day we met in his temporary office at Columbia Pictures. He was instantly likable. Goodwill virtually oozed from his warm eyes.

We introduced ourselves and sat down to talk. At that precise moment, the office door behind me opened and a giant figure entered the room. He apologized for the intrusion in a voice whose very familiarity elicited shivers. As I turned in my chair and glanced behind my right shoulder, John Wayne towered over me. His head seemed to graze the ceiling.

I scrambled to my feet as Gilroy ambled to his. Wayne still loomed large. He wore a brown corduroy sport jacket and a V-neck sweater. Even without a cowboy hat or boots, John Wayne could fill a room without half trying. His presence was mesmerizing. The office was charged with electricity.

Wayne was accompanied by producer Mike Frankovich, who introduced the superstar to Gilroy. Gilroy in turn introduced me as a writer from St. Louis.

"St. Louis," Wayne repeated in his famous semicroak. "I'm supposed to talk to a writer from St. Louis tonight. That's not you, is it?"

No, it wasn't.

"Tell me about St. Louis," the Duke asked. "Tell me what I should know so that I can impress this writer." (As if John Wayne needed to impress anybody.)

My mind blanked.

In desperation I muttered something about Budweiser beer, stuttered a few impotent phrases about the Cardinals. "How'd they do this season?" the superstar asked. I hadn't a clue.

As my lame recitation trailed off, Wayne politely excused himself. It so happened that Gilroy's office connected to this building's only private toilet; that's what had induced the Duke to cross our path. While he made use of the facilities, we three stood waiting outside the door like sheepish schoolboys. Frankovich explained that he was meeting with Wayne about their impending picture *The Shootist.* (It would be the Duke's final film.)

I would think of this chance meeting with Wayne seven years later while talking to Colleen Dewhurst on a film set in Arkansas. She recalled having costarred with Wayne in *McQ* in 1973. "I adored him," she said. One year after making that movie, she won the Tony Award for her lusty performance in the Broadway revival of Eugene O'Neill's *A Moon for the Misbegotten.* The night of the ceremony, she stayed in New York City rather than drive back to her upstate farm an hour away.

The next morning, when she called home to check on her two boys, eleven-year-old Alex answered the phone with the news that Mom had received lots of congratulatory telegrams, all of which he had opened and read. He wanted her to guess the author of one in particular. It stated THEY PICKED THE BEST GIRL, MY LOVE.

"Who do you think that's from?" Alex asked.

"That'll be from John Wayne," Dewhurst told her son.

Alex was amazed. "You're right! It's signed THE DUKE. How did you know?"

The answer came easily. "Because," one of America's most forceful actresses reasoned, "only to Mr. Wayne would I be a girl."

By now, the Duke was back in the room. He thanked us for the use of the hall and went on his way. I confessed to Gilroy that I needed a moment to unwind from the suddenness of this unexpected visitation. To my surprise, he admitted that he was as taken aback as I was. Gilroy and I were strangers, but as we began to talk, that brief encounter with a legend had endowed us with a temporary sense of camaraderie.

From Noon Till Three was my reason for being there. I asked about the novel's evolution.

"This was an idea that I'd been carrying since I was twelve years old," Gilroy said. "Everybody knows about the famous Coffeeville, Kansas, raid with the Daltons and the Youngers. There have been many movies about it. It was the day this gang tried to raid two banks simultaneously. And the gang got wiped out.

"That story's been told. But what interested me when I read it as a child, and what has always interested me, was one member of the gang named Bill Doolin. He became an outlaw of some renown. He had misgivings about the job, but he didn't know how to get out of it. As the gang was on its way to Coffeeville, his horse stumbled and broke a leg. There was no other horse available, so they left him in a farmhouse while they went in.

"What always interested me was: What did Bill Doolin do in that farmhouse? Now, I don't use Bill Doolin or that gang. But my novel is called *From Noon Till Three,* and its jumping-off place is just such an arrangement—an outlaw left behind at a woman's ranch while the rest of the gang goes in to rob a bank.

"After trying to write it various ways, I suddenly saw that telling the woman's version first and the man's version second allowed me to tell the story. But if you try to translate that twice-told tale directly to the screen it does not work at all. So for the film I found a way to tell the story without one flashback, without one voice-over. I tell the whole story from beginning to end and I capture the same essence as the novel."

Charles Bronson and Jill Ireland seemed unlikely actors to be associated with Frank Gilroy material. How did he feel about the film's casting?

"I can frankly say that Charles Bronson and Jill Ireland were not on any list I had when we were casting ideally," Gilroy answered. "But somewhere they came upon the property, liked it, and wanted to star in the film together. Well, that's a tremendous amount of leverage for any project. He's probably the number-one box-office draw in the world. At the same time, I was rather leery of him. If the working styles of a star and his director don't jell, you're in big trouble. So I approached him warily. Because it's a huge commitment. Huge! You're committing a year of your life and your health and your sanity. If a movie goes bad, it's just horrendous. And I have not reached the point where I can walk through anything. I operate from my enthusiasm, and that enthusiasm has to be genuine. I can't falsify it, so I have to be very careful.

"Now I have my picture, I wouldn't trade them for anybody in the world. There are great dividends to the two. They trust each other, and we developed a lovely friendship. It was not easy forming it. I rehearsed them for two weeks, which was crucial to the project."

And something they might not have been used to?

"Not used to and very fearful of. The first day was terrible for all three of us. They were not used to that kind of theater discipline. At lunchtime Charlie said, 'You know, Frank, you do a couple more pictures, and you'll give up this rehearsing stuff.'

"And I said, 'Charlie, I'm hoping that from now on, after this experience, you'll insist on rehearsing.'

"They had a good time doing the film. It's an easy picture to watch. You're meeting me four days before we start to score the music. We're about four weeks away from being ready to preview. And it's worked out lovely. At this point I'm very pleased, but I'm not going to kid you and say it's not a dangerous occupation. It could have gone a different way."

When did Gilroy know he was going to be a writer?

"I never *suddenly* decided," he said. "I just sort of knew it. I think I first started to write when I was fourteen. [He was born in New York City in October 1925.] But I didn't do much about it. When I was in the Army, a couple of my stories got published in the Army newspaper. I was twenty-one when I got to Dartmouth, and then I had a great deal of ambition. That's where it all began for me. I wrote my first plays there. Besides doing good schoolwork, I had two full-length and six or eight one-act plays produced in my last two years. I was in the jazz band. I ran the six-day-a-week newspaper. Plus all the committees. That was the only time in my life I've been as busy or as challenged as when I'm making movies."

The crucible of his life was World War II, during which he served in the Army for two and a half years. In 1957 he wrote *Who'll Save the Plowboy?*, essentially a three-character play about disillusionment among World War II veterans. Produced Off-Broadway in 1962, it ran for fifty-six performances and won an Obie Award.

"Some people say that's my best play," Gilroy suggested. "That play has a lot of uncharted terrain. Even I am not exactly sure of the investment I have in it."

The Subject Was Roses, a three-character drama that also focused on a World War II veteran, opened on Broadway in 1964. The drama bounced from theater to theater for a year before finally winning the Triple Crown (Pulitzer Prize, Tony Award, Drama Critics Award). It eventually ran for 834 performances.

"A lot of people seem to think that we started off, then after a few weeks we caught on," Gilroy said. "That's not really the truth. We caught on enough to live. Then we sort of hovered—and we hovered and we hovered. We were in five different theaters.

"Numerous kooky things happened. At one point we were in the Little Theater, out of money, ready to close, and just then they wanted to break our lease. So to break it they gave us enough money to enable us to move to another theater and run. And that's the way we just kept going. We always paid the actors, but none of the rest of us took anything.

"You see, we opened in late May 1964, right after all the prizes had been awarded, and we felt that if we could last a year we might win those prizes. Finally we waited a year, and then we did win all the prizes, and *then* we really took off. So it took a year. But we always had a good time. It was a project endowed with great love."

What did it mean to win the Triple Crown?

"The box office went up."

But personally? How does reputation affect you? Is anything owed to a playwright after he wins a series of awards?

"I don't know," Gilroy replied. "I don't know. If one goes to Ireland, one feels tremendously like a writer, even if he hasn't done anything well. But if you're a proven writer, there's something very nurturing in the atmosphere there. Here, it's like, what did you do yesterday? What have you done for me recently? That's part of the American ethic, and one just accepts it. Nothing's old in America. You do what you do and you survive however you survive. It's very tough, and if you start thinking that people owe you something, you can go around feeling very sorry for yourself.

"Most of the prizes don't linger. The Pulitzer Prize lingers. It's mentioned anytime anyone introduces you, and you also know that the first line of your obituary in *The New York Times* is already written. Winning the Pulitzer came as a surprise. I don't think I was really thinking about it too much."

Gilroy seemed to be implying that he had no intimation of immortality.

"No, I don't," he concurred. "What's out of my hands is out of my hands. You do the best work you can do, and you try to keep going. Anything beyond that has no meaning for me. That doesn't mean I try any less, but immortality is a wasting concern that defeats you. How the hell can you sit down and write with that on your mind?

"To be honest, as I think about it now, there were a couple years after I won the Pulitzer Prize that did bother me. I don't know if it's immortality, but you're trying to live up to something, maybe to other people's expectations. And those were bad years for me. That's where *That Summer—That Fall* comes from."

Based on the Hippolytus legend, *That Summer—That Fall* starred Jon Voight, Richard Castellano, and Irene Papas. It opened on Broadway in March 1967 and closed twelve performances later.

"That's my least favorite of all my work," Gilroy conceded. "I probably shouldn't have written it. But I thought to myself, 'That's a Greek legend, that's worthy of me.' And it took me a while to get over that. You've *got* to get over it, because it will just kill you. Instead of doing what you want, you're saying, 'That idea isn't big enough for me.' That's a lot of baloney. That's a lot of crap. But the other play I did after *Roses* I like."

The Only Game in Town is a three-character love story about a Las Vegas gambler and a chorus girl. "If I'd been able to eliminate the third character, I would have," said Gilroy, who writes best when he writes tight and lean. Starring Barry Nelson, Tammy Grimes, and Leo Genn, it opened in May 1968 and closed after sixteen performances.

"It's a funny thing about that play," Gilroy said. "Suddenly it has started to surface. It was *the* hit of Paris last year. It was a big hit in Germany. It opens soon in six other countries. The play is taking on a whole new life. I flew over to see the two hundred and fiftieth performance in Paris. Now that I've seen it again, I can say that it's really a lovely play. There's nothing deep about it, but it's very pleasing to watch. If done properly, it's rather moving. My interest in it has been rekindled."

The Subject Was Roses is a "highly autobiographical" play. But what about *The Only Game in Town*, whose protagonist is a gambler? Did that play come from Gilroy's past?

"I spent time in Las Vegas," he quietly replied. "I never lived there, but . . ." His voice trailed off in the first lengthy pause of the afternoon. ". . . gambling was a large part of my life at one point. The research for that play was very costly. I said to somebody, 'I wrote the play to break even.' "

Gilroy next returned to the material he understood best, World War II, but not for the theater. In 1970 he published an intensely personal book titled *Private.* It is an accumulation of brief, present-tense, almost flashlike memories, sparely told (sometimes in just one sentence), that take a youth from Army induction through the war in Europe and home again. *Private* almost seems to have been written *for* its author. Surely Gilroy could not have envisioned large sales?

"No," he agreed with a laugh. "I never think that way. The best rule I ever heard is: Please yourself, and hope you'll please someone else. I know no other way to operate. I'm very open to opinions. In a movie, particularly, you have to be. I'll change anything if someone can convince me that they have a better line, a better thought. But my starting point is always that I have to please myself. It stops you from going crazy, because to try to guess what critics are going to like, or what the public's going to like, would be suicidal. I'd have nothing to cling to.

"*Private* was the most personal thing I've ever done. I was always fascinated by Brady's wet-plate photography in the Civil War. So I thought I would try to construct in words—I almost called it *Wet Plates* at one point instead of *Private*—word-pictures that would be as vivid as photos. I would distill my brain and what I remembered I would put into words. Exact words. Never an extra word. They would be like snapshots, and yet they would have a cumulative effect.

"How can I tell you how hard I worked? Seven years! I mean, six months would go by and then I would have a burst. I could go for a week sometimes and at the end of the week have one sentence. I'm thinking of one just now that I remember I spent a lot of time on. It will sound so goddamned simple. 'As we leave the town, the church bell sounds. The world fills in behind us.' Now, you'll never know what that cost me. We were a reconnaissance troop, and as we would leave some German town, they would ring the church bells and the people would come out of their houses. So, 'As we leave the town, the church bell sounds. The world fills in behind us.' You'll never guess the amount of time and blood and guts invested in that book.

"I didn't expect it to be a best-seller, but the small sale was a disappointment. It's not now, because it has a very narrow but continuing life. Some teachers use it. But it was hardly reviewed. I've seen three reviews. Yet people who like it will go out of their way to write me. They'll say I touched their experience. You know, writing that book was the most difficult task, and I defeated myself because I made it look so simple and easy that people thought I must have whipped through it.

"I'll tell you an analogy that has occurred to me. Years ago, when I was a kid in the Bronx, the only way the billiard champ of the world could make money was to tour. He'd come to the local poolrooms once or twice a year and play a local hero.

"When I was eleven or twelve, the world's champ was a man named Conti. And one afternoon Conti came up to our poolroom. I remember his tuxedo and his manager. And he played our guy. So our guy ran a few balls, and Conti then took over. He's running off these balls, and suddenly we start to lose respect for him. The reason we're losing respect is that every shot Conti makes, we could have made. This one's easy, that one's easy, the next one's easy. Until finally, of course, it dawns on you that the art of it was that he controlled the cue ball so perfectly that he was always left with a shot where this one's easy, that one's easy, the next one's easy.

"And sometime after I'd done *Private,* and I had this same sort of reception, I thought, 'My God, Frank, what they don't know is that to make it seem simple is where the art comes from.' But I tell you, when I was most discouraged about *Private,* I would always cling to the idea that if I accomplished nothing more, it would be a legacy for my great-grandchildren."

Another disappointment in 1970 was the film version of *The Only Game in Town*, for which Gilroy had written the screenplay.

"George Stevens directed it. We used to go hunting locations, and George was always giving me his viewfinder. I said, 'Why are you doing that?'

"And George said, 'You're going to direct one day. I can tell.'

"A very shrewd man. He had an intuitive intelligence. I learned a lot from him. That was his last picture, and he wasn't in the best health. He had tremendous odds. They never should have gone to Paris to do it, and Elizabeth Taylor was ill during the filming. But that film clinched it for me. I thought, 'I can handle movie directing.' "

So he directed *Desperate Characters*, based on the novel by Paula Fox. Typical of so many Gilroy projects, this somber portrait of an upper-middle-class New York City couple battling alienation was a solid film, not a popular film.

"That was no great surprise or disappointment," he said. "I knew going in that it was an intellectual sort of picture. To ensure ourselves against this, we made it for so little that the movie ended up in profit. I made that whole picture—with Shirley MacLaine and unions and everything—for $350,000."

Some critics have called this MacLaine's best performance. "Yes, I've heard that too," the director confirmed. "I shouldn't be the one to say it, but it pleases me when I hear it. In addition to Shirley we had two excellent actors, Ken Mars and Gerald O'Loughlin, and a fantastic actress, Sada Thompson. I can't say enough about Sada."

What company made the film?

"These things happen by fluke, by accident, which is the way most good things happen. I was trying to raise money for the film, and I had a screenwriter friend named John Gay who was up in Oregon doing *Sometimes a Great Notion* with Paul Newman. John

Gay and his wife are our closest friends, so we'd been up there visiting them.

"I had the screenplay with me, and John liked it. He said, 'Leave a copy. I want to look at it again.'

" 'Well,' I said, 'don't show it to anybody. Until I get the money, what's the sense?' And I took my boys down the Colorado River and disappeared from the world for ten days.

"When you surface, you come up in Las Vegas. When I told Paula Fox that, she said, 'Oh, Frank, that must be like getting hit in the face with the laundry of the world.'

"So John Gay called me in Las Vegas. He said, 'You're going to be mad. I've been a bad boy. I showed your script to somebody, and she wants to do it. Big star.'

"So I said, 'Who?'

"He said, 'Shirley MacLaine. She was up here visiting and she heard about it and finally she—' She can be very persuasive, Shirley. So he said, 'Aren't you excited?'

"I said, 'I've never met her, but Shirley MacLaine in this role? What the hell do I want to do a picture like that? She's a little dancer.'

"So he said, 'Well, think it over overnight.'

"The next morning I called him. I didn't have any of the money ready but I thought, 'What the hell's the sense of doing a picture if I'm going to do it wrong?' So I said, 'John, thank her, but I'm going to pass.'

"And John Gay said, 'Do what you want to do. You're going to do that anyway. But you know I like the script. I'm telling you she can do it.'

"Now, from my friend that's a very big endorsement. So I said, 'John, I'm going to L.A. right away.' That's where she was then. So I came out here and spent several days with her. Right away I could see that I had the wrong impression of her. She's a full-blown woman, very bright, nothing like the featherbrained twits she used to play.

"So finally I said, 'Look, you want to do it. You game on me, I'll game on you. We'll go together.'

"Then, of course, everybody wanted to give me the money. But she was doing a television series with Sir Lew Grade in England. For him, $350,000 was like nothing. 'Yeah, go ahead. Go ahead and do it,' he said. So we did it, and it was a very happy experience.

"It was all location. Things that would take them a week to film out here—in New York they'd set up the cameras on Fifth Avenue, I'd say, 'Go, Shirley, go,' and she'd walk down the street. We got all the traffic shots in six minutes.

"It was very funny when we took it over to England to run it for Lew Grade. I remember being in the screening room with him and his saying, 'My God, those cars! I thought for my money I'd get two people sitting in a room. Look at that!' "

What is it that makes a man grow up in the theater, then say, 'I want to try something else,' and go into the movies?

"Every playwright would have to answer that for himself. With me, it's a very natural thing. After all, I grew up going to movies. I didn't come to plays until I was nineteen or twenty.

"The point is, plays or movies, I'm still primarily a writer. I'm only a director as it grows out of my writing. I simply found I was spending more and more time working in movies and I wasn't enjoying it. Writing for films is a very limited experience. It's not like a play. With a play, to be the writer is to make a total investment and to have total control. But if you're just the writer of a movie, if any part of your vision ends up on the screen it's a miracle, because it goes through so many people, so many filters.

"It comes down to a unity of vision. Groups don't have visions. A person has a vision. The initial and essential vision, if you're the writer, is yours. Then, if you're also the director, you can really make that vision come through. In future, any film I'm interested enough to write, I'll also direct. Though I have no desire to direct my own plays."

Those were the cerebral reasons, the rational explanations. But Gilroy went on to describe the visceral satisfaction of directing.

"For me, film-directing is a very personal and private thing," he said. "It's a supreme adventure! It's the physical adventure I've been looking for, the way other people want to climb mountains.

"All my life I've been looking for something that would challenge me completely. Writing challenges you physically as well. But there was always some other part of me left over. And let's face it. If you're a playwright, you get a genuine play idea—if you're lucky—every four years or so. And you do them pretty swiftly when they're good. That leaves great gaps of time. What do you do with that time? There was a large part of me that was not being used and which was then using me destructively.

"So finding the directing thing—it's the headiest trip in the world. And if it's your own writing, and if it's going well, it's the headiest adventure." Gilroy broke into a hearty laugh, then, in almost giddy frustration, added, "I can't tell you what it's like.

"Also, directing really replenishes me as a writer. Because suddenly I'm out with people. It complements the lonely part of my life as a writer beautifully.

"You're seeing me now after a very good experience. You're seeing me also tired. I feel rather depleted. Now I need a rest time to build up, because it takes so much out of you physically. But I finally have found something that challenges my energy."

Two hours had elapsed since we'd begun to talk. As I prepared to leave, I asked one final question. Had Gilroy thought beyond his current project?

"No," he answered. "I have a policy: I never make a commitment in advance. It's interesting that now I'm getting about one offer every week to write and direct movies. You don't know how the word gets out, because we've hardly shown this film to a soul. But I'm not looking for another job.

"Everything you do, if you do it wholeheartedly, changes you. And in the midst of changing, you should be very careful what you commit yourself to. So now I want to go home. I haven't been home in six months. I want to take a couple of months to get my head straightened out. Plus, I have a couple things I might want to write."

Gilroy looked across the desk with a satisfied grin and said, "My whole life has been improvisation. My strength has always been that I have no image. It's a great strength. I don't say it kiddingly. I like Arthur Miller and I like Edward Albee. But they're both burdened by a certain image. Do you think they can go out and do a Western? I can do whatever the hell I want. I've busted every rule, so no matter what I do it doesn't surprise anybody. Now I just do what makes me feel good."

Something went wrong with *From Noon Till Three.* Its release was delayed by more than a year. Then, though it garnered good reviews, United Artists couldn't figure out how to sell it: It was too sophisticated for the Charles Bronson audience, and the sophisticated crowd couldn't be induced to attend a Bronson movie. So the perplexed distributor all but threw the film away.

Nevertheless, two years later, in 1978, Gilroy was back busting the rules again. He released another picture, which he had produced, directed, and written. This time he distributed it too. *Once in*

Paris . . . , with Wayne Rogers starring as a Gilroy-like screenwriter, found a small but devoted following.

In 1979 the playwright was back on Broadway. *Last Licks,* starring Ed Flanders, lasted fifteen performances.

In 1985 he released yet another small film. *The Gig* also starred Wayne Rogers. Again, theater releases were minimal (though the film found an appreciative audience on cable).

And so it went.

In 1991, when the Roundabout Theatre Company mounted a new production of the Pulitzer prize–winning play *The Subject Was Roses,* a brief article in *The New York Times* identified Gilroy as the author of three novels and as the writer-director of five films. The column then quoted the writer as saying, "I'd like to walk into a room sometime and be introduced as the author of something other than that play."

Perhaps that's why Gilroy was so giving during our conversation. We had more to talk about than just *that play.*

Then too, John Wayne didn't hurt a bit.

CHAPTER FOUR

WINNERS AND LOSERS

"In terms of the Hollywood hierarchy, I suppose I have more power than a makeup man."
—WILLIAM GOLDMAN

"If you're an unknown writer—and also a woman, I might add—you can say something, but, my God, that doesn't mean anybody listens to you."
—MARY MERCIER

Early in J. D. Salinger's *The Catcher in the Rye*, when Holden Caulfield has read Isak Dinesen's *Out of Africa*, he says, "What really knocks me out is a book that when you're all done reading it, you wish the author that wrote it was a terrific friend of yours and you could call him up on the phone whenever you felt like it. That doesn't happen much, though."

No, it doesn't happen often. But it happened to me in 1969, when I read *The Season*, William Goldman's mercilessly candid examination of Broadway. And it's happened again, nearly every time I've read one of his books.

I was eager to talk to him. But, although he's not your J. D. Salinger–caliber recluse, I was unable to make contact. I pretty much gave up trying.

Then, in September 1976, a minor miracle. Or at least, a major coincidence. After reviewing Goldman's newest thriller, *Magic*, for the *St. Louis Post-Dispatch*, I received a congratulatory letter from his mother in Chicago. A friend of hers who lived in St. Louis had mailed her my review.

I promptly wrote back, acknowledged her kind words, and casually mentioned that I'd like to talk with her son but did not know how to reach him.

Mrs. Goldman mailed me her son's home and office addresses and phone numbers. "I hope you meet him, he's very nice," the loving mother wrote. She then added, "But *don't* tell him where you got this information!"

In early 1977, prior to my next trip to New York, I wrote to Goldman. In my letter, I mentioned how his enthusiastic endorsement of the ill-fated play *Johnny No-Trump* had kindled my interest in Mary Mercier's drama. (In *The Season*, Goldman champions *Johnny No-Trump*, which closed after one performance, as "the best new American play of the [1967–68] season." I read the play and shared his conviction. In 1972, when I was working at the Cleveland Play House, we mounted its first professional production outside New York City.)

Five days after I had mailed the letter, my telephone in St. Louis rang: "This is William Goldman. I have your letter. I haven't given any interviews in seven months, and I don't like giving them at all. But I'll talk to you because of *Johnny No-Trump*."

He was that abrupt.

I asked if we could set up an appointment.

"Oh no," he answered. "I'd only get nervous and find a way of backing out. Here's my phone number. Call me when you get to New York."

We spoke briefly about the Broadway play *Blood, Sweat and Stanley Poole*, which he wrote with his brother James in 1960 ("I've blocked it out of my mind"), but he was uncomfortable engaging in small talk, and the call soon ended.

When I arrived in New York that February, I phoned.

"You want to do this thing today?" he asked with apparent resignation.

Sure.

"Come at two."

Goldman maintains an office in a residential Upper East Side highrise. When the elevator doors opened on the twenty-second floor, I was confronted by a gloomy forty-five-year-old author. He looked like a contemporary Sydney Carton awaiting the guillotine. Clad in a brown turtleneck sweater and brown slacks, Goldman was a tall, handsome man with bushy graying hair, hound-dog eyes that could look very sad indeed, and a drooping mustache that on this day seemed to be drooping more than usual. Even before I emerged from the elevator, it was clear that Goldman was unhappy about my presence.

As we walked down the corridor to his apartment, he cynically lamented, "There are only two reasons to give an interview. One is for me to say nasty things about other people. The other is for you to advance your career." It was the only cynicism of the afternoon; everything else he said was straight-on, direct, and honest.

After I had absorbed his splendid East River view, Goldman began to talk about this penthouse suite in which we now self-consciously sat.

"I've been a writer for a long time now," he said, "and often people say to you, 'It must be very lonely,' meaning, 'Ah yes, communing with your thoughts.' And that's bullshit. What's hard about writing is being alone in the room physically. The silence.

"I don't do many interviews because I don't like them. As I just said, you end up saying things that hurt people. That's really the problem. If I keep a low profile, it's not unintentional. But I remember once there was a reporter here from a British paper, and I made this same simpleminded point about the silence. This happens to be a quiet room, that's why I have it. I said to him, 'Let's both of us sit for thirty seconds. We'll just be silent, and you'll see what I mean.'

"And a few seconds later he said, 'Ah yes, I can—'

"I said, 'No, no. You're not being quiet. Just let's sit.' And he couldn't. Reporters, you see, are basically social. They go out and they *talk* to people and they go back and they write 'em up. But for me, it's hard to write all the time. It's the silence."

The longer the book, I reasoned, the more consuming the silence. I asked Goldman if his massive *Boys and Girls Together* had been the most difficult of his novels to write.

"Yes," he confirmed. "It's more than six hundred pages. It's my only long novel. I will never write another. My first three books had not been long, and I wrote it because I thought it would be interesting—said he naively—to try and write a long novel, because it has different problems. Long novels are harder than short novels, in terms of brute work. They take years. But as you age, you change, so your point of view toward your characters also shifts.

"I wrote *Boys and Girls Together* because, at the time, all of my friends were screwing up in New York, it seemed. It was going badly for everybody. The city was . . . affecting all of us, and I wanted to get that down.

"But writing that novel was a horrendous experience. It was three years of my life, off and on. I wrote maybe the first three hundred pages, then I stopped. I knew I was going to have to stop. I did a play and a musical on Broadway, and that took a year. Then, when I went back to the novel, I found that I was blocked. I no longer knew how to do it. I couldn't get back into it.

"And one day I was reading the *Daily News*. The Boston strangler was current at that time, and this newspaper article offered the new theory that maybe there were two stranglers. And the notion hit me, 'What if there were? And what if one got jealous of the other?'

"And as I walked to my office, which was literally a five-minute walk—this has never happened to me before—the book simply jumped into my head. Start to finish. The whole thing. *No Way to Treat a Lady*. And I remember getting to my office and frantically scribbling down an enormous number of chapters. Then I talked with some friends who knew of my problem. I said, 'This novel just happened. Do you think I should try and write it, or am I getting farther away from *Boys and Girls Together*?' And the decision was, give it two weeks. If you can do the book in two weeks, you'll at least be grooved again. And if you take more than two weeks, you'll be putting yourself off. In other words, I knew it would be a short novel.

"There's a point to all I'm saying. At any rate, I wrote the book very quickly. I then was unblocked. I then was writing again. I went on to finish *Boys and Girls Together*. And *No Way to Treat a Lady* became the way I got into the movie business. It was like a hundred-and-fifty-page novel with fifty chapters. Cliff Robertson must have read it in galleys or typed up somewhere, because he somehow thought it was a screen treatment, and he came to me with a beautiful short story called 'Flowers for Algernon' and asked me to write the movie. I had always been a movie nut, and I said that if I liked the story I would be very flattered to.

"I read the story and I *loved* the story, and I tried to write the screenplay. I wrote the first draft. He read it, *immediately* fired me, hired another writer, did a *totally* different thing. The movie's title was *Charly*, and Robertson won the Academy Award."

* * *

"I never fired Bill," Cliff Robertson countered during a chance meeting in Ixtapa, Mexico, just prior to this book's publication. "Here's what happened. Back in the late 1950s I did several shows on live television, things like *Days of Wine and Roses* and *The Hustler*, that went to other actors when they were made into movies. I came to the conclusion that in order to get a great role, I had to develop it for myself. So I optioned the short story 'Flowers for Algernon,' by Daniel Keyes.

"I met Bill through my distant cousin, Carol Hall, the composer. I paid him thirty thousand dollars out of my own pocket, which was no small sum twenty-five years ago. I remember that after Bill finished his script, I picked it up and he asked, 'Do you want to read it right here?' I said I had another commitment. I left, walked two blocks, went into a delicatessen, and immediately sat down and read the script.

"It wasn't at all right, so I let the matter drop. Several months later, on the very day when I finally got the project moving, I had a call from Bill, who offered to do a rewrite of his original script, for free. I thought it was a wonderful gesture. I told him, 'I wish I could, because I believe in your belief. But I just today shook hands with Stirling Silliphant, who's agreed to write the script.' Bill understood and gracefully bowed out. But I never fired him."

The two accounts are in essential agreement. Robertson's disclaimer only concerns the use of the word *fired*. So are we dealing here in semantics? To a degree. But it's also a painful reminder that silence can be deafening, not only during the tortuous process of writing, but also during the excruciating periods after the writing is done.

But back to William Goldman. As he recalled his dealings with Cliff Robertson, suddenly this reluctant interviewee seemed to be unblocked from talking. While I didn't want to discourage him, I had to point out that he hadn't yet explained how he got into the movies.

"I can go even more," he continued. "I got into the movie business *because* I wrote the first draft of 'Flowers for Algernon.' In the middle of that, Robertson had contracted for a movie. I'm going back about ten years, so it's hard to remember this clearly. But I think he had contracted for a movie that originally was written for

Rex Harrison, and they needed to have Robertson's dialogue Americanized. He had not yet read my screenplay of 'Flowers for Algernon,' but he insisted that I do the job.

"So I went to London, and I Americanized the movie, which eventually was called *Masquerade.* I wrote Robertson's part and did some other doctoring. While I was over there, *Boys and Girls Together* was published, and a producer took a movie option on it. Just then there was a current movie called *The Professionals*, and this producer said, 'I'd like to make a ballsy movie like *The Professionals.*'

"And I said, because I was a nut for this writer, 'Read Ross Macdonald. If you like him, I will find a Ross Macdonald story and do a screenplay for you.' He called me after the weekend and said, 'I like Ross Macdonald very much.' So I reread all the Ross Macdonalds, like a jerk, working backwards, until I finally got to his first Lew Archer book, *The Moving Target*, which became *Harper.*

"And that was basically how I got into the movie business. Once *Harper* happened, I was simply involved in it, and I've been involved in it more or less ever since. Sometimes I get too involved in it. But in my mind I'm secretly, inside myself, a novelist who happens to write screenplays. One of the few things that's very pleasant about writing is that screenplays give me something else to do between books."

Goldman made a clear distinction between his two careers.

"You have to," he emphasized. "Screenwriting is a world unto its own, with different values. One of the things that I like to make very clear is, you must never confuse the good, the true, and the beautiful with successful screenwriting. Good and bad is not important in the movie business. All that's important is successful or unsuccessful. Lots of marvelous movies fail at the box office, and lots of pieces of shit are very successful. And a lot of people get mixed up, because they think that because they've had a success, they also have quality.

"That happens to a lot of those people out there. That's one of the reasons I don't like it out there. One of the terrifying things about being 'hot' in Southern California is that you can lunch for a year on deals, and it has nothing to do with writing. The deal becomes obsessive. It's a terrific place for producers, but it's not a good place for writers."

Prodding the Goldman chronology forward, I reminded him that his next script after *Harper* was *Butch Cassidy and the Sundance Kid.*

"No," he corrected. "That's the next one that got done. I did two that were not made, a *Harper* sequel and the adaptation of a really good, tough novel by Stephen Linakis called *In the Springtime the War Ended*, about deserters in World War II.

"What happened to that movie is a typical Hollywood story. The studio, Twentieth Century–Fox, approved *everything*. They spent a lot of money on it. Then, when we were just about to go down to the wire, they said to the producer, 'We have to cancel, because we're making a very expensive movie called *Patton*, and we need all the military cooperation we can get.' The military, I gather, was not very happy with Linakis' story about deserters."

But don't you now have the power to get that screenplay filmed? I innocently asked.

"No," Goldman fired back. "I have no power whatever."

With one success after another, you can't take a screenplay someplace and—?

"In terms of the Hollywood hierarchy, I suppose I have more power than a makeup man. But in terms of actual power, of what I call go-power, the muscle, being able to make something happen, a screenwriter is only very, very occasionally the muscle. Neil Simon. That's unusual, because Neil's *just* a screenwriter. He's not a 'hyphenate.' There are a lot of writer-producers or writer-directors, who will be the muscle. But I don't ever want to be—"

A director?

"Oh! Never! The *only* thing that is unusual about me is that I would rather die than try and be a film director."

At this point I read a statement by Frank D. Gilroy into the record: "The initial and essential vision, if you're the writer, is yours. Then, if you're also the director, you can really make that vision come through."

Goldman slid away from the quote, acknowledging, "It works for Frank. First of all, I can't do it. Second, I don't know how to deal with actors. I have no desire to deal with actors. Third, in my heart, as I said, I'm not really a screenwriter. I'm *really* a novelist. I have a certain facility for screenwriting."

Recalling Gilroy's comment about all the filters a screenplay must hurdle, I asked Goldman if he ever was bothered by his "vision" not ending up on the screen.

"Look," he replied, hammering home his point of view, "I *do not choose* to be a director. I do not choose to be a producer. I choose to be basically a gun for hire. You can hire me, and I'll do a screenplay for you, and if you want to use it, you use it. If you don't, you hire somebody else. I will make you a total commitment for doing what you hired me for. I've never done a screenplay I haven't wanted to do.

"The reality is, I'm only involved in a certain part of the film-making process. If I *wanted* my quote, vision, unquote, up there I would try and do more. The reality is, I don't want it."

Goldman's reference to his limited role led me to wonder if he ever was on the set during filming.

"This is personal with me," he said. "I don't think I belong on the set. I think I make people nervous.

"How can I put this? It's basically an adversary situation between a writer and a director, okay? Directors like to think that what the papers print about them is true. They like to think that they're really brilliant and magnificent and all things to all people. They *don't* like writers a lot because (a) we tend, many of us, to write better than they do; and (b) we are a constant reminder that it's not their baby. I very often have had arguments with people, and my relationship is not very strong by the time that we actually go to the floor."

What does that mean, go to the floor?

"Shoot. You can divide a movie into three parts. The first part is the writing and the casting. Casting is crucial. If you miscast a film, you can try and salvage it, but it's not gonna work. The third part is the editing and the scoring, and the middle part is the shooting. As a general rule, a lot of people would say that the middle part's the least important.

"Being on the floor is also very boring. The most exciting day of your life is your first day on a movie set, and the dullest day of your life is your second day on a movie set. It's so slow and so technical, and you want to die 'cause there's nothing to do. You just sit there.

"But movies are basically a bruising operation. Plays are too. I once spent a day with Moss Hart. He was at the peak of his career, and a very charming man. And he said, 'You know, I was involved with *My Fair Lady*. It's the biggest hit of all time,' which it was at that point. And he said, 'I think I'm the only one who's still speaking to everybody.' Well, that's not unusual. It's not just in failures that people end up not speaking to people.

"Any group endeavor is bruising. You get your feelings hurt, and no one is ever armed. In a group endeavor you have to try to get rid of your ego. Otherwise you're gonna get killed. Movies, of course, are very much a group endeavor. This is the basic truth that nobody understands, because they don't want to understand. People are always looking for heroes. They want to think that it really *is* a film by Otto Preminger. Well, that's madness. It's not a film by anybody. It's a film by about a dozen of us. All of us are important. And who is most important varies from film to film. I'm very significant in a film that I'm involved with. But so's the cameraman, and so's the cutter, and so's the director, and so are the performers, and so's the producer. When you think a movie is good, or a movie moves you, it's because the *mix* worked. If the mix works, you're lucky."

You might not feel you belong on a film set, but as a playwright you certainly would belong in the theater during rehearsals.

"Absolutely. But in the theater the words are crucial. There's a whole misconception about moviemaking in general, but about screenwriting particularly. People think that what the screenwriter does is make up the dialogue. And sometimes that's true, and sometimes it's not. Dialogue is not usually terribly important in a movie. There are very few *All About Eve*s, where the dialogue is crucial.

"For the most part, what makes a movie work is if you've structured it properly so that it has a rising line and goes from A to Z without people getting confused. What's really important is the emotion of the character."

Still flaunting my naiveté, I suggested that one of the reasons *Butch Cassidy* was a hit was because it was so funny. We had never before seen a Western with such clever writing.

"I don't mean to say that dialogue is unimportant," Goldman clarified, "but a lot of things made *Butch* successful. George Hill directed it beautifully. It was a beautiful-*looking* movie. The casting of the two men was extraordinarily fortuitous. Katharine Ross was terribly helpful."

But didn't William Goldman receive the highest fee ever paid a screenwriter up to that time because someone knew the material was good?

"That screenplay went out twice," he said. "The first time was about a year before it was sold. The version that was sold was more compact, but the first version was essentially there. It began the same place, ended the same place. Same story. And everybody said, 'Don't send them to South America. John Wayne does not run away. A Western hero stands and fights the Superposse.' What everybody said was, 'When they're chased by the Superposse they should get their gang together and have a big shootout.'

"And I said, 'But the whole thing was, they went to South America and made it happen all over again.'

"And they said, 'We don't care what really happened. Western heroes don't run away. This is a Western without a confrontation scene. It's a Western with very little action.'

"Now, none of those things were set about by me intentionally when I began to write it. I was very moved by their story, emotionally. I'd read about them in a book in the late 1950s, and I thought, 'Gee, how sad that these two strangely talented people should have died in that terrible place not knowing the language.' And the length of that journey—emotionally, not geographically—I found very touching. And I researched them for years and years. I worked on it for years and years.

"I remember, the summer before we started shooting we were talking with George Roy Hill. And what I wanted for *Butch Cassidy* was that in twenty or thirty years when people talked about *Shane* and *The Gunfighter* and *High Noon*, I wanted them to mention *Butch* . . ." He paused, almost embarrassed at having verbalized such a lofty ambition to a stranger. Then he rallied and continued.

"That was the image that you go for. Sure, the dialogue is helpful. It's a very competent screenplay. But it ain't art, and it must never be thought of as art. Now, I'm not trying to shit-kick here. Obviously, I get paid what I get paid because I do a certain job, and I think I do it competently. But I won't go any further than that."

So on the one hand you sit here telling me you're only competent, but at the same time you want the finished product to be a classic.

"I want it to be as good as it can be *of its kind*. I'm not denigrating screenwriting. But it's a craft, like carpentry."

I asked the screenwriter if he expected to be nominated for an Academy Award for *All the President's Men*.

"That's out of my hands."

If you're not nominated next week, will that bother you?

"We'll have to see what happens. One of the only healthy things I've ever done was when I won for *Butch*. I was watching the awards on television. I did not think I was going to win, because *Bob and Carol and Ted and Alice* had won the critics' award in New York. And when my name was announced, I remember the *first* thought that went through my head—and this is really true—was, I thought, 'Thank God, now I never have to win it again.' And that was *instant*. So any awards additionally that one gets, obviously it's very flattering.

"It's better to be nominated than not to be nominated. It's better to win than not to win. But the reality is, you can't take awards too seriously or you'll make the fatal mistake of taking *yourself* too seriously. It's so wonderful to believe you're wonderful, but you must not do it or you will go crazy.

"Going back to that day with Moss Hart, he said to me: 'I've done a lot of theater work. I've written and produced and directed. But every time I go out of town with a show, I get sideswiped by something I hadn't expected.' And basically I think that's true. I think every time you sit down to write a novel, it's really the first time.

"The life of a creative artist is very tenuous. You never know when it's over, and you always have that sense of panic. You always continue to think, 'Jesus Christ, what if I *don't* get this done? What if I've written my last book?' So if you begin to take yourself too seriously, it can be *very* dangerous."

Then what criteria do you use to measure your own standards of quality?

"I'm peculiar. I don't like most of my writing. There's usually one scene in each book that I like a lot, that I think, 'Gee, I'm proud of that.' But not much more. If you've read a great deal, as most of us have, you're aware of what a really marvelous novel is. You've read the Russians, and you've read those people whose writing thrills you. And you have your own story in your head. Then, when you put it down on paper, it comes out like toothpaste." He pressed his right thumb against the air, as if he were trying to squeeze toothpaste from an empty, twisted tube.

What's the one scene in *Marathon Man* that you're especially proud of?

"The one scene I like in the novel is the run, when the two fantasy figures come down and flank Babe and run with him. Now, that's not the way it is in the movie, although that's the way I wrote it in the script's first draft. But John Schlesinger, who directed the movie and who is a consummate craftsman, did not like it because he felt he could not make it play. Now, that is not in any way, shape, or form an iota of criticism. What I mean is, we *all* of us only deal with what we can make play. John felt, and he may well have been right, that the run in the book is a literary conceit and wouldn't play in the movie. He felt, and I think he *may* be right, it was a break in style. We hadn't set up in the course of the film that the Dustin Hoffman character has these fantasy figures.

"Even somebody as gifted and as serious as Schlesinger is still just like anybody else. We all of us deal with what we can make play. In my own case, I have a sense of structure, and I have an ear for dialogue, and that's all I've ever really had any confidence in. I have been asked, 'Has movie writing affected your novel writing?' and I don't think it has. As far back as my first novel, it's all dialogue.

"If you came to me and said, 'You must write a sequence in a book in which you describe two women on a shopping spree. They can't talk much, but you have to describe their clothes and what they buy and what Madison Avenue looks like,' I would panic. Because (a) I don't write women particularly well. And (b) I don't know what clothes are like. But John Updike, who writes *so* brilliantly, has the most phenomenal vocabulary and can describe anything. He could write that sequence standing on his ear.

"What I'm saying is, we all of us have our strength. We deal with what we can make play. Schlesinger told me he didn't believe that scene. I think basically what he felt was that he did not believe he could make the audience believe it."

Did Schlesinger's decision make you wish you had a different director?

"No. You're very lucky to have somebody that gifted on a piece of material like that. All you can hope for in the movies is that you have somebody who's serious, who isn't just doing it because he needs the job. Because there are so few people who *are* talented, they're usually busy in advance. I mean, whatever the successes or failures of *Marathon Man*, that's Laurence Olivier playing that part. There's a lot of talent in *Marathon Man*. It's a very classy picture."

What has been your biggest film disappointment?

"It's hard to say. I don't expect much. A movie that I think could have been very strong, but it was rewritten and altered, and I don't think happily, was *The Stepford Wives*."

Your name is still on the film, but you don't include it in your list of credits.

"That's correct. I left my name on, because I had been paid a lot of money for that, and I felt it would have been bad form for me to do otherwise. I find it loathsome when you see performers bitching about a film they're in while the film is still current. If you're being paid a million dollars, your job is to shut up. Let the man who's given you all that money try to have a return on his investment. Then you can say, a year or two later, 'No, I did not like the film.' "

I asked Goldman about the evolution of his theater chronicle *The Season*.

"*The Season* I wrote because I had gotten too deeply involved in movies. I had made a ton of money on *Butch*. I wanted to get away. I didn't have a novel, and I thought, 'Gee, wouldn't it be nice to try and write some nonfiction.' Originally, I just wanted to write an article. The first idea I had was—this is how things develop—I was at that time a great fan of Good Humors, and they were coming out with all kinds of new and different flavors. And I got the idea of interviewing the Good Humor man who invents the new flavors and new coatings, as if he were some kind of mad scientist. So I called up Good Humor, and I got to the public-relations man, and I explained what I wanted. He said, 'I'll get back to you.' He never got back to me, because I realized he thought I was a nut.

"Then I got an idea of writing about the various private sanitariums in this country as if they were colleges sending out recruitment brochures. 'We think you will like it here at . . .' It was going to be called 'The Hatches.' In the middle of it, I realized that the most famous was Menninger's, and if Menninger's didn't go along with me I would have no article. And then I thought, 'Shit, what can I write about that no one can stop me on?' And I'd been involved with the theater, and I knew that in the theater there was always somebody who would talk.

"For the original article, I wanted to interview everybody who was involved with a show in an important position, before and after. But I realized very early on that all failures have the same song. It's always a case of people not communicating, people not understanding, people lying. It's always the same wail, and I realized that my premise was not valid. But by this time I was into it. It became obsessive, and it evolved into whatever *The Season* is.

"*The Season* I enjoyed writing. I don't *like* writing very much. But doing *The Season* was social. I was interviewing people all over town. People would call up and say, 'I can see you for twenty minutes now,' and I'd run over. And I loved it, because I wasn't *here*, sitting alone in this office."

When I suggested that there had never been a theater book with the gut honesty and insight of *The Season*, Goldman said, "I hate, loathe, and despise most writing about show business, because it's so false and the writers are so ignorant and uncaring. They just want to say, 'Sissy Spacek is the hottest girl in Hollywood,' as if that's some sort of justification. So I was determined to write as honest a book as I could. It was a year and a half of my life, and a lot of people still won't speak to me because of that book, and it really shocked me.

"I was so shocked by people's responses I stopped going to the theater. For about five years I didn't go at all. I had hoped that somebody would say, 'Well, at least it's down now. This is what Broadway is like at this point in time.' And it was, for the most part, atrociously reviewed—as I am generally in New York—and so many people *hated* it, and hated *me* for writing it, I just simply pulled back."

You stopped going to the theater because you were afraid to run into people?

"I think that had a lot to do with it. I mean, there were actresses who would say, 'If I ever see him, I'll hit him.' Things like that. There was a wild reaction to it. It was very difficult for me to move in that area."

I reminded Goldman that *The Season* introduced me to Mary Mercier's lovely play *Johnny No-Trump*, which had died aborning. What happened there? I asked.

"I think it was just the fact that the play came in so quietly. It had no power connected with it. Sada Thompson was not then Sada Thompson. And Pat Hingle was what he always is, which is a good, solid actor, but he doesn't sell tickets like Rosalind Russell. So the critics were allowed to pick at it. That same play, word for word, wouldn't have been any better done if it had come in as a David Merrick production, with Elia Kazan direction, and a star. But it's my contention that if the play had come in with power, then people would have overlooked any flaws, because those who saw it were so moved by it.

"But you always tend to want to not like things in the theater if they're serious. There was a great story about *Death of a Salesman* where the husband turned to the wife and said, 'I'll get you for this.' Most of us really want to laugh and sing and dance and not be told that life can be sad."

Some critics carped about the mother's unexpected death at the end of the play. Was that its fatal flaw?

"No. Had *Johnny No-Trump* been an Arthur Miller play, had it been Harold Pinter, the critics would have said, 'Do you see the mastery of having the sudden flash of reality at the end? Life is a mystery, and there is no future because of the possibility of sudden death. That's what Pinter is telling us.'

"What I find so painful is that critics don't realize that you can say pretty much what you want to say about Harold Robbins or Barbra Streisand, and they will survive. But when you're dealing with a new writing talent, a young talent, the possibility and the daydreams of success are so great that when they fail it can be so terrifying that they'll never go to bat again. Always the critic's first responsibility ought to be toward the artist, but especially so with new talent. Because you can kill it.

"I suppose I have a very strong sense of what I think is fair and unfair. There's a line in my novel *The Princess Bride* where somebody says, 'Life isn't fair. It's just a lot fairer than death.' Just the unfairness of how Mary Mercier was treated bothered me so terribly, because everybody's saying, 'Where are the new playwrights?' and there *is* one, with this extraordinary play, and she got kicked in the teeth."

This September, ten years will have elapsed since the start of the season you wrote about. If you were to update your book, what changes would you describe?

"Primarily, the tremendous decline of talent. I mean, we're almost through the 1970s, and who's the best new playwright? That's a Broadway book, remember. It's not dealing with Off-Broadway. Talent doesn't come to Broadway anymore in the way that it used to. I'm hoping there's a resurgence, because Broadway is certainly commercially now bigger than it's ever been. The problem is that production costs have become so phenomenal that the old New Haven–Boston out-of-town tryout tour is no longer affordable.

"So what we've got basically now are revivals, and it's just like the movies, and it's just as dumb as the movies. It's just as stupid to revive *My Fair Lady* as it is to film *French Connection II*. You think there's an audience out there for it. The reality is, there isn't *enough* of an audience out there for it."

How did you justify your sequel to *Harper*?

"I was ten years younger. I don't think I would do it again. In other words, I don't think I would write a sequel to *Marathon Man*. It's curious I should say that, because I once did write a sequel novel. *Father's Day* is a sequel to *The Thing of It Is* . . . Well, I was younger then, too."

What about your early writing? Did you have any trouble selling your first novel?

"I graduated from Oberlin College in fifty-two, did the Army for two years, then went to graduate school at Columbia University for two years. It was then the summer of 1956. I was twenty-four, and I'd always wanted to be a writer. I'd shown no signs of talent. I got my worst grades in writing classes. I was the fiction editor of the literary quarterly at college, and I couldn't get a story of mine in the goddamn thing. Now it was late June of 1956. I lived in Chicago at the time, and it was fish or cut bait. So in desperation I wrote *The Temple of Gold*, literally not knowing when I went to bed each night what was going to happen in the plot the next day.

"I had met a guy in the Army who had found a young agent, so I sent the book off to the agent. He knew an editor at Knopf who said, 'It's too short. If you double it in length, we'll consider publishing it.' So I doubled it in length, and it was published. It came out when I had just turned twenty-six. So I would have to say no, I did not have a great deal of trouble getting it published. It happened to be flukey."

You never had a single rejection on it?

"No. But if I had, I would never have written anything more. Since I had shown no signs of talent, and since no one was saying, 'Keep at it, Bill, you've really got the goods,' if *The Temple of Gold* had not been taken, I never would have had the courage to inflict another novel on anybody. I know this is true."

Were you *that* lacking in confidence?

"I'll give you a theory of mine. I really believe this. I think we tend to gravitate toward affection. The last short story I ever wrote was the first one that I thought was any good. It was called 'The Simple Pleasures of the Rich,' and I thought, 'For the first time you've written a *good* short story.' And I got something like seventy-eight rejections over the next five years. Finally, out of sympathy somewhere, it got taken—years later. But I remember thinking, 'That's as good as I can do. If they don't like that, I'm going to quit trying. That's too hard over there.'

"I think we go toward softness, toward where there's affection for us. That's why, if you have a certain success in films, you'll probably stay in films."

Is that why you don't write for the theater anymore?

"Yeah. I didn't like it. I *did not like* the out-of-town experience, the pressure, the whole thing. I'm basically a private person. I stay in my room and do my work and that's my life. And being in one of those turmoil situations I found hateful. Some people love it. For me it was not a happy thing."

Yet staying in that room meant living with the silence. Goldman already had identified the solitary part of his work as unpleasant. What did he like best about his work?

He thought for a moment, then said, "I don't know. I am so constantly aware of my own inadequacies as a writer. I am not one of those people who thinks, 'Oh, boy, I can't wait to get to my typewriter, I'm gonna write something terrific today.' Because it's too hard to write a book. It's too hard. I really like *The Princess Bride*, and I really like *Wigger*, which is a children's book. Those two were wonderful experiences, compared to what it's like ordinarily. For the most part, what you do is . . . you live in a constant state of panic."

Yet you are a highly disciplined writer.

"It's very important for me to come to this office," he said. "No matter how neurotic this sounds, it's very important for me to try and think that what I'm doing is really a grown-up endeavor. In other words, a banker is a grown-up thing to be. A doctor is a grown-up thing to be. They have offices to go to. I may just come to this office, read the newspaper, have coffee, and then go off to a movie, but it's important that I get out of the house.

"One of the differences between being a writer and a doctor is that if you're a doctor, you live your life in a straight line. You get out of medical school and you're in debt. Nobody wants you. You get a few patients. They tell other people. Suddenly you're busy a month in advance. Your income goes up and up, and you go out in a straight rising line. Artistic careers, on the other hand, are very jagged, and you don't have that many times at bat. If you're involved in a musical like *A Chorus Line* and it comes in big, you're set for life. If you have a percentage of *Johnny No-Trump*, you can't buy coffee. So there's enormous pressure."

But once an artist is set for life, why does he keep working in these bruising, pressured, collaborative endeavors?

"Striving is a terribly important part. I recently saw a book advertised about how to survive various losses. Loss of a mate, loss of a job, loss of a child. And in this list, after 'loss of success,' in parenthesis it said '(loss of striving).'

"You know, when you suddenly have great success thrust upon you, it's very disconcerting. *Especially* in America, because the heights are so phenomenal here. If John Gielgud gives a bad performance, the English tend to say, 'Johnny wasn't really very good in that, but he'll be fine next time.' In *this* country, when Jason Robards gives a bad performance, we'll say, 'Well, he's past it.' We live in a pop culture, fast turnover, and I don't know how people in the public eye cope with it. But one way is to keep striving."

You were just talking about a couple of your books you like. How much influence has an editor ever had on your writing?

"My late editor was a marvelous man named Hiram Haydn who

I revered. He was the head of Phi Beta Kappa, was a professor at Western Reserve in Ohio, got into publishing very late. I was devoted to him. I went to him in 1959 and was with him beginning with *Soldier in the Rain*, which was my third novel. He died in the early seventies. The last book I did with him was *The Princess Bride*."

Which was the one prior to *Marathon Man*, I half-stated, half-asked.

"That's right," Goldman confirmed. Then he added a startling revelation. "I don't think I ever would have written *Marathon Man* or *Magic* had Hiram lived. I don't think he would have liked them or understood them."

And his disapproval would have been enough for you to not write them?

"I think so. You know, *No Way to Treat a Lady*, which is the *one* thing I've ever written that got raves from the New York critics, was published under a pseudonym. I already told you how I came to write it. Well, when I gave it to Hiram, he said, 'I don't know what to do with this.' He said, 'Why don't you try and get it published somewhere else under another name?' And so I did.

"He had a great influence on *Boys and Girls Together*. I had no structure for it, which is not usually the way I am. And Hiram kept saying, 'Just keep writing. Just keep writing. We'll structure it later.' He was eventually enormously responsible for the structure of the book. That was a case where he was certainly influential."

One last question. What has been the happiest period of your life?

"I think I've been very fortunate, though I tend to be so negative about everything anyway that even if a period was good I wouldn't like it. My forties have been better than my thirties, and my thirties were better than my twenties, and God knows, anything was better than my teens."

On that positive note, we stopped. Goldman had promised me an hour and given me nearly three. When I suggested that interviews aren't so painful, he said, "One of the terrifying things when you do interviews is that somebody will ask, 'This is your first movie script, right?' And you get people: 'What else have you done?' Well, it's not my job to tell them that. I've talked to performers about this. They *hate* being interviewed so much because the questions are so inane. And when somebody asks them a good question, they simply open up. People who are interviewed a lot—not like myself, but people who really are—they're desperate, *desperate*, to be put down accurately on paper. Because most of what you read is how much money they make and how cute they are or how tall they are or how big are their—what their figures are like. And no one gets them down. It's because most interviewers don't take the time to do any homework. But basically, I think, most of us will open up if anybody takes us seriously."

One week later, William Goldman *did* receive an Academy Award nomination for *All the President's Men*.

One month later, he won his second Oscar. This time he was there.

Later that year, his film adaptation of Cornelius Ryan's *A Bridge Too Far*, directed by Richard Attenborough, was released. When we spoke, Goldman had been high on the film; its less-than-enthusiastic reception must have been a disappointment.

Almost unnoticed in the extensive publicity campaign was a slender paperbook titled *William Goldman's Story of "A Bridge Too Far,"* which included a forty-five-page essay on filmmaking. This wise, witty essay was the seedling for *Adventures in the Screen Trade*. But while that was germinating . . .

In 1978, the movie version of *Magic*, also directed by Attenborough, was released.

In 1979, his Hollywood novel *Tinsel* was published. It was a nasty piece of writing, as if the subject matter determined the style.

Although *Tinsel* was Goldman's eleventh novel, he had never had a best seller. (*Marathon Man* had found its audience in paperback.) The novelist was persuaded that if he would participate in the publicity campaign, the book would sell. Suddenly this once-hidden writer was everywhere. *Tinsel* went straight onto *The New York Times* list.

Then, three years of deafening silence. . . .

In 1982 another thriller, *Control*, was published.

In 1984, *The Color of Light*.

In 1985, *Heat*.

In 1986, *Brothers*, which was billed on the dust jacket as "the sequel to *Marathon Man*." (So much for his remark that he'd never write another sequel.)

But more important than any of these novels, sequel included, was the 1983 publication of *Adventures in the Screen Trade*, his almost-but-not-quite companion piece to *The Season*. That book had been written from the Broadway periphery; this new Hollywood book was written from the eye of the hurricane. At its core it was subjective and personal, and its pages howled with hurt and pain. Screenwriter Goldman may view himself as a novelist, but it's in the area of *reportage*—in both *The Season* and *Adventures in the Screen Trade*—that he has produced two masterworks.

He's continued in this vein. *Wait Till Next Year* (1988), which he wrote with columnist Mike Lupica, is "the season" in sports. *Hype & Glory* (1990) chronicles his experiences as a judge at the Miss America Pageant and the Cannes Film Festival.

William Goldman is now at the pinnacle. The publicity for *Misery*, his film based on Stephen King's novel, focused on King, director Rob Reiner, and Goldman rather than the actors. In 1991 the writer even lectured at Oxford University.

But the man hasn't changed a bit. He's still as unsure of himself as ever, as the following incident suggests.

In August 1987, just prior to the release of *The Princess Bride* (which finally was filmed, fourteen years after the novel's publication), I wrote to Goldman and requested that he contribute to a story I was compiling in which I asked a dozen writers to respond to the following queries:

If you could meet one nonliving author, who would it be? And what question would you most want to ask that person?

A week later I received his response.

"I've thought a lot about the first question and obviously, the answer you should give is Shakespeare, or, if you're feeling really snobby, Dante or Milton or Virgil. Except I wouldn't pick them. I'd pick Chekhov, and I think I can tell you why. All the great writers, and you can throw in any of the other immortals, it doesn't matter, all of them have one thing in common: They are beyond me, in terms of talent, poetic skill, whatever. Of all the giants in Western lit, only Chekhov—at least for me—seems approachable. We always snooker ourselves, writers do, that today we're going to get it right, only we never do. Well, sometimes I think if I'm really lucky for a week or a month, I might write something as good as Chekhov. It's all impossible, of course, but he seems—part of his genius—to be like the rest of us.

"And I wouldn't ask him a question. I'd just thank him and shake his hand."

The reply was vintage Goldman.

MARY MERCIER

Mary Mercier doesn't write plays anymore, and that's a shame. But she wrote one, and it's worth remembering.

At its heart (which is large), *Johnny No-Trump* is a family play in the tradition of *The Member of the Wedding* and *Ah, Wilderness!* This poignant character study of a sensitive teenager's quest for maturity is laced with humor and humane honesty. The lovely comedy-drama is set in February 1965, in a small Long Island town on the weekend of John Edwards' sixteenth birthday. John lives with his mother, Florence, a divorced schoolteacher; her brother, Harry; and their aged mother, Nanna.

In Act One John announces his decision to quit high school, get a job, and become a poet. The announcement is greeted with derision from his Uncle Harry and concern from his mother.

In Act Two John is packing to leave home before his birthday party begins. His father, Alec, an unsuccessful artist, arrives early (at Florence's request) to talk to John about his sudden decision. Bettina, a teenage neighbor, stops by and flirts with Alec. Johnny taunts her until she leaves. When his mother defends Bettina, Johnny cries out, "How dare you understand a stranger and not me!"

After Florence goes to the store for some bread, Uncle Harry offers the boy his trust as a birthday present. While the three men celebrate their own private birthday party, Bettina returns with the tragic news that Johnny's mother has been killed at the street corner by a passing truck. Alec leaves to identify the body, and the boy and his uncle are left to face the future together.

With Don Scardino in the title role, Pat Hingle as the uncle, Sada Thompson as the mother, James Broderick as the father, and Bernadette Peters as Bettina, the play opened at Broadway's Cort Theater on October 8, 1967, to some glowing reviews:

> "A beautiful play . . . witty and intelligent . . . poignant and tragic. In her first play, Mary Mercier has wrought the miracle of creating life out of ink and paper, and she has done it magnificently. . . . *Johnny No-Trump* is a winner, and it may be a winner again when the Tony Awards are given out."—Stewart Klein, WNEW-TV

> "The play has honesty, humor, and infinite compassion. . . . It is so much better than any other American play in several months. . . ."—George Oppenheimer, *Newsday*

"Possibly the most honest and unpretentious dramatization of the conflict between young and old Broadway will see this season."
—A. D. Coleman, *The Village Voice*

"An absorbing play about recognizable characters . . . it has humor, pathos, and compulsion. . . . An interesting and moving play, and a promising first work for Miss Mercier."
—Hobe Morrison, *Variety*

"The first interesting American play of the Broadway season. . . . Mary Mercier can write. There's verve in her writing, and some quite touching scenes as well. . . . Mary Mercier is a playwright with a future."—Edwin Newman, WNBC-TV

But Stewart Klein was wrong about the Tony Awards, and Edwin Newman was wrong about Mary Mercier's future.

Why?

Because Clive Barnes thought the play was a cliché. At the beginning of the 1967–68 theater season, Barnes (a dance critic from England) succeeded Stanley Kauffmann as theater reviewer of *The New York Times*. *Johnny No-Trump* was the second American play of Barnes' first season, and he was ambivalent. "I personally would have preferred to have written it than, say, *Cactus Flower*," Barnes wrote, "but that does not mean it will run as long."

He was right about that. The morning after its opening night, *Johnny No-Trump* was closed.

Twelve days later Clive Barnes wrote in *The New York Times*, "The season, even this early, has regrets as well as its triumphs. Personally I regret that *Johnny No-Trump*, not a brilliant but a promising play, superbly acted with a lovely cast, led by Pat Hingle, was abruptly taken off by its producer before it had a chance to get a word-of-mouth resuscitation. This was Broadway at its most savage."

Two days later, Walter Kerr's enthusiastic eulogy appeared in the Sunday *Times*. "Beyond doubt," he concluded, "Mary Mercier's confidence has been damaged: one-night runs suggest total ineptitude and are perforce humiliating. Worse, she has been cheated of experience: she hasn't been able to hear many people respond to her play. She is at this moment a failure rather than a discovery, and she hasn't even been able to learn much for her pains. Yet she *is*—or should have been—a discovery, she is plainly talented, she is already capable of a blunt and crackling speech that insists upon being listened to, of managing open and moving confrontations between scratchy, well-meaning, strong-willed people, of giving breath and resilience to the people themselves. Her structural gaucheries were almost unimportant; she has a voice."

In 1969 William Goldman's *The Season* was published, and several of us "discovered" the play. In 1972 Susan Jacobs' *On Stage: The Making of a Broadway Play*, a short but highly informative chronicle of the *Johnny No-Trump* production, was published. Later that same year, Marilyn Stasio's *Broadway's Beautiful Losers*, an anthology of neglected but worthy plays, included *Johnny No-Trump*.

When we staged the play at the Cleveland Play House in 1972, Peter Bellamy wrote in the *Plain Dealer*, "*Johnny No-Trump* is a grand slam of a play—tremendously touching, human, and superbly done." Tony Mastroianni echoed that praise in his *Cleveland Press* review: "New York's loss is Cleveland's gain." A series of morning performances attended by responsive high-school students was particularly gratifying.

Mary Mercier accepted our invitation to attend the production. Then, a few days before opening night, she canceled. Something to do with an unexpected free-lance writing assignment. I suspected it had more to do with a reluctance to rekindle unhappy memories.

Sada Thompson, on tour in Cleveland with *Twigs*, attended one of the Play House rehearsals and spoke to the cast about "inexorable deadlines that make art in our lives so chancy."

A year later I talked with Pat Hingle. "The key to that play is the boy," he said. "Don Scardino gave one of the finest performances I've ever seen on any stage. The wonderful thing that happened in that play was that the house changed from a matriarchy to the men taking over. That boy entered a man's world. It's a rare thing to see on the stage."

As he recalled the Broadway production, you could hear six years' ache in his voice. "We did capacity business in previews," Hingle said. "Then, when the *Times* review came out, the producers panicked. But I'll tell you something. Later that same season I was cast in another new play, *The Price*, by Arthur Miller. If you go back and check, you'll discover that *Johnny No-Trump* got much better reviews than *The Price*. But this time we had Arthur Miller's name. Nobody panicked, and *The Price* ran for more than a year. When I think back on the whole *Johnny No-Trump* experience, it's one of the saddest things that ever happened to a play."

I first met Mary Mercier in the early 1970s, prior to the Cleveland production. As we talked in the lobby of the Algonquin Hotel, I was immediately struck by a frail, birdlike quality that inhabited her: One sudden move and she might take flight.

In November 1977, ten months after my session with William Goldman, Mary Mercier and I met again. She lived in Los Angeles now; she'd put New York behind her. Her once-dark hair was dyed blond; she'd put on weight. The former Mary Mercier was not easily recognizable; only that sweet, birdlike vulnerability gave her away. She still seemed ready to fly away at the first harsh word.

We met at Actors Studio West, where she worked as executive secretary. As we sat on an old couch in a combination living room–rehearsal hall and chronicled the anatomy of a casualty, four actors in a nearby room rehearsed a scene from Edward Albee's *Who's Afraid of Virginia Woolf?* Their distant voices provided a sadly ironical counterpoint to the story I was hearing: It was, after all, the Edward Albee management that had produced Mary Mercier's play.

Let's start at the beginning, I suggested. Where were you born?

"Cardiff, Wales," she replied. "My father's an artist. I was brought up partially in Wales, also in Monmouthshire and a little bit in London. Then, when I was a teenager, I came to Los Angeles. But there was little theater here, so after a few weeks I went to New York to become an actress and pretty much stayed there until I came back here a couple of years ago."

She found work Off-Broadway. Her first Broadway play was *The Fun Couple*, which starred Jane Fonda and Bradford Dillman. Mary Mercier understudied a featured role acted by then-unknown Dyan Cannon and also played a small part. In New York she married actor Gene Wilder. He worked steadily on Broadway, though during their marriage he was not yet widely known. In 1967, the same year his film career began with *Bonnie and Clyde* and her playwriting career began and ended with *Johnny No-Trump*, they separated, and later they were divorced.

The play actually was born four years earlier.

"In 1963 I acted at the Spoleto Festival," she said. "On the way home I stopped off in Rome. I was walking around that gorgeous city when these characters began to form in my head. I think a writer does a lot of work of that nature before he really sits down. Because I remember, when I came to write the first scene it really wrote itself. All that preliminary work was done in my mind, and that started in Rome."

How long between the time you came home and the time you sat down to write?

"Fairly soon. I remember that when I finished the scene I thought, 'I've done this so fast, maybe something is wrong. I'd better put it away and take it out in a month. Let a little time elapse before reading it over.' Because, after all, I did not grow up wanting to be a writer. It sort of surprised me that I had really written a scene. So I waited awhile, and then I took it out and read it through, and I thought, 'Well, this is actable, this is playable on a stage.' And after that I began to continue with the rest of the play.

"By 1965, in between acting jobs, I had it written. It came in bits and pieces. I never did sit down and just totally write the play. There was always something else going on. I was still at a point when I was not thinking of myself as a writer. In fact, I finished the play in order to see if I *could* finish it."

She might not have been thinking of herself as a writer, but she was writing as one . . . as a writer who acts.

"I love to listen to the way people speak," she said, "especially when they have colloquial flair, a kind of richness of language. I remember thinking that I wanted to differentiate characters through language. People use different slang at different age levels. An older man will use terminology that was in vogue twenty years ago. A teenager uses words that you've hardly heard of yet. Those kinds of things.

"I think I learned a lot from working in not very good plays and trying to figure out what should have been in the scripts to make them workable. Not all scenes will have a thrust to them, a real intention, a real conflict, a real characterization. Very often an actor is stuck trying to add that to a banal script, because the writer has not done all that work.

"Also, technical things. If you're an actor you know never to give anybody a quick change. But so often writers do that. Often problems that occur in production are because the writer did not understand the actor's point of view."

So we're up to 1965, and you had finished the play. What happened next?

"I let a few people read it for reactions. Several teenagers read the play, because I wanted to know if they found it truthful. Then some actors read it, and they began telling me to try to get a workshop production. That's the most I ever thought would happen to it. But the play went to five different workshops and was rejected by all of them."

Over how long a period of time?

"Well, I tell you, I was not exactly running around ambitiously with this play, because I was still acting, and I went out of town constantly with my husband."

What did he think of the play?

"He liked it very much and thought I should pursue a production. He was highly encouraging.

"Now at this point I bumped into my director from Spoleto, Ivan Utall. He had come back to New York and was working for a literary agent named Bertha Case. So he read the play and then took it to her. She read it and then called me in, and it was decided that she would send it out for a professional production. And she got five offers. At this point I didn't understand what was going on at all. It seemed bizarre that I couldn't get a workshop but I could get a commercial production. Kermit Bloomgarden made an offer. Norman Twain was another. But the Richard Barr office got it because they were the first to call back.

"Meanwhile, at the same time the play was being sent out, a director named John Stix took it to The New Dramatists and I heard one cold reading. Pat Hingle read the role of Uncle Harry. That reading put me into *shock*. There was no real audience; just a few people were there. But sitting through it and listening to what you'd written was very strange.

"But then, to me, the whole experience has always been a strange one. I suppose if I had wanted to become a writer, if that had been in my plans, I would have understood things better. But I never did understand why I ever sat down and wrote the play. Today I love to paint, I love to draw, and I wonder why it was that I didn't go to those in between acting jobs.

"Anyway, it was not long after that cold reading that I had the news that producers were interested. So my agent said, 'Let's not pursue a production at The New Dramatists. Let's get a professional production.' I must say Bertha Case was always a strong supporter. So she was very disappointed the way it turned out. At any rate, the Barr-Albee office took a one-year option, which, as I recall, was renewed."

Did Edward Albee have much to do with the production?

"I didn't see him around that much. During the actual production he was in Europe. And for a lot of the time so was the other producer,

Clinton Wilder. So it was really Barr who was left producing the play.

"A lot of directors were discussed. But Joseph Hardy had just done *You're a Good Man, Charlie Brown* Off-Broadway, so he was successful at the time. And he was available and he seemed to have a feeling for the play. I think it was his first Broadway show."

Can you remember your first meeting with him?

"No, I can't remember my meetings much. There weren't that many, because although the Barr people make an extraordinary statement like 'The playwright is God to us, Mary' "—she burst into a sarcastic, derisive laugh, then continued—"it doesn't bear out in fact. Maybe Edward is God over there, and maybe if you're a successful playwright you can pull your weight. But if you're an unknown writer—and also a woman, I might add—you can say something, but, my God, that doesn't mean anybody listens to you. They pretty much treated me as if I had just come in from Hackensack. They didn't particularly know me as an actress or think of me as anyone with any kind of theater experience. So if I made a suggestion—Lordy knows, I learned not to do that too much. Because no one listened. Unless you have a director and a producer who are determined to carry out your vision, it's very difficult."

But doesn't the playwright have certain rights through The Dramatists Guild?

"The Guild is always saying how strong its contract is. But if someone in production says he's going to cut this or change that and the writer disagrees, there's little that can be done. The only strong playwright I've ever personally witnessed was Graham Greene, when my husband was in *The Complaisant Lover.* That was only because all the people paid him great respect and allotted him that power. It's not because he was aggressive. They *gave* him that power."

Were you happy with the cast that was assembled?

"Well, I tell you. That particular outfit considers it a waste of time to audition actors. They feel that they can cast it on paper. I beg to differ with that, because the first two people that they suggested were Hume Cronyn and Jessica Tandy. That to me wasn't intelligent. They're fine actors, but they're not in any way right for my play.

"Pat Hingle had done a very good cold reading, so I had seen something of what he would do with the part. I suggested Sada Thompson. I knew she could play the role because I had seen her do very good work in Molière's *Tartuffe* a couple years before at

Lincoln Center. I don't know how casting people think, but if I see an actor do a very good piece of work, then I always think the actor will be good in many things. I also suggested James Broderick, because I had seen him do well in a play-reading at The New Dramatists.

"Finally they did agree to some auditions for the boy. I liked Don Scardino. They wanted a boy called Richard Thomas, who has since gone on to do *The Waltons*. Richard Thomas at that time was very stiff. If the kid in my play had come from a military school, Richard would have been right. But he did not have that loose teenage quality that you need for Johnny. So I asked for Don Scardino, and they gave the understudy to Richard.

"Bernadette Peters got her part from the audition, which she did very well. And the old lady, Anne Ives, got her part from an audition. Later they cut her part, though it always was my personal opinion that they didn't cut out a character; they cut out a salary."

At this point, I read a statement from the press release which accompanied *Broadway's Beautiful Losers:* "Mary Mercier's lovely and delicate play was closed the same night it opened by the producer's lack of faith in his own production and the author's reluctance to compromise."

Do you think that's a fair assessment of what happened?

"But you see," she implored, "I was never asked to compromise. Once Barr and Albee option a play, that's it. They do not want rewrites. Any rewrites are done prior to option. Then they read the play again and decide. After The New Dramatists reading I rewrote the opening of the second act to the extent of maybe three pages. After the Barr people read it I was told that I was lucky they had accepted it. Because the play that they option is the play they want to do.

"With my play, the difference of opinion centered on the cuts. At a rehearsal one day I heard what to me were giant cuts being rehearsed. And Joe Hardy said, 'Don't worry, if you don't like it this way, we'll put the dialogue back in.' But when it came time for me to say, 'Now can we see it the other way?' they didn't want to do it.

"You see, they were very concerned over time. They did not want a play that probably would have run two hours and thirty-five minutes. As they did it, I think it went two hours and fifteen minutes. That's twenty minutes missing, twenty minutes of arbitrary cuts. If only they had asked me for twenty minutes' deletion I would have pruned it from top to bottom to cut away twenty minutes without interrupting the flow. When you write something you try to make certain that it flows from one scene to another. But they would chop out whole sequences and create a jump."

Were you at rehearsals?

"I would sit in the back. I was not forceful during this period. That was a big mistake, because in every production that I've ever been a part of, it's always been the same: The one who wins the argument is the one who shouts the loudest and the longest. It does not matter whether they have intelligence or whether they're right. They win that fight and get what they want. I once saw Franco Zeffirelli give up because a producer could shout louder and longer, not because the producer was right.

"After each rehearsal you have a little conference. And pretty much, Richard Barr would vote with the director. Charles Woodward was coproducing along with Barr. He was learning the business. His comment to me after it was all over was 'You got buffeted by everybody.' I simply did not have enough votes at any conference for my side. This nonsense about the playwright being God, forget it!

"What I should have done, really, was to fight for my own work, because I felt that there were moments in my play that should not have been jumped over. I would rather hear as criticism that the play is too long than hear that a scene came out of nowhere. That's why the mother's death seemed so sudden. But originally the mention of death was all through the play. The opening scene even begins with death as a joke. It was all there as foreshadowing."

From the time they optioned the play until it opened, was the death at the end ever a topic of debate?

"No. All that talk came up after the fact. That's when Richard Barr suddenly decided there was a problem about the ending. He had forgotten his own policy as a producer, which is that the play you option is the play you're going to do. If they had asked me to rewrite the ending, there would not have been a production.

"You see, the play was planned as a trilogy. One of the reasons I was disappointed that we didn't get a run out of the production was because I wanted to be able to write the second play so that the references would not have to be totally explained. People would know them from the first play. I'd have been able to write a lot closer to how people really communicate, which is verbal shorthand.

It would have been a very interesting challenge to write a play in which there is so much that we never say to each other, yet it's all said, it's all there."

Have you outlined the next two plays?

"Oh yes. The next one was going to be two or three years later, when Johnny was eighteen or nineteen. The third one would occur ten years later, when he was an adult. And Uncle Harry would carry through.

"So you see, that was another reason why I didn't want to change the ending of the first play. Because the death was a strong enough force to change people's lives. An accident can totally change your life. And what I wanted to say in the next two plays could not be said if the first play had simply ended with a party. Their lives would have continued going along in the same direction. But dramatic changes happened to both Johnny and Uncle Harry with the death of the mother."

What was going to happen to them?

"I'm not going to say, because I may still get to it. The thought even has occurred to me that I might be better off telling the story as a novel, not three plays. But I *will* tell you that the death at the end of the play is nothing compared to the death of the spirit. So if people thought that the *play* had a downbeat ending . . ." Her sentence trailed off into a lonely laugh.

The previews grew to capacity business and were extremely well received. Did you go into opening night thinking you had a success?

"The response from the five previews and the good word-of-mouth was enough to make Barr and the others believe they had a show that would run," she answered. "Maybe not for two years, but I'm sure they thought it would be successful."

And did that anticipation warm up everyone's personal relationships? Did you go into opening night with everyone on speaking terms?

"We were always on speaking terms, because I hadn't argued with them. That was the problem!

"After the opening-night performance there was a party at Joe Hardy's house. I remember one very nice notice coming over television. Then they call up and find out about the *Times*. It was certainly not what they term 'a money review.'

"The next day we all met at this place where they plan what the publicity campaign will be. Richard Barr said that he had decided that he could not run the show. And nobody spoke in favor of fighting for it. Not the director or the other producer. No one suggested in any way that we fight for the show.

"I asked if it couldn't be run at least for the week, but I really felt that Richard was so angry about the *Times* notice that he could not make a rational decision. I think he made a bad business decision in anger. I think Richard was wrong, because afterward I was told that television commentators who had seen previews had offered to help fight for it. I think that if he had accepted their help, it might well have proven to be a good business venture for him."

What happened to you at that point?

"I felt physically ill when it was all over. I just wanted to go home and not be bothered with any of it. And I really did totally ignore everything to do with the play after that. There were a lot of letters written to me that I didn't answer for maybe a year.

"For a few years, any reference to the play was very painful. I did not like to be reminded of it. Now I can take it in stride. I can talk here. That would have been very difficult the first couple of years. As an experience in one's life, the thing hurt me very deeply. Sometimes people say, 'Wasn't having a Broadway show and an opening night the most exciting thing that ever happened to you?' Oh, no."

We sat silent for a moment, the quiet broken only by the muted, arguing voices of George and Martha. Then Mary Mercier continued.

"If only it took ten minutes to write a play." She was silent again. "But the writing and the preproduction and the rehearsals total three years. That's a chunk of your life to suddenly have thrown away on the basis of one journalist's opinion. And that's what it came down to. Mr. Barnes' opinion is all that they listened to."

Who's accountable for that, Mr. Barnes or Mr. Barr?

"It certainly takes a very strong producer to fight the Broadway system, though some people have. You know, Hollywood doesn't always know how to make a picture, but they know how to sell one. Have you ever read a movie press kit? Do you know the detail they go into? Tie-ups with department stores, you name it, in order to promote that film.

"Yet on Broadway you find people who know how to put on a play but don't know how to sell it. In New York, by opening night a producer might have four cents in the bank and absolutely no wherewithal to promote a product that he is now trying to sell. I don't think that happens in many other businesses. In the case of my play, there wasn't even a poster! Things like that were to be paid for out of monies coming in at the box office. But they really should be in advance. You can't just wait and hope that the guy at the *Times* gives you a terrific notice."

To what extent did the experience destroy your self-confidence as a writer?

"It did a certain amount of damage, inasmuch as, while I still get ideas, I no longer put the time in."

Did you lose your confidence in the script?

"No. Nor did I think it was a bad production. Some playwrights at the end of a failed production will blame the actors. My actors did really good ensemble work. I had no complaints about them at all. And it was well directed. Apart from the cuts, the work that *was* done was good work. So, despite what the critics said, I did not come away feeling that I had written a terrible play or that it was a terrible production.

"There were times when the critics made me feel ashamed of what I had done, but that's different from feeling that I had written a bad play. Made me feel ashamed to the extent that I thought maybe I should have done it in a workshop, in a more humble situation, rather than on Broadway. To that extent I remember feeling shame. But I don't remember having the feeling that I had written a rotten play that deserved to be off the boards.

"Even if my play had run a month I would not have felt the tremendous letdown of having it close after opening night. My God, one month isn't a long run for a play, but I would have been very satisfied if that's all that had happened."

"All failures have the same song," William Goldman had said. "It's always a case of people not communicating, people not understanding . . . It's always the same wail. . . ."

But *Johnny No-Trump* wasn't a Broadway failure; it was a Broadway casualty.

And it was not alone.

Some personal selections for that unhappy list include:

Great Day in the Morning . . .

In 1962, Alice M. Cannon's vibrant play, produced by George C. Scott and Theodore Mann, directed by José Quintero, with Colleen Dewhurst in the leading role, vanished after thirteen performances. ("Years from now people will realize what a great play it is," Dewhurst told Howard Greenberger in *The Off-Broadway Experience*. Three decades have passed, but the play is still obscure.)

Peterpat . . .

In 1965, Enid Rudd's two-character comedy, with Dick Shawn and Joan Hackett, disappeared after twenty-one performances.

America is relentlessly in search of the new play. Regional theaters and universities sponsor New Play Festivals and high-paying competitions. But perhaps, somewhere in this vast land, one little theater could remove itself from this rush to judgment and instead devote itself to reconsidering lost works.

True, America is preoccupied with fast turnover. But couldn't one theater, somewhere, concern itself with breathing fresh life into dead drama?

And what of Mary Mercier? I see her name from time to time in cast lists of television shows and feature films. I think she was in one of the *Airplane* comedies.

A few years ago, during a visit to Los Angeles, I called Actors Studio West and asked for her.

"This is Mary," the voice that answered the telephone cheerily replied.

"This is Dennis Brown."

Silence.

"From the Cleveland Play House."

Silence.

"We did *Johnny No-Trump*."

Silence . . . then, "I remember."

Numbed by this withering cold, I began to flounder: "I've been, uh, wondering what you've been doing."

"We just closed a show here."

"Would it be out of place to stop by and see you?"

"I might be busy."

"I'll call you first."

"Yes, that would be all right." But no warmth.

The brittle conversation came to an abrupt end.

Perhaps the call had been a misjudgment.

Perhaps during the last decade she simply had forgotten about me. (That had not entered my mind, because her play is still so fresh in mine.) I concluded that she had closed the book on that chapter of her life.

I didn't take her coldness personally. But I also stayed away.

A PORTFOLIO OF PHOTOGRAPHS

The following photographs, except where noted, were taken in roughly the same period of the 1970s during which Dennis Brown interviewed his subjects. The photos of William Inge and of John Patrick were taken at a slightly earlier time. Horton Foote was interviewed in the late 1980s, and his photo corresponds to that time period.

LANFORD WILSON
Used by courtesy of Dennis Brown.

Lila Vigil Photography

JASON MILLER

FRANK D. GILROY

WILLIAM GOLDMAN

MARY MERCIER, far right, with (from left) Bradford Dillman, Jane Fonda, Dyan Cannon, Ben Piazza, Delos V. Smith, Jr., and Ivor Francis, in *The Fun Couple. From the New York Public Library Theater Collection.*

EDWARD ALBEE

Photograph © 1992 by Jill Krementz

TENNESSEE WILLIAMS
Photograph © 1992 by Jill Krementz

Charles Fuchs

EDWINA DAKIN WILLIAMS

DAVID MERRICK
From the New York Public Library Theater Collection.

Jerry Bauer

ALAN JAY LERNER

WILLIAM INGE
From the New York Public Library Theater Collection.

RICHARD WILBUR
Used by courtesy of Dennis Brown.

Suburban News Photo

JOHN PATRICK

David Spagnolo

HORTON FOOTE

CHAPTER FIVE

MOTHER AND SON

"I love her very deeply, but she's not culpable, really, for the mistakes she made. But they were terrible mistakes. . . ."

—TENNESSEE WILLIAMS

"Ah'm just like any othuh mothuh who thinks her son is of course a genius always."

—EDWINA DAKIN WILLIAMS

Tennessee Williams, the small *New York Times* advertisement announced, would appear from noon till two at the large Doubleday Fifth Avenue bookstore to autograph copies of his just-published *Memoirs*.

No one was prepared for what followed.

By 11:45 A.M. the autograph line snaked throughout the capacious store. The shop was so jammed that all activity was halted except for the selling of the Williams book. Outside, four policemen were dispatched to control the mushrooming crowd, which threatened to disrupt midday traffic.

Williams' tardy arrival at 12:27 P.M. was almost anticlimactic. As he entered the store and was guided to a table next to the front window, two persons began to applaud. The other hundreds waited quietly for the line to begin to move.

"Would you like something to drink?" the store manager promptly asked, as if he thought the offer was expected.

"A light white wine would be nice," Williams replied in his soft Southern drawl. The bottle sat prominently by the writer all afternoon; Williams never finished his first glass.

On the street, throngs of people pushed to the store window. So many others rushed for the revolving door that the police closed the store. A hastily formed line of customers simply seeking admittance stretched for more than a block.

When the store temporarily reopened at 12:45, the bedlam at the counter as crowds raced to buy *Memoirs* resembled a scene that Robert Riskin might have written for a frantic 1940s comedy. *Magic Town*, maybe?

Doubleday executives and employees were so busy congratulating one another that they almost neglected to note one problem: They were about to run out of books. Urgent calls were placed to the warehouse, then to other bookstores.

By cab and by messenger, in cartons and in shopping bags, in stacks of eight and ten and twenty, books began to arrive from throughout Manhattan.

Two o'clock came and went, and the winding line continued. At the center of the vortex Tennessee Williams sat inscribing copies of *Memoirs*, impervious both to the frenzy at the book counter and to the hordes of staring onlookers outside the window. Impeccably dressed in a three-piece gray tweed suit that matched the color of his mottled hair, he rarely looked up from writing. As fans showered him with praise, the playwright smiled above his blue bow tie—but kept his eyes on his work.

A ruffian rushed into the store, shouting, "He's a fake! He ain't real!" Williams remained undaunted. An admirer placed a large red rose next to the wine bottle. Williams ignored it.

"No personal inscriptions, please. Mr. Williams does not have time to write personal inscriptions," a clerk intoned over and over. For the playwright, the afternoon was a chore not unlike working on an assembly line. But for each person on that line, the afternoon was an adventure. How else to justify an interminable wait, climaxed by fifteen silent seconds in the presence of an impervious celebrity?

And how difficult it must have been, in fifteen seconds, to reconcile that small, seated, signing figure with the American theater's most scandalous poet. . . .

He was born in Columbus, Mississippi, on March 26, 1911, and was raised in St. Louis.

He left there at age twenty-eight to seek recognition as a writer. Five years later he left an envelope at his agent's office, upon which he'd scribbled, "Here's a rather dull little play." Today, that description of *The Glass Menagerie* sounds ridiculous. Yet anyone who's ever borne a play's labor pains knows the loss of confidence that occurs when you finally release it to strange eyes.

One year later, in 1945, when *The Glass Menagerie* opened on Broadway, the American outcast had found a new voice.

The Glass Menagerie was followed by *A Streetcar Named Desire* (Pulitzer Prize), *Summer and Smoke*, *The Rose Tattoo*, *Camino Real*, *Cat on a Hot Tin Roof* (Pulitzer Prize), *Orpheus Descending*, *Sweet Bird of Youth*, *Period of Adjustment*, and *The Night of the Iguana*. In the 1950s, when the eminent theologian Paul Tillich was asked to define existentialism, he replied, "Read the plays of Tennessee Williams."

I was scheduled to talk with Williams on that November 1975 afternoon following the autograph session. I'd decided to attend the event to ensure that our meeting occurred.

At 3:05, just as the line was beginning to wane, a large book shipment arrived. "I can keep going; I'm not tired," the sixty-four-year-old writer assured his agent. Soon the line was almost back to its original length. At peak times, people stood for more than an hour.

Only one man, who cut past the crowds and charged straight to the table, compelled Williams to look up from his task.

"Why, David, where did you come from?" the startled playwright asked producer David Merrick.

"I was just walking down the street and came in to see who was responsible for this riot," Merrick replied. Williams giggled with embarrassed glee.

As the dapper producer continued down Fifth Avenue, I abandoned my observation perch at the sales counter and darted after him. I introduced myself as a writer from St. Louis, then asked him about his well-known disfavor toward that city. He agreed that his dislike of his hometown was at least as publicized as Tennessee's. "Of course, that doesn't have anything to do with why I produce his plays," said Merrick, who is just eight months and one day younger than Williams. "But we both grew up there, and I think we both felt that we received no encouragement from the city."

The producer apparently is something of a frustrated playwright. According to one popular rumor, back in the 1930s, while he was attending Washington University in St. Louis, Merrick placed second in a playwriting contest in which Tennessee Williams was only a runner-up. Before I was able to ask about that, Merrick resumed his brisk march down the avenue. I followed and hastily blurted out that I would enjoy the opportunity to talk to him at greater length another time.

"Give me a call," Merrick volunteered. "I'm in the book." The producer strode on, and I returned to the seemingly perdurable spectacle inside the store.

By the time Williams signed his final autograph at four o'clock, more than eight hundred books had been sold. A new sales record had been set hours earlier; the previous most successful signing had totaled not quite two hundred copies. "You mean I attracted more people than Jacqueline Susann?" the amazed playwright asked. Yes, he had, he was assured.

Now he was clearly tired. "Not my hand," he explained, "my head." But he consented to talk over a late lunch.

As we walked along West Fifty-Seventh Street to the Russian Tea Room, idly discussing his mother's former home on tree-lined Wydown Boulevard in St. Louis (he had her house in mind as he wrote *Period of Adjustment*), time and again he lurched to the right side, stumbling so markedly that I would have to support him. He began to apologize, but it was his written words—not his spoken ones—that I heard. I thought of the sentence in *Memoirs* that reads, "I was always falling down during the 1960s and I would always say, before falling, 'I'm about to fall down,' and almost nobody, nobody ever caught me."

At the Russian Tea Room, after we were seated against the wall deep in the rear, Williams continued to talk about the city in which he was so unhappily raised.

"Nearly all the really dreadful experiences of my life have occurred there," he said, "such as my sister's mental breakdown. It was an awful change in environment from Mississippi. Had we gone to Detroit or Cleveland, anyplace, it would have been the same, I suppose. It really was such a radical change in my life.

"And you know, St. Louis is a very materialistic city. It really is. It's very middle-American. Of course, when I was a kid the South still had an aura of romance about it. Not a *Gone With the Wind* sort of thing, but people still had *time* for each other. And they didn't judge you by the kind of car you drove or the street you lived on, although"—Williams burst into a garish laugh that sputtered and hissed like a blinking neon sign—"we lived on respectable streets in Mississippi."

After the playwright signed over half the royalties of *The Glass Menagerie* to his mother, she could have afforded to return to Mississippi. She remained in Missouri.

"She likes St. Louis, strangely enough," her son said. "She never complained about St. Louis at all. And my brother loves it. I'm the only one that complained."

He complained as loudly as David Merrick, who has told reporters he won't even fly over the city.

"I don't blame him," Williams said. "I was so surprised when he appeared at that book-signing, because, you know, he closed my latest play in Boston."

Williams' latest play was *The Red Devil Battery Sign*, which is set in Dallas shortly after the assassination of John Kennedy. The production, with direction by Edwin Sherin and a cast that included Anthony Quinn, Claire Bloom, and Katy Jurado, closed in Boston in June 1975, ten days after it opened.

"I can't get mad at David," Williams continued. "There's something disarming about him. I think, actually, he did me a favor by closing it there. The play wasn't ready. Although David had been sitting on it for two years, I had been so preoccupied with other things that I hadn't read it carefully. For some reason I was resisting. I was resisting psychologically the true material of it, which is the moral decay and corruption that has developed in the United States ever since the Korean War, you know? Since we began to interfere in the internal affairs of nations on other continents. And really, it was not the reason that our administrations were telling us. It was *all* for industrial profits. The Vietnam War, the Indo-China thing, it was really . . ."

His voice trailed off into silence. A moment later he recovered his focus and plunged ahead.

"Now, I am not . . . I never thought politically before. I don't even vote. I've never belonged to any party of any kind, and I don't subscribe to any 'ism' at all. But I've just become recently, in the last few years, very conscious, very conscious, of this corruption, you know, of morals, and of the decay of democratic ideals which I think began as far back as Korea, which manifests itself through our political system, and which surfaced most dreadfully with the Kennedy assassination, you know."

Just then, Williams was distracted by the approach of a lone, hunched black man. Only after the intruder hovered over our table did Williams interrupt his discourse long enough to look up.

"Jimmy!" he exclaimed. "How are you?"

"How are you?" James Baldwin replied. The two men spontaneously laughed in mirrorlike unison, for each knew that he had nothing to say to the other, yet social amenities among the elevated must be observed.

"Good to see you," Tennessee Williams said.

"What are you up to?" James Baldwin asked.

"Oh, I'm leaving Sunday," Tennessee Williams replied.

"It's very nice to see you," James Baldwin repeated.

"You're looking great," Tennessee Williams added.

"You are too," James Baldwin followed.

"Thank you."

"Thank you," Baldwin copied. "Take care. *Ciao*."

"*Ciao, ciao*."

Amidst the volley of *ciao*s, James Baldwin wandered away. Tennessee Williams resumed his monologue, as if he never had been interrupted.

". . . which surfaced most dramatically with the Kennedy assassination. People think it is, you know, unpatriotic to mention these things. I have the contrary view. I think one *must* mention these things, and be aware of them.

"*The Red Devil Battery Sign* is my first play in which political things are elucidated and emphasized, despite the fact that it is primarily a love story. But the love story involves itself very much with moral decay, which is the one thing that I've been talking about."

Continuing his theme of social concern, he said, "Recently I was asked if I cared whether in a hundred years people think *A Streetcar Named Desire* is a better play than *Death of a Salesman*. I said the thing to wonder was whether or not there *will* be any literature in a hundred years. Whether there will be any form of art, or whether people will just be concentrating all their energies upon trying to survive on a planet that has been virtually reduced to cinders by the holocaust of nuclear war—which is what we're constantly inviting, it seems to me. Why are we distributing nuclear materials to Egypt and Israel and all these little countries? I heard some very good newscaster say that the great nuclear holocaust will not be set off by Russia or America, but probably by some relatively unimportant country. Some little country."

Talk turned to the playwright's *Memoirs*. In years to come, I would recognize some of the seams where Williams had patched it together. In years to come, it would be judged harshly, yet always with an underlying sadness for what might have been.

"So disappointing," William Goldman termed it.

Elia Kazan, Williams' most understanding director, while never raising his voice, said, "His autobiography was terrible. Terrible, terrible, terrible. He had much more to him than is in that book. A far deeper person and more concerned person than is in that book. He was full of love for people, despite the fact that everything in society at the beginning had attacked him and made him feel ashamed. He was resilient and strong-willed. He was very tough, very strong, and completely devoted when he was devoted. A wonderful man.

"He wrote in that book that I bullied him about changes in *Cat on a Hot Tin Roof*. I never bullied the son of a bitch. I've had quite a few good friends, but he was one of the best. I really miss him."

But on November 11, 1975, the book's official publication date, we were more prone to share the opinion of Christopher Lehmann-Haupt, whose review had appeared that morning in *The New York Times:* "This is so distinctly Tennessee Williams talking that it never occurs to us to judge him objectively." Publication day was too soon to judge harshly. Williams hadn't had a theater success in fifteen years; on this day, there was an unheard sigh of relief simply that the book was done.

"I think when you're going to write your life," the playwright said, "there's no way to do it but honestly, you know? You either do it honestly, or you don't do it at all."

I observed that Williams wrote that the two qualities he inherited from his hard-drinking, hard-gambling, hard-carousing father, with whom he got along not at all, were—

"Total honesty and total truth," Williams interrupted. "Yes. Honesty of speech and honesty of behavior. It got him in a lot of trouble."

In *Memoirs*, Williams treated his father with much more sympathy than had Tennessee's mother in her autobiography twelve years earlier. "She didn't appreciate him, it's true," he said. "But remember, she didn't have the benefit of psychoanalysis, in which so much was revealed to me about my respect for my father and the trap that he fell into. It's hard to treat one another that way. I love her very deeply, but she's not culpable, really, for the mistakes she made. But they were terrible mistakes, mistakes of excessive devotion to children, to the point of obliteration."

At the beginning of *Memoirs*, Williams wrote, "You have to know that you've been lucky" in the theater.

"Yes, I did write that," he said. "And yet in truth I think there's no such thing as luck, really. You make your own luck. You do it through work, through working as hard as you possibly can. And I have a somewhat mystic feeling that providence enters into the affairs of people somewhat."

So you don't feel that luck was involved when *The Glass Menagerie* received such a spectacular response?

"No, indeed."

Or that lack of luck was involved when *Orpheus Descending* was attacked by the critics?

"No. All these things—I don't regard them as pure luck. No. And I don't know how to identify the other factor. There's another factor besides luck. And even besides your own efforts, I think, there's another factor. I don't quite know what it is."

Williams was shattered by the poor reception given to *Orpheus Descending* in 1957.

"I had to go to an analyst for the first time," he said. "It contains some of my best writing, but as a whole, you see, it's overloaded. There were too many elements in it that overloaded the play. And it ended with such violence. The audience and the critics were not yet conditioned to violence of the sort that *Orpheus* presented."

He paused, gazed across the restaurant, then turned to stare at me before declaring, "They are now conditioned to violence."

Our conversation occurred on the eve of the American Bicentennial. At the time, numerous Williams plays were being revived. I asked if he thought *Orpheus Descending* was ready for revival.

"Yeah," he said. "It hasn't been given any major revival. But it needs considerable work before it's revived. There's too great a density of highly overcharged scenes. One piles on top of another. It needs to be 'cooled' a little, you know. If there ever is serious talk of reviving it, I would like to weed some of it out, you know, and diminish some of the elements."

Williams began to paraphrase the play's most memorable speech.

" 'There's a kind of bird that don't have no legs, so it has to sleep on the wind.' Brando delivered that speech so beautifully. I think of Brando's connection with it because he made the film version, *The Fugitive Kind*. That was the best speech in the play. He and Joanne Woodward had the best speeches. Unfortunately, Anna Magnani didn't have such speeches. She had the passionate scenes, but not the great speeches.

"But she was hindered a great deal by the fact that she had to learn English like a parrot, you know? And Brando—I don't think through malice, but through his natural style—was unable to read a line precisely as it was written. And she would be expecting a certain line as her cue, and he would say 'um' or 'ahh,' and so she wouldn't get her cue. This drove her into a frenzy, and she would call me at midnight."

Williams accelerated into a high-octane imitation of Magnani that could be heard throughout the restaurant: " 'You're *keeling* me! Why are you letting him *keel* me?! He's trying to *keel* me! This man is trying to *keel* me!' But he wasn't. He just wasn't able to act otherwise. That was his style of acting. She had her own style, too, and he had his. But they didn't jell.

"You know, she was madly in love with him at first. I remember we spent a week writing and rewriting a love letter. She had me and two others working on that love letter. It must have taken ten drafts to get it right. And he didn't even answer it."

She did send it, though?

"Yeeees, she sent it! He never answered back. That ended"—Williams lapsed into gales of laughter—"the love affair. Poor thing."

The anecdote was out of keeping with Williams' description of Magnani in *Memoirs* as being dominant with men. "She *was*, with Italian men," he explained. "She knew how to dominate them. But Brando was very difficult to dominate. I don't think anybody ever tried to dominate Brando."

Williams wrote in his autobiography that writing was his life and "its failure would be my death."

"That's rather melodramatic," he said with a laugh. "That's kind of like something that might be said in a melodramatic movie. But I can be very melodramatic sometimes. Well, in a sense it's true. I think if I never had anything but failure, it would be devastating and destructive. It would be like dying young.

"I distinguish between two kinds of failure. One is commercial failure and the other is artistic failure. And even when things don't make it commercially, sometimes I have a conviction that artistically they were worthwhile. And very often it happens that a play will fail one time, as in the case of *Summer and Smoke*. It failed originally, you know, because of bad direction. And then it was revived with great direction by José Quintero, and it made a star of Geraldine Page.

"I've worked with great people always, of course. I've always worked with great people. And I don't know where I left off and they began. But I don't think commercial failure, or what they call a flop, is going to annihilate me anymore. It will be annihilating at the moment it occurs, because I'm very affected by success and failure and such things. It will be very painful. But it won't stop me."

Williams wrote in *Memoirs* of his estranged relationship with writer Donald Windham, "We were both so absorbed in our love that we neglected our friendship."

"He was my closest friend in the early forties," Williams said. "It wasn't love between Windham and me. It was just a very deep friendship. You see, if you're a writer, you give seventy percent, at least, of yourself to your work. And what you have left over, you have to give to whomever you love, you know? And only about ten percent is left for ordinary social occasions and concerns. But one of the friendships I most regretted having lost in the shuffle was Windham. I thought he could have been more understanding."

I quoted a line from Williams' book, "All close friendships are turned later to poems," and asked if he meant that as a literal statement.

"I meant it when I wrote it," he said with some umbrage, as if he thought I had challenged him. "I don't see any reason to retract it. They *are*. Close friendships *are* like poems."

Metaphorically speaking?

"Actually," Williams defiantly replied. "Because people rarely reach a real meaningful relationship in friendships, one which is really close. When that happens, they become poems to me." Again he paused. He thought for a moment, only a moment, then added, "Not all poetry is sentimental poetry, you know. Some poetry can be pretty savage."

Williams and his young companion (an unnervingly silent lad who had spent the day clutching a shoe box) rose from the table. They were headed for Times Square to see a new French film starring Alain Delon. "I looooove Alain Delon!" Williams squealed for all to hear.

Before you go, one last question. In the book you say, "I've made a covenant with myself to continue to write." How do you define the word "covenant"?

"A binding spiritual agreement that we will respect. I have no choice but to write. What else can I do?"

Of the many Williams revivals in the mid-1970s, the most notable was *Sweet Bird of Youth*, with Irene Worth as the Princess and Christopher Walken as Chance Wayne.

In April 1976, two months after *Sweet Bird of Youth* closed, six months after my meeting with Williams, I met with Walken in his Upper West Side apartment. Walken stalks a living room just as he stalks a stage. Your eyes never leave him. After he came to rest in a canvas director's chair, he spoke about Tennessee Williams.

"Williams is one of those people who's able to talk about things that most of us cannot articulate," he said. "He's one of those writers who talk about the darker corners of the soul, and the less visible and more ambiguous parts of a personality—things about people that don't get talked about too often. In *Sweet Bird of Youth* the Princess talks about herself and her fear. Discussions of fear are very tricky, and he handles them so well. Another writer who can do that is Albee. I can't really think of anybody else. That conversation between the two men at the end of *A Delicate Balance* is one of the scariest things that I've ever heard. And it's about something that really doesn't have a name. That sort of writing fascinates me."

Why is it, I asked, that a Williams play seems greater in its whole than it does in its parts?

"It's true. You read it and think, 'Oh, Christ, how am I going to say that?' Then the whole play somehow comes together and makes a certain kind of sense. *Sweet Bird of Youth*, really, is surreal. It's like a nightmare. It's not really about this place with these people. It's all sort of hanging there somewhere inside his mind. Everything is so fragile with him, fragile and smokelike. His characters, in the most positive Elizabethan sense, all seem to be shadows, and they really do dissolve into air when it's over with.

"You know how you see a play, and you sort of recognize somebody? A character reminds you of someone you know? I don't think that's ever true of Williams. His characters are always just who they are on the stage, and they're too outrageous to be anybody you know. In a sense that's his greatness, because he does build larger-than-life people. Very few writers can do that. These characters are heroic in their own way and exist completely in themselves.

"With a play like *Sweet Bird*, in rehearsal you try to say the lines naturally. And then you have to finally face the fact that it's poetry, and that it has to be dealt with as poetry, whatever poetry is. I suppose poetry is a condensation or a distillation. It's not the way you or I would say it. It's the way you'd say it if you were . . ."

Walken paused, searched, then spoke again. "It's the way you'd say it if you were . . . an angel."

Another five months passed. Back in St. Louis, in September 1976, I arranged a visit with the last of the belles.

Though at age ninety-one Edwina Dakin Williams was a solitary, fragile figure, confined with her memories to a simple two-room apartment, the world still knew Miss Edwina by her stage name. She was, of course, Amanda Wingfield, the delicate, well-intentioned, but tyrannical matriarch in *The Glass Menagerie.*

When Miss Edwina's son wrote that masterpiece in 1944, he described Amanda as "a little woman of great but confused vitality clinging frantically to another time and place. . . . Certainly she has endurance and a kind of heroism, and though her foolishness makes her unwittingly cruel at times, there is tenderness in her slight person."

Thirty-three years later, there was still foolishness, and tenderness, and she was still clinging with all the brittle energy she could muster to her memories of that long-ago time and place.

In the company of her younger son, the always-affable Dakin, Miss Edwina spent several hours reminiscing about her childhood, about her children—and especially about the gay, gal-*lant*, romantic Old South.

Her father was an Episcopal minister who frequently moved from parish to parish. So, although Miss Edwina was born in Ohio, in 1884, her girlhood was spent in Tennessee and Mississippi. Her fondest and most vivid memories harkened back to those gala turn-of-the-century parties when she was the belle of the ball.

"Mah fathuh was a very beloved clergyman in each parish," she explained in a lazy, elongated drawl that made even the shortest sentences seem to roll on and on like ol' man river, "and of course that made me very populuh, because a new girl in a new place is always very interesting, you know.

"Ah had a very gay time. Ah think Ah had about the gayest youth of any person imaginable. We'd have elaborate parties. Ah don't know of any place in the world that was gayer than the South, even after that terrible war. Of course, that was a *terrible* war. They called it Civil War, but it really wasn't a civil war. It was war between the states. The boys volunteered to fight for the South when they were only fifteen years old. It's very sad, Ah think, that fifteen-year-old boys would be called into the war." As she recalled those teenage boys she was born too late to know, her eyes filled with tears.

Most of the time, though, her eyes shone as she recounted the gay days and nights in Vicksburg and Port Gibson and New Orleans. She spoke in a frail, canarylike voice which added music to her flights of fancy. She concluded each story—each sentence, almost each phrase—with an airy, gossamer, ethereal laugh which was not unlike a nervous tic.

While theatergoers know she was the model for Amanda, it's less widely realized that she also was the prototype for Miss Alma in *Summer and Smoke* and its rewrite, *The Eccentricities of a Nightingale.* Miss Alma is a minister's daughter who loves to sing and play the piano. Her constant laugh is her most eccentric mannerism. *Summer and Smoke* was Miss Edwina's favorite play.

Despite the fact that she'd lived in St. Louis since 1918, her Southern accent still was so strong you could bundle a bale of cotton with it. In her tiny mouth, most *r*'s were dropped at the ends of words, though final *g*'s (as in *interesting*) usually rang loud and strong. If *g*'s were the one concession to her life lived upriver, New Orleans still was pronounced as a four-syllable city, and "gallant" was pronounced "gal-*lant*," with stress given to the chivalry rather than the first syllable.

"They had wonderful spirit," she chirped on. "They were the most gal-*lant* people Ah've ever known in time of trouble, and they were the most helpful to each othuh, the most sympathetic with each othuh in their sorrows. Ah think they're more sympathetic with each othuh's sorrows than we are up here. In the midst of all the troubles they were having, if they wanted to have a big card party, they *had* a big card party. They didn't seem to be cast down by their troubles any, and yet they had their tragedies."

But why dwell on unhappiness when there were so many gay times to recall?

"Mardi Gras was a very favorite time to have celebrations," she said. "We'd choose partners and have a *big* evening of it. One thing the boys did make a point of was trying to please the girls. Often our beaux would take us for a trip down the Mississippi. At Port

Gibson, the steps from the plantation to the levee are very long and steep. One time, Ah remember, Ah slipped on the top step and slid all the way down. That was an ignominious descent.

"Of course we always had a chaperone. Not that we needed one. We were not the type to cut up any. It's amazing the freedom Ah was given. It was expected of me, naturally, to behave myself."

If she wasn't dancing or boating or horseback riding, she was talking. As Dakin pointed out, "Southern ladies of her age used to entertain gentlemen callers by conversation. There was no TV or radio then. I've met quite a few of Mother's peer group, and they're all capable of talking all afternoon without anyone else being there except as an audience."

"Ah like to talk," she said. "That's one of mah failings. Ah used to give a number of interviews. Ah'm not giving a very brilliant one now, because Ah had a bad fall the other night, and so Ah don't feel in a very brilliant frame of mind."

When I suggested that we curtail our conversation, she demurred. "No, Ah like to talk. Ah may be a little too talkative. Oh, yes, Ah'll talk to you. When Ah was a girl, we could talk all evening. The servants would bring in these big logs, you know, for the fireplace, and we had our own entertaining. Of course, when we entertained beaux, we had plenty of assistance. There used to be slaves, you know, and they were still devoted to the families. Every household had plenty of help. They had the amount of service so the girls didn't have to do anything they didn't want to do. But one thing Ah *could* do was play the piano. Mah beaux would come to hear me play and sing at the piano."

Eventually, Miss Edwina married one of those beaux. They had a daughter, Rose, and a son, Tom. Eight years after Tom's birth (and after the family had moved to St. Louis), Dakin was born. Without her servants in a new city, the Southern belle quickly realized that marriage was fraught with responsibilities which she was unprepared to assume.

"Mother never knew how to cook till she moved to St. Louis," Dakin said.

"Oh, Ah made delightful angel foods, Dakin. That's one thing Ah *could* make, was cake."

"She may have learned how to make angel food in Mississippi, but that's the only thing she knew," Dakin countered. "I'll never forget one time when I had to wear my only pair of long white pants to some special event. Mother was ironing, and she scorched the seat out of them."

Miss Edwina laughed, then confirmed the incident. "Ah wasn't altogether a domestic," she said. "You could hardly say Ah was domestic." She paused, then added for good measure, "Ah didn't *want* to be domestic."

In the late 1930s, two significant events occurred. First, Miss Edwina's elder son changed his name from Tom to Tennessee. He did so because his University of Iowa fraternity brothers were amused by his Southern accent. But to Miss Edwina, her son's name would always be Tom.

"Tom was in a very low state financially at the time," she said, "so he took the position in his fraternity of waiting on tables, which was very amusing to us because he wasn't too handy in the kitchen when he was younger."

The second incident was not amusing. Miss Edwina subjected her daughter to a lobotomy. "There's a picture of Rose over there," she said, pointing to a nearby endtable. "You can see what a beauty she was. She had auburn hair. Great long auburn curls and great big blue eyes. Ah think a great many people were struck with Rose's beauty and how much she resembled Mary Pickford when she was growing up.

"When Ah was a girl, Ah'd sit home expecting the beaux, and they came. Unfortunately, poor Rose didn't have so many. She lived in a different age. Rose was a very beautiful girl, a very sweet girl, lovely disposition. But she was satisfied with one beau at a time."

Once again, tears welled in Miss Edwina's eyes. She gazed at a fading red rose which sat in a slender vase on the coffee table and said, "Our poor little rose . . . it looks very forlorn and sad." For once, her sentence was followed by silence rather than laughter.

Tennessee modeled the painfully shy Laura in *The Glass Menagerie* after Rose, just as he modeled Amanda after his mother. Though for decades Miss Edwina had conflicting emotions about Amanda, she now was reconciled to the truth that she was indeed its genesis.

"Ah always enjoyed that part," she said. "The first time Ah saw the play was at the Chicago opening. Tom wrote and asked me if Ah'd come up and give him courage. Ah think they were astonished that it turned out as well as it did. Tom wasn't prepared for all the curtain calls, and Ah don't think he was too well groomed for them, either.

"Laurette Taylor was Amanda. She was real genius. Laurette seemed to enter into the pathos of the charactuh. Amanda was a many-sided person. It's a very appealing part."

Her second-favorite Amanda was Helen Hayes. Dakin attempted to sway his mother's opinion, but she held firm. He then suggested that one reason for Miss Edwina's loyalty to Miss Hayes was because both women were physically small.

In her youth, Miss Edwina never weighed more than ninety-eight pounds. Now she weighed even less. "Ah was considered very delicate," she said, "but Ah haven't been weighed in a long time. Dakin, you better take me and weigh me. You don't know whether yuh dare take me or not, do yuh, Dakin? He doesn't know whether he dares take me. Ah might weigh too little."

Throughout the successful late 1940s and early 1950s, Miss Edwina and Dakin traveled to New York for each opening night. "Oh, yeeees," she exclaimed, "Ah was the honoree at a party every opening night. Tom always gave it for me himself. We had big times at those parties. Tom was very devoted to me."

This was the period when she hobnobbed with celebrities like Marilyn Monroe, Gloria Vanderbilt, and Elia Kazan. When I recently mentioned her name to the director, he began to laugh, not unkindly, at her memory. "She's a good old Southern girl grown up," Kazan said, "flirtatious, and never stopped talking, dominating anybody she was with. She was all right. She was just a typical, almost a grotesque, caricature of a Southern belle grown old."

Dakin and Miss Edwina attended their final opening night in 1969. *In the Bar of a Tokyo Hotel* was one of Williams' many commercial failures of the 1960s and 1970s. "That was the trip when Mother lost her seal coat," Dakin said as Miss Edwina hooted. "Tennessee had ordered her a fur coat from Bergdorf Goodman. The morning after the opening, we had breakfast in his room. The reviews were devastating, and Mother made the mistake of saying, 'Why don't you take up some other line of work?' It made Tennessee angry, and he canceled the order for the coat."

Between laughs, Miss Edwina chimed in, "That was a tactless remark, wasn't it?"

In addition to drawing on his mother and sister for inspiration, Williams also included his grandfather in *The Night of the Iguana*. The two men were great friends.

"Mah fathuh was a very beloved clergyman. He was the oldest living alumnus of Sewanee," his only child said, referring to the

University of the South, which is located on a Tennessee mountaintop. "Sewanee is the only quiet, peaceful place Ah know of in the world today. That's where we're plannin' to go. Ah've got my bags packed already. Ah can't wait to get to Sewanee."

Dakin is the one member of the family who is not in any of the plays. "Nor do I anticipate being in any," he said. "Though, if Tennessee ever dramatizes his Barnes Hospital experience, I'll unquestionably be one of the villains."

In late 1969, not long after the seal-coat incident, Dakin had Tennessee committed to the psychiatric division of St. Louis' famed Barnes Hospital. "I very definitely think my efforts saved his life," Dakin said. "He was on the verge of death from overdoses of drugs and excessive alcohol. Now that his health has improved, he is furious with me. I probably would feel the same way if I were in his position. It's only natural that you resent somebody who has locked you up and saved your life. You don't stop to figure, 'If he hadn't done it, I wouldn't be here.' A person thinks only, 'This kid brother of mine had the nerve to interfere with my life and lock me up, where I was subjected to all kinds of indignities—' "

"Talking about indignities," Miss Edwina interrupted, drawing the conversation back to herself, "Miss Mary gave me the greatest indignity Ah've ever had done me in mah life."

"Miss Mary is her nurse," Dakin clarified. "The other day she told Mother she didn't smell good and made her take a bath."

"She yanked me out of bed when Ah was asleep," Miss Edwina fumed.

And made you take a bath?

"Well," she backed off, "in proper places. Now, Dakin, don't you forget about mah bags for Sewanee."

There was, of course, no impending trip; there were no packed bags. There were only fantasies, which spilled over and obliterated realities, as relentlessly as a flooding river claims delta soil.

Even *Memoirs* fell prey to her flooding fantasies. In his autobiography, Tennessee Williams had written explicitly about his homosexuality. "Mother's reaction to *Memoirs* was that the publisher must have put in a lot of things that Tom didn't say," Dakin said with a wink.

"Ah thought it was very poor taste," Miss Edwina confirmed. "The strange part of it is, he told all these terrible things he was supposed to do, and he didn't do them. Tom's a very good conversationalist himself. He inherits that from me. But all his life, he just seemed to like to shock people. It gave him great pleasure if he could shock somebody.

"Oh yes, that was their favorite sport. Misquoting Tom was the favorite sport of the reporters. If they wanted to hear something shocking, he'd really give them something to be shocked with. And it wouldn't be true at all, because Tom was a very shy person. Sometimes he'd cover up his shyness by pretending to be otherwise, but he was a very shy person and always a gentleman. That's why he always had a nice young man with him as his companion. He always had a very devoted friend with him."

Tennessee had not seen his mother in four years. Nor had he phoned recently, preferring instead to keep check on her through intermediaries. In a recent newspaper interview, he had said of her, "She had the gift of gab. . . . I still find her totally mystifying—and frightening. It's best we stay away from our mothers." Eleven years earlier, during one of his rare visits to St. Louis, mother and son had met jointly with a local reporter. The interviewer asked her, "Exactly what is a 'gentleman caller'?" Before she could summon a reply, Tennessee wryly interjected, "It's one who stays a short time."

As the mother of a major playwright, Miss Edwina had enjoyed a celebrity status all her own. Now, she discounted it. "Ah don't think Ah am anything special," she said. "Ah'm just like any othuh mothuh who thinks her son is of course a genius always. And Ah not only thought so, but other people thought so too. Ah still think so. Ah think he's a genius. He's one of the few geniuses Ah know who is extremely modest, so modest that he tries to make other people think he's a rogue."

Age and illness had taken their obvious toll. A series of strokes had forced Dakin to place his mother under round-the-clock nursing supervision. Yet Miss Edwina did not worry aloud about her restricted future. So long as she was able to watch Lawrence Welk—"he really puts on the good plays"—on Sunday nights, she was content.

She still had her memories, and they were all the world she needed. "Ah'm very proud of my age," she asserted. "Ah'm proud Ah've weathered all the things Ah have."

What was the most difficult time of your life? I asked.

"Well, of course, when my children were born, there was difficulty. When Rose was born, that was a most difficult time.

"But mah times are my own now. That's one good thing about

growing older. Your time is your own. Before, mah life belonged to the gay times. Ah had so many gay times. Ah had a marvelous girlhood. Everywhere Ah went, Ah was the belle of the ball. When Ah was eighteen, Ah made mah debut in Vicksburg *twice*. Ah'm not exaggerating. Ah was *really* the belle of the ball, and the boys would stand in line to get a chance to take me out. Ah'm telling you the truth. Ah'm not just making up anything. Ah went to every dance in Mississippi, and Ah thoroughly enjoyed it, too. And Ah loved to take part in plays. Ah guess Tom has his love of plays from me. And Ah was very talented. Ah was very, very talented. Yes, indeed. Ah didn't miss a thing."

Four years later, at age ninety-five, Miss Amanda passed into silence. Her rebellious but ultimately dutiful son returned to St. Louis for his mother's funeral.

Three years later, at age seventy-one, he returned again, this time for his own obsequies. The mass was held at the cavernous St. Louis Cathedral, mere blocks away from the original apartment building that he'd described in *The Glass Menagerie* (and which some savvy real-estate owner had renamed "The Glass Menagerie Apartments"). Just as the coffin arrived from the funeral home, a gentle rain began to fall, and it continued to fall until after the burial.

Against Williams' wishes, Dakin buried his brother in St. Louis, the city he had so dreaded, next to their mother. It was a cruel, seemingly unforgivable act. But the plays of Tennessee Williams testify to the need for forgiveness . . . of strangers and lovers, of mothers and sons, and of brothers too.

Countless words were written about him; countless others were spoken. But in all that torrent of elegy and dirge, for me the most meaningful statement, the truest thought, was a simple sentence I'd read four years before. In a 1979 *Playboy* magazine interview, Marlon Brando, who had found his own legend through *A Streetcar Named Desire*, said of Tennessee Williams, "If there are men who have a clean soul, he's one of them."

Amen.

CHAPTER SIX

A CERTAIN AMOUNT OF SPLEEN

"I created myself, and I'll attack anybody I feel like."
—EDWARD ALBEE

It's the oldest interview question in the world, and I don't think it appears in this book: Who were you influenced by?

But in her scrapbook of memories, *People Who Led to My Plays*, Obie Award–winning playwright Adrienne Kennedy answers that tired chestnut of a question in a fresh and original way that subtly lures the reader into confronting his own influences even while reading about hers.

The links in her chain of inspiration include nursery rhymes, fairy tales, comic strips, Bible stories, movies. In high school she discovered Tennessee Williams and *The Glass Menagerie.* She felt an intense identification with the crippled Laura, who lived in her fantasyland of glass animals. Kennedy writes, "From my extreme empathy with her I learned that I too felt frightened and crippled, which was totally puzzling to me. Why? Why did I feel like Laura? Why? I was popular in high school, had a boyfriend and went out constantly with my friends to movies, picnics and the Friday-night Y-canteen dance. Why?"

As the years passed, new influences included such actors as Marlon Brando: "He was the first movie star that both my white and Negro friends had loved equally, at a time when we seemed to have little in common. . . ."

Now add music and art: Beethoven, Van Gogh, Debussy.

Add a finally emerging sense of black pride: James Baldwin, Richard Wright, Langston Hughes.

Add Duke Ellington: "I learned from hearing his music that there was an immense poetry inside my life as an American Negro if I could find it."

The book ends in 1961, as she is about to join a playwriting workshop at Circle in the Square, at which her first play will be performed.

The final page contains a brief biography of Kennedy which states that she has been "influenced by American dramatists Tennessee Williams and Edward Albee." Williams, yes, but her text does not progress to Albee.

Nine months after the memoir was published, in an article in *American Theatre* magazine, Kennedy elaborated on Edward Albee's contribution to her maturation. He taught the Circle in the Square workshop which she joined in 1962. In the article, she remembers Albee as "shy and frightened. . . . There was a hole in his sweater, which gave him the air of a struggling writer."

When Kennedy decided to drop the class rather than allow her play (which she deemed too revealing) to be performed, Albee told her, "Do you know what a playwright is? A playwright is someone who lets his guts hang out on the stage. . . ."

Later in 1962, *Who's Afraid of Virginia Woolf?* exploded at the Billy Rose Theater and ran one and a half years. When I met its author in April 1976, the drama was back on Broadway with Ben Gazzara and Colleen Dewhurst in an Albee-directed revival.

"What shall we talk about?" he began. Albee was slick and confident. He exuded an assured authority.

He was not what I'd expected.

I'd expected to confront the image he'd imparted when he'd first become a celebrity fifteen years earlier.

I'd expected him to be wearing that same threadbare sweater he wore to Adrienne Kennedy's workshop.

I'd expected to meet an introspective, brooding intellectual ("shy and frightened") whose pale complexion would be lit by an overhanging Tiffany lamp.

Perhaps a cat or two would be coldly glaring from his ascetic shoulders.

To my surprise, Albee was forceful and robust, with a deep clarion voice. He was expensively dressed. He possessed a full head of thick, shiny dark hair. (No more close-to-the-skull crewcuts for him.) There was nary a cat in sight.

He projected the presence of a matinee idol. Heat emanated from him; only the warmth was missing.

We sat facing each other across a desk in his spacious West Forty-seventh Street office. The walls were lined with framed posters from Albee productions. His name grew successively larger on the posters, till finally it was indistinguishable from the titles. EDWARD ALBEE'S WHO'S AFRAID OF VIRGINIA WOOLF? blended together, the way SIDNEY SHELDON'S WINDMILLS OF THE GODS and JUDITH KRANTZ'S MANHATTAN read as one phrase.

"What should we talk about?" he began.

Let's begin with something simple. Let's talk about your biography, as it appears in theater playbills. Why is it that you begin with your date of birth and then skip ahead directly to the list of plays?

"Fair enough," Albee countered. "You always want to know when a man was born. And I began writing plays thirty years later, okay? Fine. It's true. What should I have put in? The schools that I got thrown out of? When I started fucking? How many dogs I have? Those are the things that people can fill them up with, but why? I learned a long time ago reading theater bills that the shortest listings are usually about some of the more interesting people. Excessively long, flowery nonsense is an ego trip. I put down all the pertinent facts."

Well . . . not quite *all* the pertinent facts. For the fact is that the facts of Albee's life are cloaked in innuendo; the events of Albee's life are shrouded in mystery. Even as far back as that first "pertinent fact," there are question marks.

Edward Albee was born on March 12, 1928. According to reports, his parents promptly abandoned him. The infant was placed in a foundling home in Washington, D.C. The playwright has stated that he has never tried to uncover the identity of his real parents.

The baby was adopted by Reed and Frances Albee, heirs to the theater fortune amassed by vaudeville king Edward F. Albee. The impresario died in 1930, two years after his name had been given to his foundling grandson.

Edward Franklin Albee III grew up uneasily amidst the affluence of the Albee mansion in Larchmont, New York. He was no more happy at the private schools he dropped out of or got thrown out of. ("I did not write *The Catcher in the Rye*," he once told a reporter. "I lived it.") At age nineteen he broke with his parents and moved to Greenwich Village, where his rebellion and odd jobs were subsidized by a bequest of $50 a week from his grandmother.

One of your jobs was as a telegram-delivery boy. Is it true that you had to deliver telegrams announcing deaths, and that you would allow people to read them and then reseal them?

"The thing was," Albee explained, "if they didn't accept them, they didn't have to pay for them. I thought it was the proper thing to do."

A telegram figures prominently in *Who's Afraid of Virginia Woolf?* In one of the play's more surprising speeches, George declares, "I ate it." That's hardly more unexpected, though, than a delivery boy allowing people to read telegrams and then reseal them. (Imagine Martha asking, "Where's the telegram?" and George replying, "Well, we put it back in the envelope and the messenger boy returned it to the office.")

"I think the thing that bothered me most about those telegrams," Albee said, "was that private hospitals never used to do that. It was only public hospitals, and it was always the very poor people whose families were dying in the charity wards. And they'd get these collect telegrams. And I thought there was something grotesque about the city sending out *collect* telegrams. The information of the death wasn't bad enough. You had to *pay* to get the bad news. That offended me deeply, or at least it offended my sense of logic, if not propriety."

What would you say when delivering such a telegram?

"Well, I would say, 'Look, this is very bad news, and they want you to pay for it. Read it, copy down what it says, and give it back to me.' There was the anticipatory numbness that people know. Tincture of grief, and all that. You know, you deliver telegrams—especially on the Upper West Side of New York City—and you see an awful lot of poverty and unhappiness. And there are just some things you don't want to contribute to. It seemed like the natural thing to do."

* * *

Just prior to his thirtieth birthday, Albee wrote a two-character one-act play, *The Zoo Story*, which opened Off-Broadway in 1960 and ran for nineteen months. It was followed by *The Death of Bessie Smith*, *The Sandbox*, and *The American Dream*. Albee had found his métier.

In October 1962, when his first full-length play, *Who's Afraid of Virginia Woolf?*, opened on Broadway, critics cheered the play's engrossing theatricality. Albee was crowned as our newest Very Important Playwright; the cover of *Newsweek* served as his pedestal.

Virginia Woolf just as quickly became the subject of controversy, which helped it to rack up a profitable twenty-month run. Along the way it won the Antoinette Perry and Drama Critics Circle awards.

Was *Virginia Woolf* also well received in London?

"Oh, yes. It ran against a trend. There aren't many serious American plays that are successful in London."

Why do you think it ran against the trend?

"Oh, who knows? Possibly to a certain extent because of the scandal that accompanied it. I'm sure it ran an extra six months here because of the theoretically dirty words that it had in it. Then, the fact that there was a big scandal, with the Lord Chamberlain's office in London requesting thirty-eight changes. It was considered vile and impolite and obscene. I was startled by all of that, because it didn't seem any of those things to me. Since nothing was gratuitous, nothing struck me as being out of place. But those things don't hurt a run, you know."

Your next play, *The Ballad of the Sad Cafe*, in 1963, was adapted from the novella by Carson McCullers. It's curious how *Ballad* has been ignored. When your third play, *Tiny Alice*, opened, it repeatedly was referred to as your first major play since *Virginia Woolf*. It was as if *The Ballad of the Sad Cafe* had been expunged.

"That's sort of a compliment, as a matter of fact," Albee suggested. "I think that unconsciously, at least, it comes partly from the fact that I made the piece sound so much like Carson McCullers that I vanished. And that's why *it* vanished. I got some of my best reviews, as a matter of fact, from the oddest people on that particular adaptation. A lot of people liked it a lot."

Then problems arose. His next dramas traveled in new directions, away from safe "theatricality" and into areas that sometimes puzzled, confused, and even bored audiences. When *Tiny Alice* opened in

1964, many perplexed critics tended to equate confusion with controversy. Hence, *Tiny Alice* became controversial. But this was not dirty-word controversial, and this time audiences stayed away. So Albee gave a press conference to clarify the confusion. He not only "explained" the drama but also waged a frontal assault on the critics.

"It is indecent to fault a work for being difficult," Albee charged. "It is the height of immodesty for a critic to assume that what he finds confusing will necessarily puzzle an audience. . . .

"It is not enough for a critic to tell his audience how well a play succeeds in its intention; he must also judge that intention by the absolute standards of the theater as an art form. . . . The Broadway theaters that are full each night are full of entertainments that succeed entirely in their intentions, even though these intentions are relatively low on any absolute scale. It is far easier for a play that attempts the point of twenty on a graph of one hundred to achieve the point of nineteen than for a play that attempts eighty to reach even forty. But we all know that forty is higher than nineteen.

"Yet, at the end of each season the critics lament the lack of serious and ambitious plays. The odd thing is that these same critics have spent the season urging their readers to rush to the nineteen-point plays. Well, perhaps they are better plays *to* their audience, but they are not better plays *for* their audience. And since the critic fashions the audience taste, whether he intends to or not, he succeeds, each season, in merely lowering it. . . ."

Surely you're familiar with the myth that theater critics build up a playwright and then take great pleasure in knocking him down.

"It's not a myth," Albee bridled. "It's true, and there's nothing new about it."

But you haven't been knocked down.

"They keep trying. I simply plan to outlast them, that's all. Of course it's not a myth. Critics do like to flex their muscles, create a Frankenstein monster, and then dismember it. That's what they enjoy doing. Williams they used to attack for not writing *Streetcar* over and over again, and then when he tried to write a play like *Streetcar* they attacked him for repeating himself."

Is being on the cover of *Newsweek* part of becoming the Frankenstein monster?

"I suppose there was a kind of suddenness to my eruption that may have disturbed a few of them," he conceded. "And then after the general stupidity of the reviews of *Tiny Alice* I did give this famous press conference in which I said that even though the critics were confused, that's no reason to assume the audience would be confused. Well, then they figured that I needed a little knocking down. They'd created me and how dare I attack them. I mean, indeed! They didn't create me, I created myself, and I'll attack anybody I feel like."

So you understand now that when I referred to a myth, I was referring to the fact that the critics really *don't* always have the power to knock someone down.

"No, they don't. But they like to play at it.

"You've always got two or three kinds of critics. You've got the sensible, responsible men who have been involved in the theater and know something about it, like Harold Clurman and a few others. Walter Kerr to a lesser extent, but certainly to an extent.

"Then you've got your ex-reporters, who don't come to the theater with anything more than a certain amount of intelligence and who over the years develop expertise. And if they can retain their enthusiasm, they're useful critics. The two best examples are Richard Watts in New York and Elliot Norton in Boston.

"Then, every once in a while you have a man who is capable of writing a few words himself, like Brendan Gill—who's not a *bad* critic. But then you've got the ambitious men, the ones who are fundamentally on an ego trip. The John Simons of the world. Who's the one who quit criticism and is now misrunning the Yale Drama School? Brustein, Robert Brustein. Those who are fundamentally on ego trips, who think the world should be seen through the shattered lens of their own imaginations.

"You've got all sorts. You've got very good critics and terrible ones. But whatever one may feel about critics, none of it would matter if we had an audience that was educated at all in the theater and was willing to make its own decisions and understand that what a critic says is an opinion and not a fact. Then there would be no problem at all."

Judging from your past interviews, the thing you're most concerned about is the problem of writing for an audience that refuses to (a) listen, and (b) change.

"Yes, and the important word there is 'refuse' rather than 'be unable to.' The *refusal* to do it."

Is that a conscious act?

"Whether it's conscious or not, it's certainly deliberate. It's not very important, though. Nothing's very important. The critics aren't important. Commercial success isn't important. The theater is something that exists outside of all these day-to-day hazards in the minefield."

Do you have days when you think that even being around the theater is unimportant?

"Well, no. I like writing plays, and occasionally I like seeing them. I think I like writing more than I do seeing them, except for my own. Though there are some other playwrights whose work I also like.

"No, I'm happy I'm a playwright. I just don't like all this crap one has to go through: the theater owners, and the critics who are interested in their own egos, and the audiences who want to be patted on the back rather than waked up."

Yet you insist on remaining in New York. You never offer your new plays to regional theaters. You keep producing them on Broadway.

"So long as the public taste in the rest of the country is determined by what's done on Broadway, then there's a responsibility on a lot of people's parts to stay here."

Can't the taste be moved geographically if enough important people lend their support and presence to regional theaters?

"You go to a regional theater and you end up being lost. I could go to Seattle for a year, or I could go to Houston or various places, and nobody would hear from me again except the people in Seattle and Houston. It wouldn't affect anything except for that particular moment."

In 1966 *A Delicate Balance*, Albee's first original play after *Tiny Alice*, won the Pulitzer Prize. Many viewed the award as mere compensation for the committee's collective lack of spine in refusing the prize to *Virginia Woolf*. When the Pulitzer Prize announcement was made in May 1967, Albee called another press conference, this time to explain that he had considered declining the current Pulitzer.

"I have decided to accept the award for three reasons," he said. "First, because if I were to refuse it out of hand I wouldn't feel as free to criticize it as I do accepting it. Second, because I don't wish to embarrass the other recipients this year by seeming to suggest that they follow my lead. And, finally, because while the Pulitzer Prize is an honor in decline, it is still an honor, a considerable one."

Soon after the opening of *A Delicate Balance*, Albee became entangled in one of his more bizarre adventures, when he rewrote Abe

Burrows' libretto for a new Broadway musical based on Truman Capote's *Breakfast at Tiffany's*.

You once told an interviewer that while working on *Breakfast at Tiffany's* it "was fascinating to watch a dictator being disappointed in preconceived notions."

"A dictator?" Albee asked, puzzled. "I don't think I could have said that. I can't imagine what it means." A bulb lit in his eyes. "Oh! What I probably meant was that what I succeeded in doing in *Breakfast at Tiffany's* was to take a nice, mediocre little musical and bring it back to some of the harshness that Truman Capote had originally intended. And the dictator I was talking about was the audience, who at the intermissions of the previews in New York were running around saying, 'Where's David Merrick? How *dare* he give us anything like this?' *That* dictator."

Was it a harsh musical, then? Did you make it more serious?

"I was on my way. I don't think the two weeks that I was given to redo the whole thing was enough time. It was sort of done in a half-assed fashion. But it could have been pretty exciting. New songs. New dances."

You write so sparely. Doesn't that lend itself to the writing of a book for a musical?

"The problem is, a libretto fundamentally has to be written on the level of a comic strip, and that gets in the way of some of my circumlocution."

All Over premiered five years later, in 1971. It was a contemplative drama that had the misfortune to open during one of this country's most strident periods, as Americans were taking to the streets to protest the Vietnam War. One month before *All Over* opened, critics had been enthusiastic about the Phoenix Theater production of Daniel Berrigan's political tract *The Trial of the Catonsville Nine*. Most of those same critics were impatient with and dismissive of Albee's quiet play.

The New York Times gave the playwright a forum from which to respond. "There is a misunderstanding about what political theater really is," he complained in a lengthy interview. "In 1968, I went around campaigning for McCarthy, and during my speeches I talked in *specific* political terms. But when I write a play, I'm interested in changing the way people look at themselves and the way they look at life. I have never written a play that was not in its essence political.

But we don't need an attack on the specific or the conscious. We need an attack on the unconscious."

Alas, these comments appeared late in the piece. Earlier paragraphs contained catty exchanges between Albee and his coproducer, Richard Barr, which attacked various other plays, playwrights, and performers. These were the paragraphs that caught the public's attention.

How well do you remember that interview you gave to *The New York Times* five years ago after *All Over* opened?

"The one out in Montauk where I attacked everybody? That was all right. I don't remember regretting saying any of the things that I did. I said some of them with a certain amount of spleen and a bit of alcohol in me. It was kind of cleansing to do it."

You also talked about your concept of political theater. Do you consider *Virginia Woolf* a political play?

"A political play? Political in the broadest sense of the term, of surviving without false illusions. Dealing honorably with ourselves. In that sense it's political. Sure. If anybody wants to find the analogy, let them. I don't care."

But you thought *All Over* was a highly political play.

"Yes."

And I assume you thought *Seascape* was a political play.

"I daresay I did."

Seascape, which reached Broadway in 1975, concerns an aging couple alone on a beach. After a lengthy first-act discourse about their lives together and apart, they are prepostrously confronted by two great green lizards, Leslie and Sarah, who have left the seas because "we had a sense of not belonging anymore." The two couples haltingly attempt to adjust to one another and finally conclude that trust and friendship must come with time.

When *Seascape* opened in 1975, the Vietnam War was winding down, and Vietnamese refugees were beginning to enter America. This time, Albee's play—with its call for understanding between alien forces—could be viewed as the timeliest of political dramas. *Seascape* survived only a sixty-three-performance run, but it garnered for Albee (who made his directing debut with the drama) his second Pulitzer Prize.

* * *

Do you think there's any validity in relating *A Delicate Balance* and *Seascape*?

"Yes. That line in the third act of *Delicate Balance*—'Everything comes too late, finally'—that's the connective tissue between the two. Where choice is no longer possible, change is no longer possible. In that sense they're related. But then again, that relates a lot of my plays to an extent, I guess."

I was thinking of a relation between the two lizards in *Seascape* and the intruding couple, Harry and Edna, in *A Delicate Balance*.

"I certainly didn't do a conscious relation there."

People who were no longer at home in their normal environment and were thinking about imposing themselves elsewhere, where they may or may not be interfering.

"I don't think that the lizards, Leslie and Sarah, were determined to impose themselves on anybody. They were up there blinking, not quite knowing where they were or what they were about. Edna and Harry were indeed going to impose themselves. They knew the territory. Leslie and Sarah did not know the territory."

In his first Broadway role, Frank Langella won a Tony Award for his performance as the lizard named Leslie. Three years later, when Langella was starring in the title role of *Dracula*, his second Broadway play, I asked him why Albee's drama had elicited such inordinate hostility from audiences.

"Because they were shown an incomplete evening," Langella replied. "The play as originally written, as I originally agreed to do it, was three and a half hours long. It was in three acts, and Edward revealed much more of himself and more of the play's human characters. The lizards were fairly unchanged. But one whole act was cut the first day of rehearsal, and then, through the course of the run out of town, more and more of the man's role was cut so that he became almost unrecognizable from what the original character had been.

"Most people who came back to see me after those performances were terribly hostile to Edward and to the play. Whether they had enjoyed our work in it or not, they were all angry. And over the years I have come to the conclusion that *that's* what they were angry about—that they somehow sensed that they weren't being given a complete evening, that they were being teased. I don't think Edward set out to do that. I just think that at some point, perhaps given his temperament, he felt he'd revealed too much of himself in the original play and decided to cut it.

"If I had been a member of the audience at *Seascape*, there's a good chance I would have just hated it. But while I was in it, I thought that what he had to say was extraordinary. Fascinating. I still do. But *so much* of what he had to say that was really brilliant is somewhere in Edward's study on a shelf. Maybe one day we *will* get to see that."

You tend to write four hours a day and then stop. Is that because after four hours you're drained?

"My brain gets tired. Or my concentration vanishes. Or I get a headache. Or I want to do something else. I find usually four hours is enough. Then I can go and correct for fifteen minutes. But I concentrate rather heavily when I'm working, so my brain gets tired."

Yet we hear these stories about Noel Coward and others writing all day long.

"I've never known whether any of those things were true or not. I don't know whether Tennessee Williams still gets up at eight in the morning, has a pitcher of martinis, and writes until midnight. I doubt it. Whenever I see him, he's not at home. He's out. He's not writing. So I don't know."

How much of writing is not writing?

"When are you not writing?"

When you put your work in the drawer because you have to get some distance from it, I suggested.

"Then you write in a different fashion. You're looking and listening and sifting and distorting facts of truth and all that sort of thing that's the function of a writer."

What about when you're writing during the four hours and you find yourself staring out a window because the words just aren't in your head?

"What you're doing then, I guess, fundamentally, is moving things from the general to the particular. Sometimes that takes a while. You're writing down a particularization of what you've been generalizing about in your mind. So getting it down properly, and, you know, focusing in—yes, moving from the general to the particular—is exactly what I mean. Why should I try to expand on it?"

You speak at a lot of universities, don't you?

"I don't love doing it, though it is nice to get out. Last week I was at the University of Tennessee and the University of Indiana. The kids seemed pretty bright. The questions were reasonably intelligent.

"Young audiences I do find are the most interesting, and the most interested. When we were doing *Virginia Woolf* this time in New Haven, thank God for the Yale audiences. Those kids made a big difference in giving the actors confidence. Young audiences are absolutely fine. I walk past the TKTS booth in Times Square every day coming to and from the office and there are always young people buying discounted tickets. There *are* more young people going to the theater all the time.

"Now, there are a lot of young people doing lots of things wrong. They're cutting off politically. They're doing all sorts of terrible things. But they're going to the theater too, and they're still the best audience. They're the most honest audience. They haven't predetermined the nature of the theatrical experience they want to have quite so much. And they haven't learned how to close down, cut off, not listen. They haven't learned those things yet. They will fairly soon, but they haven't yet."

When you first had success, you constantly were being asked if there was an Albee style of writing, to which you would reply, "No, there's not an Albee style. I think you'll see that as the years go by." In fact, we've seen quite the contrary. You *have* developed a writing style. Harold Clurman calls it writing from the other side of the tomb.

"I daresay there is a style, but I don't think about it. I really don't. I'm always startled when people say, 'Here's an interesting play. The fellow tries to write like you.' Or, 'This one imitates you.' I can never see it. It's dangerous for a playwright to think of himself in the third person. Extremely dangerous."

Since our conversation, Albee has continued to be pummelled on Broadway.

In 1980 *The Lady from Dubuque* lasted twelve performances.

In 1981 his adaptation of Nabokov's *Lolita* lasted twelve performances.

In 1983 *The Man Who Had Three Arms* eked out sixteen performances.

Silence for a long while. Then I heard he was mounting his plays at an English-speaking theater in Vienna.

In 1989 he directed another production of *Who's Afraid of Virginia*

Woolf?, this time in Los Angeles, starring Glenda Jackson and John Lithgow. The revival did not continue on to Broadway, as some had expected it would. Instead, Albee directed still another production of *Virginia Woolf*, this time with the Los Angeles understudies, at the Alley Theater in Houston.

One senses that, while the New York critics have not scored a knockout, Albee and his wounded spleen have retreated to a distant corner of the canvas.

Yet I think of him often.

Of how he, more than any other playwright, was so unlike what I'd anticipated.

Of how sure of himself he was, and of how ready his answers were.

"Do you know what a playwright is?" he asked Adrienne Kennedy. "A playwright is someone who lets his guts hang out on the stage. . . ."

Now, whenever I think of him, my mothlike mind settles on the bright light of a comment in Walter Kerr's review of *Tiny Alice* in 1965. "Every once in a while," the critic wrote, "you meet a man who is so knowing that you never get to know him."

CHAPTER SEVEN

SOLITARY MAN

"It's fatal if the producer starts bragging about his creative contributions."
—DAVID MERRICK

"I don't do interviews," the producer said as he offered a reluctant hand. "But come on in."

The amenities concluded, David Merrick led me into his insular private office on the fifth floor atop the St. James Theater. The office was much more colorful than he was. It was bright scarlet.

Red walls, red doors, red drapes.

Not garish. Not ostentatious. Just very red.

I'd never expected to be sitting in that firehouse. Merrick had been maintaining a low profile for several years; interviews had become a rarity. Indeed, in 1973 a *New York Times* reporter sarcastically wrote that an interview with the reclusive producer "was no more difficult to arrange than tea with the Queen at Buckingham Palace."

My pursuit was initiated in late 1975, when I chanced upon him at Tennessee Williams' New York City book-signing party.

Back home in St. Louis, I began to research Merrick's early days—just in case we should ever meet.

It wasn't easy.

Some people refused to talk to me, while others actually seemed afraid to talk.

I encountered numerous contradictions and unanswered questions. The only for-sure fact is his November 27, 1911 birthdate—though when he became a producer he claimed that he had been born in 1916. Reports differ as to how many children haberdasher Samuel Margulois and his wife, Celia, had; most agree on five. David, the last, was ten years younger than his next-elder sister.

Merrick's youth is a confusing haze. His parents were divorced when he was ten (or was he seven?), and the boy was raised by his sister Sadie and her husband, Sam J. Margulis.

Did he eventually live with more than one sister?

Did his parents remarry and then redivorce?

In how many city apartments and houses did he live?

"I have the soul of an alley cat," Merrick once told an interviewer. If so, it was shaped in St. Louis alleys.

To help make ends meet, the youth sold shoes, was a stock boy for the Margulis family's garment firm, had a paper route with the *St. Louis Globe-Democrat*, and during Christmas holidays signed on at the post office. "Dave was a worker," Sam Margulis' brother Al told me. "He tried to make a buck." Perhaps it would be more accurate to suggest he *needed* a buck. One former acquaintance recalled that Merrick's family was "dirt poor."

Dave became a loner, but he also became a leader. He was senior-class president at Central High School. When he was graduated in 1930, the caption under his yearbook photo read, "His spirit is their power." The yearbook cites him with more activities than any other male student. Dave's stiff frown scowls out from the yearbook's various club photos. His only smile: the debating-team picture.

That 1930 yearbook includes a short story by Margulois titled "An Artistic Success." This tale of deception and double-cross in the art world prophetically begins, "When a man has reached heights of authority on artistic matters . . . his words have weight."

High-school classmate Thekla Knoernschild told me: "Ten years ago someone from *Time* magazine wanted juicy stories about David. There were none. David was then as he is now—not really aloof; he just minded his own business. You respected him but you couldn't get close to him. None of us were in a high socioeconomic status. But he was always an immaculate dresser." Another classmate described how Margulois constantly would tug at his suit-jacket sleeves in order to cover his frayed shirt cuffs.

Under the guidance of a demanding drama coach, he performed in the class plays. Stagestruck, he continued to act during his college years. At the YMHA, he appeared in productions of, among others, Clifford Odets' *Awake and Sing!* and Elmer Rice's *Counsellor at Law*. "I've always thought Dave was a frustrated actor," Al Margulis said. "Actually he was a very good actor." A friend from those YMHA days told me that as an actor Merrick refused to take direction.

One of his Washington University Law School classmates, Melvin Newmark, was quoted in *Newsweek* in 1966 as saying: "We all thought he was a drip. If you would have picked the man least likely to succeed, you'd have picked David Margulois." When I called Newmark, he was eager to set the record straight. "I was misquoted," he claimed. "I didn't say Dave was a drip. I said he was a nebbish.

"He didn't make a big impression on anybody. He faded into the background. The thrust of my remark was that we should all be such successful nebbishes."

Midway through law school Margulois transferred to St. Louis University. He was graduated from St. Louis University Law School in 1937.

On January 16, 1938, alley cat David Margulois married a girl from the right side of the tracks, Leonore Beck, despite her family's vigorous opposition. "Her family continually snubbed him, and Dave resented it," said Irwin Mohr, probably Margulois' best friend at the time. "Dave was always fiercely ambitious, and he resented anyone who didn't accept him."

Ironically, David's disapproving mother-in-law was responsible for the upturn in his fortunes. When she died in the early 1940s, a large inheritance allowed Leonore and David Margulois to change their last name to Merrick, leave St. Louis, move to New York, and attempt to break into Broadway. (Merrick's own parents also died in the 1940s.)

In April 1976, before I traveled to New York, I wrote to Merrick and requested an interview.

No reply.

Once in New York, I looked him up in the phone book (as he had instructed five months earlier) and placed a call. A secretary took my request. When two days elapsed without a response, I phoned again.

"Didn't Mr. Merrick call you?" the secretary asked.

No. Can't you just get me a confirmation or refusal?

"I wouldn't *dream* of asking Mr. Merrick such a thing," she replied. The fear in her voice was palpable.

The next afternoon, a Friday, I interviewed Edward Albee. After I left the playwright's office, while running the gauntlet of rush-hour congestion I literally stumbled into a man on the corner of Eighth Avenue and West Forty-fourth Street. Only after mumbling an apology did I actually look at him. To my astonishment, my victim was David Merrick. I quickly re-introduced myself, mentioned the futile phone calls, and requested an interview.

"Call me Monday morning," he said, and strode away.

It sounded like another brush-off. But I did call, and it wasn't. Now the immaculately dressed producer was seated across from me on a red velvet couch. There were no longer any frayed cuffs that needed hiding.

Merrick promptly declared, "There are two ground rules: no biographical questions, and I don't talk about St. Louis."

So much for research.

Deprived of my sustenance, I nibbled at random.

Do many producers have your law background? I asked.

"I don't have a law background," Merrick curtly corrected. "I have a law education. I never practiced. That was many, many years ago. I passed the Missouri bar, but I knew that I didn't want to practice law even before I started law school. However, I've been practicing law as a producer constantly. I do all the contracts, and without that law degree I would not have been as successful as I have been. Frequently I'm off someplace in Europe and find it necessary to do contracts, and the ability to alter them or write them myself has been a very important ace for my activities."

Forget about *Clutterbuck*, the first show for which he was associate producer. His Broadway ascension began with *Fanny*, which he co-produced with Joshua Logan in 1954. Merrick's business acumen gave *Fanny* the largest operating profit Broadway ever had seen. Despite mixed notices, the musical returned its $325,000 investment in less than seventeen weeks.

I told Merrick a story Joshua Logan had shared with me. Logan was breaking in William Inge's *Picnic* out of town when fledgling producer Merrick came to Cleveland to persuade him to direct *Fanny*. *Picnic* wasn't working, and Merrick's observations motivated Logan to insert new dialogue that made the play a hit.

Is this typical of Merrick's role as a producer?

"Well, it's part of it," Merrick answered, loosening up a little. "I remember that incident. *Picnic* had been to several towns and gotten bad notices. Cleveland, again bad notices. I sat in the audience. I thought the play was quite marvelous. And I watched the audience. The women were *loving* it, but the men were sitting there with their teeth clenched. The critics were all men at that time.

"So I came to the conclusion that they hated the lead character, who was a swaggering, sort of empty-headed, fatuous athletic type. And I was having the same reaction. I remembered that type from when I was in college. We *hated* him, you know. Certainly anyone who was there to get an education, who was more of a scholar—we hated those Saturday-afternoon heroes. So the men in the audience just hated this character out of memory.

"I told that to Josh. I said, 'I think the way to get around it is just to tell the audience early on in the play that they aren't *supposed* to like him. If you give one line to the other character, and have the nice boy say that people at college used to bristle at Hal'—I think bristle was the word I used—'it might help.'

"So Josh put in one quick line. And he claimed it made all the difference. From that point on they started to get good notices. I don't know if that was the only reason, but he seemed to think it was important.

"Yes, the producer is supposed to do that, but he's also supposed to never talk about it. It's very important that any ideas coming from the producer are given to the director, and that the *artists* take credit for them—the director and the writer. It's fatal if the producer starts bragging about his creative contributions. Sometimes, if the producer wants to get his opinions to the director, he must channel those ideas through stage managers, through anybody. Even the cleaning women are sometimes listened to before the producer! But even if the rapport with the director is very good, the producer must never talk about it elsewhere.

"I recall an interview in which I was talking about a musical that I had just produced, and the reporter kept asking, 'Now, how did this develop? Who did that? Who thought that up?'

"And I kept saying, 'Gower Champion, the director.'

"So finally, after listening to fifteen minutes of the wondrous contributions of Gower Champion, the reporter asked, 'Well, what did you do in this, Mr. Merrick?'

"I said, 'Oh, I picked Gower Champion.'

"That's good enough. Picking the right people is very important."

After *Fanny*, Merrick's schedule became relentless. In 1957 he made news by opening two plays in one month. Three years later he opened three productions in a week. He persuaded stars to tour, and he adapted his shows for Las Vegas.

Through the years, significant plays by Jean Anouilh, Brian Friel, John Osborne, Terence Rattigan, Tom Stoppard, and Peter Weiss came to America through Merrick's sponsorship. But it was his blatantly commercial comedies and musicals—*Gypsy*, *Take Me Along*, *Irma la Douce*, *Carnival*, *Sunday in New York*, *Oliver!*—that made him a Broadway legend.

He told his friend Irwin Mohr that he'd be delighted if every review of a Merrick offering included the word "ribald." (Mohr also confirmed the popular anecdote that Merrick refuses to fly from New York to Los Angeles on Trans World Airlines because the flight pattern passes over St. Louis. "As far back as the 1940s I can remember Dave joking about that," Mohr said. "He never liked the city, and he had justification.")

In 1964, *Hello, Dolly!* was the bonanza that finally provided the producer with what he always had sought: financial independence. And still the hits kept coming: *Cactus Flower; Marat/Sade; I Do! I Do!; Rosencrantz and Guildenstern Are Dead; Promises, Promises; Forty Carats*.

"The producer walks a balance between business and art," Merrick said. "He's a total contradiction. He's a mathematician who can't add, a poet and a rascal at the same time. So it runs through those two extremes. But the successful producer has to be a good businessman. Most of them aren't. They want to work at the creative area. Casting. But they can't make the budgets balance and make the shows run, because their break-even is so high."

I could have noted that Merrick knows how to add very well. Instead I pressed forward.

Have you ever been totally surprised by a show's reception? You thought you had a turkey, then glowing reviews came out? Or you had something you were really proud of and it got shot down?

"Not the latter," he said. "Anything that I've been really proud of was not shot down. Sometimes it's not as big as I thought it might be. The other way around, when I thought very likely it was a turkey—now, understand, it's not that *I* didn't like it, because I've never gone into a production that I didn't think was a very possible hit; I've been wrong, of course.

"But I remember on *La Plume de Ma Tante*, they were walking out in droves. And on opening night itself the audience just sat there, not a laugh. And it was supposed to be funny. And the critics were stone-faced. After the show I went over to Sardi's and dismissed it. I had dinner with somebody who asked me how it went, and I said, 'It's a flop.' And when the reviews came out later that night, it was a unanimous-rave press. Walter Kerr said he fell into the aisle laughing. And he was the stoniest one of all.

"Of course, once the reviews come out everyone starts laughing, because they've read it's funny. On that play, after walk-outs of two weeks and not very much success on the break-in in Philadelphia, the moment the notices came out audiences started laughing before the curtain went up. And they laughed for two and a half years, and then on tour."

Which of your shows elicit the most vivid memories?

"They're frequently the flops," he answered. "My decision to close *Breakfast at Tiffany's* the night before it opened and give back a million-dollar advance sale—that sticks in the mind. We always live with our failures. On the other hand, the opening night of *Hello, Dolly!* was something sensational."

Did Edward Albee make any positive contributions to *Breakfast at Tiffany's*?

"No," Merrick said. "I'll tell you about that show. Abe Burrows was the director and the writer, and he was having trouble with the writing. Well, we got to Philadelphia. We were sold out. Our stars, Mary Tyler Moore and Richard Chamberlain, had both come off of big television careers. But the reviews were *horrendous*.

"So then we got to Boston. Mr. Burrows made the show better, and still terrible reviews.

"So just after it opened in Boston, Edward Albee saw it and said he knew how to fix it, and if I wanted him to, he would rewrite the book. He'd never written a musical, but Edward Albee is certainly a writer for whom I have great admiration.

"So I went to Abe Burrows, and I said, 'You know who's down the hall? Edward Albee, and he says he knows how to fix the show and he's willing to move into the writing of the book. Now, it's up to you. It's your decision, because I'm not going to make any change. We seem to be kind of mediocre now, but the audience likes it.'

"Abe said, 'I'll talk to my agent and my wife.' The next day he called me. He said, 'Yes, it's all right with me if you want to take that chance.' So it was all amicably done. I made the deal, and Albee rewrote it completely. Changed everything. I had to lay off and start a new production.

"When he turned it loose and we put it back into rehearsals, he had written a Pirandello kind of thing with the characters walking in and out of reality. It might have been fascinating. It might still be, had it been cast for that particular version, had the scenery and costumes been designed for that.

"Then something happened at the first New York preview. The audience, a perfectly friendly New York preview audience, started talking back to the actors. I'd never heard that before. And I looked at Albee, who was standing next to me. I said, 'Edward, I think we ought to close this very rapidly.'

"He said, 'I think so, Mr. Merrick.'

"So I folded it. My God, that caused a big stir in the press and around! The story was that I'd folded the show and was saying 'Sorry' to the public. I didn't think of that at all. It was simply that I could do it because I didn't have any backers. It was RCA and myself. So I called them, and they said all right."

You make producing sound like a solitary function. Is it not collaborative? For instance, when you closed Tennessee Williams' *The Red Devil Battery Sign* in Boston, was that also a decision you made alone, or was it collaborative?

"No, it's really a decision I have to make alone. Naturally, in the case of a closing out of town before New York, I discuss it with the author and the director and I try to get their agreement. But it's the producer's decision.

"It's always solitary. Everything is solitary. I doubt if the people connected with a show are very fond of the producer. It's a bad idea to fraternize with the actors, because it makes them feel uncomfortable, I think. The producer is the enemy, or someone on the other side. Authority."

During the past decade Merrick had been steadfastly associated with the new plays of Tennessee Williams.

"He was always a hero of mine," the producer said. "But I couldn't get to Tennessee Williams until he was well along in his career, and I got the waning days, I'm afraid. I didn't get his peak work or his best work."

Did you feel a moral responsibility to continue to produce those plays?

"Yes, I did in his case. Exactly. I thought he deserved productions. I didn't think *Red Devil Battery Sign* was any good, but I went along with it anyway. He'll want it on again. I think I did him a favor to produce it in Boston."

He told me you did him a favor to close it in Boston.

"That's right. I thought it would be killed in New York, and it was a better play by far than appeared on the stage. It wasn't my fault. It was his production. He picked the cast and the director. Anthony Quinn was all right, but Claire Bloom wasn't. The director was hopeless. It was just a very poor production, but he was determined to get it on, no matter what. Big mistake. You have to simply wait until you get the right people."

That's the second time you've mentioned the producer's role in choosing the right people. When you do it right, and the show works, everyone gets credit but you. Isn't that frustrating?

"Oh, no no no," Merrick insisted. "Not frustrating at all. Quite the contrary. I would prefer less attention than I get. The Howard Hughes approach would be mine, but unfortunately I chose a business that needs publicity and I can't avoid it. If the actors are in rehearsal, sometimes I'll go out on interviews. I don't enjoy it, but I want an audience in there when it comes time to test the play."

You may not enjoy publicity, but you certainly used to enjoy pulling publicity-oriented pranks. As you've grown older, have you consciously backed away from those stunts?

"Oh, yes," Merrick said. "Maybe I'm too lazy to do them, but they'd still work. When I was driving hard to succeed I used every device to make shows succeed. Perhaps they were rather undignified, some of them. Maybe I'm looking for a more dignified image. Maybe I should start back. The press asked me to do it. They thought they were great fun and good space-fillers. Even the critics said, 'Why don't you go back to critic-baiting? That was fun.' "

Well . . . surely not *all* the critics said that. Certainly, Stanley Kauffmann didn't. In February 1966, Merrick kept *New York Times* critic Kauffmann from reviewing the final preview performance of Brian Friel's *Philadelphia, Here I Come!* by shutting down the Helen Hayes Theater and declaring there was a rat in the generator. Was that Merrick's most expensive prank?

"It wasn't very expensive," he said. "I actually hadn't sold many tickets ahead of time, knowing I was going to do it. I didn't want people to be inconvenienced. That was a prank, but it also was very serious on my part, to get him fired. And I did. I thought he was hopeless.

"He sealed his doom at the very outset. The *Times* welcomed him with a cocktail party, and he came up to me and said, 'Mr. Merrick, you know how much I admire *Marat/Sade*. But if you had read it first instead of seeing it in England, would you have produced it?'

"So I snarled at him, 'I *did* read it first.' Peter Brook had asked me what I thought about doing it here first. And I had said they could do it best in England, because they'd probably need lengthy rehearsals and a repertory-type company. So it was done over there at the Royal Shakespeare Company.

"But that was the end of Stanley Kauffmann so far as I was concerned, that night of *Philadelphia, Here I Come!* He was a critic who admitted that he couldn't write rapidly after seeing an opening night—so I don't think he had any right to be a critic—and therefore wanted to attend previews so he could work on his review for several hours. I don't like critics at previews. I think we aim for an opening night and all that excitement that generates from the stage as well as from the audience. So I canceled the preview and he had to come to the opening. As luck would have it, the play received unanimous press except for Stanley Kauffmann. He made the mistake of panning it."

In 1966, *Time* magazine did a cover story on you in which you were quoted as saying, "It is not enough for me to succeed. It is also necessary for others to fail." Was that an accurate quote?

"It wasn't my quote at all," Merrick railed. "I thought the *Time* story was largely a hatchet job, and I can prove it. I had a friend at *Time* lift the file, and I read the quotes they had garnered from all over the world. They do an exhaustive job. And what they had done was to put about ninety-five percent of the bad ones into the story and use only five percent of the good ones, when in actual fact about ninety-five percent of what they had collected were good and only five percent were negative. Also, some of the quotes were changed. So I had a straight-out libel action. I photostated the file and sent it back. Then I went to my lawyer with it. Because I *hate Time* magazine. I hated Henry Luce and the type of journalism he created for his own benefit.

"But the libel laws of America are awful. My lawyer said, 'Well now, what do you get out of this? You have to prove malice.'

" 'That can be done,' I said.

" 'But then,' he said, 'you get to the thing called the measure of damages. How much damage did they do you?'

"They probably did no damage. I couldn't prove I'd lost a fabulous movie deal or that a play had gone somewhere else. *Time* might have been able to prove, to the contrary, that the publicity helped. So I forgot about it. We wrote them a private letter. The answer was that they didn't know why I was disturbed, that they had no malice toward me. *Life* magazine was theirs, and they told me about all the hundred-and-some-odd pages of *Life* magazine coverage of my shows, all favorable. It was an implied threat that if I followed this up, I'd be boycotted. So I dropped that one. But there are a lot of misquotes in that story."

Did you take your name from the classical stage actor David Garrick?

"Not really. My brother-in-law gave me the idea. I'd left St. Louis to try the theater, but I thought, 'I'd better use a different name, in case it fails and I have to go back to practicing law.' So my brother-in-law gave me David Merrick. I think he was inspired by a combination of David Belasco and David Garrick. Whatever, I used it, not thinking it would be my name forever. But I succeeded in theater very early on, so the name stayed."

Merrick had mentioned his hometown, so I decided to include it in the conversation.

Do you have any relatives still living in St. Louis?

"No. Nobody. There are some old friends still there. I don't have any hostility toward St. Louis. I didn't have much luck there. The moment I came here I got lucky, so I love New York and my memories of St. Louis have to do with hardship."

Why no questions about biographical material or St. Louis?

"I think both subjects are boring."

Yes, Merrick had been lucky in New York. But somewhere along the way the milk began to sour. In 1968, he announced that he was withdrawing from Broadway and offering his "energies and loyalties" to the movies.

It was not a smooth transition. Merrick found out fast that movie folk have energies and loyalties all their own.

Marlon Brando walked out of Merrick's first film, a screen version of his stage hit *Child's Play,* after the producer refused to hire Brando's pal Wally Cox for a featured role.

Merrick's next film, the strife-torn *The Great Gatsby,* sent him back to New York licking his wounds.

The Great Gatsby was a negative experience, he confirmed, "because of all sorts of reasons having nothing to do with picture-producing. It had to do with the fact that the vice-president in charge of production at Paramount, Robert Evans, really was doing the film to get an important part for his wife, Ali MacGraw. When we were in the middle of preproduction she ran off with Steve McQueen, and that was the end of Paramount's interest in the film. Evans wanted me to give it back to him so he could dangle the part in front of Ali. I thought that was a very peculiar way to try to get your wife back. It wouldn't work anyway. So he then tried to sabotage the film. We had to fight through all that. He succeeded in partially sabotaging it. But the flaws of the film and the ridiculous hype that went before it were all beyond my control."

Merrick, one of America's authorities on hype, was "astonished" at how they oversold the movie. "And not only astonished," he added, "but nauseated at the particular *kind* of sell. There are ways to promote, but that particular one—well, we won't go into that. Anyway, it turned out to be quite a successful film. It's grossed some twenty-seven million dollars, highly profitable for them and for me."

In 1979, three years after this conversation, I spoke with Frank Yablans, an independent film producer who was president of Paramount Pictures when *The Great Gatsby* was released. I asked him about the *Gatsby* super-sell.

"But you must understand the free-enterprise system," Yablans said. "The free-enterprise system is based on a misrepresentation of product. When was the last time you bought a product that was as good as the ad? As president of the company I had responsibility to stockholders and to thousands of people who depended on that corporation for their livelihood. And we had a film which in my judgment was not going to be a commercial success. So we hyped it.

"But you can go back over every single quote I ever said and I never said it was a great film. The most I ever said was that it was a good film, and it *was* a good film. I did not oversell *Gatsby*. The press did. They got snookered in, because they wanted to sell copy. They made *Gatsby* bigger than we ever could. We spent very little money on the film. That's what the free-enterprise system in this country is all about. I think it's fabulous. Because after all the copy is written, and all the advertising is sold, the people are the final arbiters of taste. They decide what will be a hit or failure."

Now, in 1976, this more subdued David Merrick was back where he belonged. His ninetieth production, *The Baker's Wife*, was in rehearsal even as we spoke. Like his first musical, *Fanny*, it was based on a story by Marcel Pagnol.

"But *Baker's Wife* is better than *Fanny*," Merrick said. "It's a better story."

Before he could elaborate, we were interrupted by a secretary. The interview was over. Merrick had promised an hour, and he had delivered an hour, to the minute.

If only Merrick had heeded his own advice—picking the right people, waiting for the right people—*The Baker's Wife* might have stood a chance.

Alas . . .

Immediately after its Los Angeles premiere, the leading lady was replaced by newcomer Patti LuPone. She came through with the sort of galvanic performance for which Tony Awards were created.

But by then . . .

The original director, Joseph (*Johnny No-Trump*) Hardy, also was replaced, and the deteriorating production could not be salvaged by LuPone's star turn.

By the time the show played a one-week engagement in St. Louis as it lumbered from San Francisco to the East Coast, morale was a shambles.

The original show was performed at night, while a new script was rehearsed by day. A huge waste of time, because . . .

The musical's star, Topol, refused to participate in rehearsals. He would attend, in order to fulfill his contractual obligation. But once there, he would merely sit, observe, and smile.

Another defiant cast member refused to attend at all. He sat daily in the hotel lobby, thereby inviting dismissal.

Merrick had told me he'd accepted less-than-generous financial terms for the St. Louis booking because "I wanted it to play there," sounding like a man who wants his hometown to see the fruits of his labors. But when it did play there, he stayed far away.

A fatal two months later, he finally fired Topol and replaced him with Paul Sorvino.

He laid off for three weeks in Boston for revisions. (Shades of *Breakfast at Tiffany's*?)

All to no avail.

The musical collapsed in Washington, D.C., in November 1976, and lost a million dollars.

"Merrick doesn't have it anymore," scoffers jeered. "He's gone soft and lethargic." "The old Merrick magic is gone."

But he still held one final ace. One last laugh.
He produced *42nd Street.*
This time, he got "the right people": Gower Champion.
And when it opened in August 1980, in an almost Machiavellian turn of twisted events, Merrick manipulated the most bizarre, headline-grabbing, perverse prank of his career by announcing Gower Champion's death at the opening-night curtain call.

"David understood," Marge Champion told me one month later on a TV-movie set in Savannah. "I don't know how he understood, but he understood how Gower worked. David tortured Gower to death. Not just *42nd Street.* Always. *Carnival. The Happy Time. Sugar.*

"The stories are legendary. On *Hello, Dolly!,* when we were in Detroit and in trouble, Gower went away. He went to Ypsilanti and said, 'Tell Mr. Merrick that when he leaves town I'll be back to fix the show.' He stayed away for three days. There wasn't anywhere to go except Ypsilanti.

"There was a love-hate between the two, but look at the shows it produced. David absolutely understood his function as the producer, which was to see it through to the end, and then promote it to the hilt."

There was so much hoopla surrounding *42nd Street,* most people have forgotten that Merrick produced a second show that same season. But lightning didn't strike twice, and Oliver Hailey's comedy *I Won't Dance* is surely the only play in the Merrick canon to have opened and closed in one performance at a Sunday matinee.

Four Sundays later Merrick was eager to dance for a national television audience at the Tony Awards. In retrospect, the selection of *42nd Street* as Best Musical seems inevitable. Yet at the time, Merrick (whose relations with the League of American Theatres and Producers often had been strained) feared that the coveted Tony would be denied him. But when the envelopes were opened, Gower Champion was the posthumous winner as Best Choreographer, and Merrick's miracle was Best Musical.

He still took pride in his independence as a producer. The three musicals *42nd Street* had bested shared no less than twenty producers. But Merrick continued to act alone.

Later that night, at the gala ball at the Waldorf-Astoria, he spoke to his rival Bernard Jacobs of the Shubert Organization. Jacobs also had received a Tony, when Peter Shaffer's *Amadeus* won as Best

Play. At the ball, Merrick looked Jacobs square in the eye and said: "Bernie, I can't believe you had the nerve to go up there and thank everybody, as if you did something. What did you do? You flew over to London, you saw the play, you bought the rights, and you flew the star to New York. You should have thanked your travel agent."

42nd Street, David Merrick's anachronistic love letter to the city where he "got lucky," kept his name before the public for another eight years and 3,485 performances. But it was just that: an anachronism. The new musicals of the 1980s and 1990s, the new works by Stephen Sondheim and Andrew Lloyd Webber, were not produced by this infuriatingly driven man who had championed the form in the 1950s and 1960s. Like his final hit, Merrick was evolving into an anachronism. Thus it ever is.

From Florenz Ziegfeld to Jed Harris to Max Gordon to David Merrick, the greatness of the most successful producers is that their productions reflect a time. Yet, when time moves on, as it inexorably must, those producers are left behind and cast aside. Few producers continue to strike pay dirt to the end of their careers.

Now David Merrick's career is winding down. In recent years, the Merrick saga has gotten sloppy. There have been divorces, strokes, brushes with the law. One senses that the solitary man is lonelier than ever. But when he goes out—though it won't be with the skyrocket flair of a Gower Champion; that's not Merrick's style—there will be few more fitting epitaphs than those simple words of Marge Champion's: He saw it through to the end, and he promoted it to the hilt.

He was a producer.

CHAPTER EIGHT

WORDSMITHS

"The higher up you go, the more sensitive you become."
—ALAN JAY LERNER

"Almost anybody going seriously into musical theater is bound to find himself used and cheated and alienated."
—RICHARD WILBUR

Alan Jay Lerner and Richard Wilbur were formed from different molds.

Lerner was all civility, style, and grace. His best work reflected an affection for the lofty, refined world of manners and decorum. His elegant, tailored wardrobe heralded the best that money could acquire at Turnbull & Asser and on Savile Row.

Wilbur sports a different style. He wears ties, too . . . on occasion. But he's a lot more comfortable in cut-off jeans, wandering through a New England meadow.

Yet they're both craftsmen constrained by meter. Lerner was a lyricist whose rhymes sometimes aspired to poetry; Wilbur is a poet who flirted briefly with lyric-writing.

First, Lerner.

Born in 1918 into a prosperous New York City family, he was graduated from Harvard at age twenty-one. A chance encounter led to his collaboration with Frederick Loewe, fourteen years his senior.

Loewe composed the music, while Lerner wrote the librettos and the song lyrics.

They suffered a couple of early misfires, then *Brigadoon* in 1947 established them. *Paint Your Wagon* in 1951 was followed by *My Fair Lady* in 1956 (nine Tony Awards) was followed by the motion picture *Gigi* in 1957 (nine Academy Awards) was followed by *Camelot* in 1960 (three Tony Awards).

Lerner and Loewe were the most successful composing team since Rodgers and Hammerstein, but after *Camelot* Loewe wanted out. Lerner's post-Loewe collaborations with other composers (Richard Rodgers, Leonard Bernstein, Burton Lane, André Previn) ranged from uncomfortable to downright disastrous. His most impressive post-Loewe accomplishment was a memoir, *The Street Where I Live.* The street where he lived, of course, was Broadway. But the street where he worked was Madison Avenue. That's where his office was, and that's where we met late one November afternoon in 1978. He sat crisp and starched behind a spotless desk.

The walls were lined with books, so I asked Lerner a hypothetical question: If you were going to a desert island to write a musical, which of these books would you take along?

"I have a few books I read all the time," he said. "I read *Crime and Punishment* every two or three years. I read *The Great Gatsby* every few years. I read *Huckleberry Finn* a great deal, and I read *Great Expectations*."

The reply surprised me. I'd been thinking more along the lines of a thesaurus or dictionary.

Do these novels help with your work? I asked.

"No. But when you want to lose the world so that you can really get into yourself to start writing, I find very often that a wonderful transition is to pick up a familiar book that you love, that always evokes an emotion in you. You start to read, and pretty soon you forget about whether the stock market is up or down or whether your children are doing well in school. And you're able to write."

His autobiography, which was fresh in the bookstores as we spoke, attempted to explain what went wrong in the professional collaboration with his friend Fritz Loewe. What went wrong, in a word, was success. Lerner's theory was that a person can survive a failure reasonably intact, but that success "steals your defenses and leaves you on top of the world stark naked."

"I think the higher up you go, the more sensitive you become," he theorized. "When you're struggling, you're like a fighter. You take the blows and you keep going. But when you reach a certain point—and I've always been amazed by it—you become more sensitive, not less.

"During our early years I could show Fritz a new lyric and he might say, 'My boy, don't write me another weather report.' Or he would play me a melody and I would say, 'Come on, you've got to be kidding.' I would never force a lyric on him, nor would he insist upon using a melody that I disliked.

"But at a certain point you have to be careful about those casual derogatory remarks. Because success triggers egos which never were there before. If you're not careful, success can give you a self-inflated opinion of yourself. What happened was that what used to be healthy compromise between us got twisted into concessions. I'd say to myself, 'Oh, I'll give in to him.' Then I'd think, 'Why the hell should I?'

"By the time of *Camelot,* the collaboration no longer worked. I railed at Fritz's ideas and held firm to my own as 'exalted artistic opinions,' which was nonsense. We were no longer a collaboration hammering and chiseling out one voice together. The comfortable camaraderie of our early years had vanished."

In his memoir, Lerner wrote of *Camelot:* "Pockmarked with flaws though the play may have been, at that moment I did not see them. Three months later I would. But there was something about *Camelot,* more than any play I have written, that was too much a part of me to be objective."

What prevented that objectivity?

"Probably two things," Lerner said. "First, the deteriorating collaboration that I just mentioned. A play had to be rewritten, and I was the only one there. Fritz was not feeling well. Our director, Moss Hart, was in the hospital. *We* were the producers. So there was no one to come over to me at the end of the day and pull me up short.

"Second, I love the theme of it so much. It sounds pretentious and I don't mean it to, but I love the naked idealism of it. You know, I have found that I always write the same play. There's always a moment in every play I write where the hero suddenly wonders whether his life has been worth it all, then discovers it has.

"And at that particular time in my life, King Arthur's discovery that everything he had done was not for naught—that so long as it lived in the heart of one child, it still lived—somehow that thought touched me so deeply that I couldn't extricate myself from the feeling. And I still have it.

"That final scene in the musical between Arthur and the young boy on the battlefield was always in the script, but I didn't realize until I saw it staged how much it meant to me. When I saw that scene in rehearsal, it came as quite a shock. I found myself crying. I had to leave. And I thought, 'This is absurd. I'm an old campaigner. I've been at the barricades an awful lot. Why is this happening?' But I was terribly moved by Richard Burton and by what was happening between him and that child.

"I suppose it was in some way related to the biological instinct of lineage. I have three daughters, and I was about to have another child. I remember thinking that I didn't care whether it was a boy or girl. I just wanted everyone to be healthy. I was at the hospital waiting for the news, when the doctor walked in and said, 'You have a son.' Suddenly, from nowhere, I burst out crying. And I later realized that there must be some very deep biological instinct within us that is concerned with perpetuating ourselves, and I suppose there's something of that in *Camelot.*

"I realize even now that it's an imperfect work, but it's my favorite. There are moments in it that I like better than anything I've ever written. I've also come to appreciate Fritz's score more and more as the years have gone by. It's melodic and haunting, with a Schubert quality to some of it."

Lerner described his post-Loewe collaborations as "absolute agony. I have never felt comfortable since I stopped working with Fritz. Ever. I have written a lot of things, and some of the lyrics have been quite good, and some of the songs I like. *But* . . . that special joy of creation that we had, I'll just never have that again, that's all there is to it."

He wrote only two musicals in the 1960s, *On a Clear Day You Can See Forever* in 1965 and *Coco* in 1969. It was not a happy decade.

"During the convulsions of the 1960s," he said, "there was a great revolution by the young people against the establishment. The two places where a rebellion is always physical first are in clothes and in music. And that's what you saw. The hair got longer and the clothes changed, and the music changed.

"When I grew up, my gods were Cole Porter, George Gershwin, Jerome Kern. But in the sixties I was *nobody's* god, nor were any of the writers of my generation a god. Those were the days of instant art, and nobody was particularly interested in the craftsmanship that is needed to create a musical theater. So now that has to begin anew. There's nothing left over from the sixties that we can use."

From 1970 to 1973, after the close of *Coco,* Lerner endured three years in which he doubted his relevance "to the point of paralysis."

"*Coco* occurred right at the period where there seemed to be no market for musicals, no interest in musicals," he said, "and I began to wonder, 'What am I doing? Who am I writing for?' Of course, I write for myself. But in the end, in a popular art form, somebody else has to be moved too, or touched. I just thought that maybe I'd reached the point where what you feel is no longer what others feel. You're out of style.

"Eventually I realized that I was miserable during those three years in large part because I wasn't working. In order for me not to be miserable, I have to write. No matter what happens to what I'm writing, if I don't write, what am I? I am what I do. I'm a writer. That's all. So I went back to writing again. I started things and threw them away. I went through all of that.

"That crisis in confidence came *after*, but not *because* of, *Coco*. I always think that you get more or less than you deserve all the time. With *Coco* we got less than we deserved. I think *Coco* was better than the critics said. Not that much better, but better. Because it was literate and it was quite witty.

"By the way, it isn't that I mind being criticized, because most of the time I think I deserve it. Often it's the *level* of criticism that irritates me—if I'm dismissed as if I'm just some pop-tune writer. Or if nobody looks at my work in the context of a lifetime of my having worked in the theater."

His only original work to this point in the 1970s was *1600 Pennsylvania Avenue*, a Bicentennial Upstairs, Downstairs view of the White House on which he had collaborated with Leonard Bernstein. It opened and closed in 1976 after seven performances.

What went wrong there?

"It was an unfortunate case where Lenny and I were writing two different shows and we weren't aware of it."

At what point did you make that discovery?

"The second week of rehearsal."

You mean to say you knew you had a failure before performances even began?

"The sad truth is that once rehearsals begin, you can never turn a bad show into a good one. You can make a good show better and a bad show not so bad, but you can't make it good. Especially not that one, because it was so far afield from what it started out to be. We just kept going slowly and meticulously down the wrong road.

"And here's another sad truth: Whenever a musical fails, the book bears the brunt."

That view was shared by Reid Shelton in a conversation we'd had ten months earlier, prior to a matinee of *Annie,* in which he starred as Daddy Warbucks. Shelton, who had toured for more than five years as Freddy Eynsford-Hill in *My Fair Lady,* also had been featured in *1600 Pennsylvania Avenue.*

"They're blaming Alan Lerner for the failure," he said. "I've never seen anyone work harder than Alan Lerner to try and make a show work. The rewrites. Doing whatever he was told.

"After it closed, the press release described the musical as an idea that didn't work, and basically that's what it was. It was an idea that didn't work—with two of the largest egos, but also two of the most talented men in the theater. Lenny has come off scot-free. People say the music was marvelous, and it *was* very, very good. Lenny *is* a genius. But his music was not indigenous to this property. There is a *brilliant* show there. But it probably will never see the light of day, because nobody is going to spend a dime on it again."

Undaunted by his growing string of failures, and convinced that a writer writes, Lerner was at work on the book and lyrics for a new musical, to be called *Carmelina.*

"Two summers ago I was in Capri," he said. "I was lying on a rock with my foot in the water and a bottle of *vino* in my hand, looking at the sun, and I suddenly thought, 'Why don't I ever have this nice warm feeling in the theater?' You have a lot of other feelings in the theater, but not this one. So I decided to try and write an Italian musical that has that kind of sunny, romantic, silly feeling about it."

Lerner had been working on the musical for two years, which for him was standard. "Most people neither understand nor appreciate the work that is involved in writing a musical," he said. "Every so often someone from the legitimate theater will attempt to write a musical, and they always have a distorted view of what is involved.

"We once had a producing group in New York called the Playwrights Company, which consisted of five noted playwrights: Robert Sherwood, Elmer Rice, Sidney Howard, Maxwell Anderson, and

S. N. Behrman. Kurt Weill told me that one November he was at their meeting, and Robert Sherwood said he had decided to write a musical.

"So Kurt said, 'When would it be for?'

"And Sherwood said, 'I suppose it would be in the spring.'

"And Kurt said, 'In the *spring*?'

"And Sherwood said, 'It's only a musical.'

"Well, it didn't get out in the spring. *Miss Liberty* got on the following fall and was a total disaster, even with an Irving Berlin score and Moss Hart directing. Because it doesn't work that way.

"I have found that a musical takes two years to write. Some of them take longer. It is a very complicated form. It doesn't purport to be a highly intellectual form. But if you do it properly, I think it's possible in the musical theater to transport people so that their souls leave their bodies for two and a half hours and then return refreshed."

In what direction is the American musical theater headed?

"I don't think anybody knows where the musical theater is going," he said, "and I think the reason for that is because our country doesn't know where it's going. Musicals don't operate in some demilitarized zone all by themselves. They are a part of the social fabric and expression. But there's no direction in musical theater. There's this kind of musical that Steve Sondheim writes, and there's that kind of musical that I write, and there's another kind of musical that Bob Fosse does. But there isn't a mainstream, and that is also true in legitimate theater.

"The only subject that I ever see anybody discussing in serious theater is death, because that's a sure thing. We've all got to roll up and die, so death is a peach of a subject for drama. But there's no concern with issues in today's theater, as there was in the 1930s, when we had a theater of protest against the failure of a system that we had all believed in. Nobody's writing about issues today, because I don't think we know where we are or where we're going."

There was an unintentional sense of irony in Lerner's response to my final question: What is the quintessential Lerner lyric?

"For me, it's 'I Remember It Well,' from *Gigi*," answered this man who felt he'd been forgotten by his audience.

"Back in 1948 I wrote a musical called *Love Life* with Kurt Weill. It was one of the few musicals that Gadge Kazan ever directed. One day he said to me, 'Every writer who's worth his salt usually has one little area of expression that is his and his alone. And you have yours. When you pursue that, you communicate. But when you step out of it there are others who do what you're doing much better.' I never forgot that, though of course I rebel against it all the time.

"But I think of 'I Remember It Well,' 'I've Grown Accustomed to Her Face,' 'How to Handle a Woman.' "

He paused for a moment, then embellished his answer: "If I'm writing an emotional song I try to capture one *precise* emotional moment—the way somebody is feeling at *this* split second. If it *is* that kind of an emotion, as a rule you try to keep the images clear and the language simple. And in a funny way that's much harder than having the whole range of vocabulary at your disposal, because then vocabulary can become an obstruction to that simple thing of 'If ever I would leave you, it wouldn't be in autumn.'

"Of course, no matter what world you're creating in your musical, be it the American gold rush in *Paint Your Wagon* or Parisian society in *Gigi*, you never can do real life on the stage. The lyrics always have to be heightened a bit. 'Auld Lang Syne' is probably the best lyric ever written, but I don't think it's stage material. It would have to be heightened. You pull the ears a little longer and make things a little larger than life for the theater.

"One thing I will say in defense of my lyrics is that, unlike some lyricists, I think I understand music. I began as a composer. I went to the Juilliard School, and I studied music at Harvard, and I've played the piano since I was about five. As a result of all that, I love the human voice and have very precise ideas about what sound I want on certain notes. Most people who write lyrics, even when they have marvelous ideas, don't understand that they are written for the human voice, which has certain requirements. Whether a lyric I write is good or bad is not for me to judge. But I know they are singable, because everything is where it ought to be."

As I was preparing to leave, I mentioned that I had been affected by the tribute which he paid in *The Street Where I Live* to his father, who had waged a courageous and gallant seventeen-year combat against throat cancer before he died. My remark triggered a revealing torrent from this usually contained man.

"What I miss most in life is gallantry," he said. "It's a lost virtue. No, it's more than a virtue. It's a lost sense of our self-respect. What has happened to the people who used to strive to make a contribution to life, and who held their heads high no matter what their conditions? That kind of gallantry is vanishing, as we systematically destroy all our heroes, one by one. The books keep pouring out to show you all the warts and pimples of everybody that you looked up to.

"I don't care what Eisenhower did with his secretary or what Jack Kennedy did in his private life. Who gives a damn? What has that got to do with the memory of a moment when we all felt so happy and good and were a little prouder of ourselves, and the world did too? Kennedy was the first president born in our century. No matter what he may or may not have accomplished, that feeling was so exhilarating and fresh, and Mrs. Kennedy was a wonderful First Lady.

"I don't want to read about all the other! I want to keep the heroes! I don't think we can live without them! What we're doing now is to let Congress run the country, and it doesn't work. We need leaders. We need people to look up to. As long as we don't look up to God anymore, we certainly need people.

"And I miss my father. I miss him every day. I never go through a day when I don't think about him."

Six months later, *Carmelina* opened on Broadway. This musical, about which Lerner had expressed such enthusiasm and optimism, closed after seventeen performances.

In his *New York Times* review, Richard Eder dismissed the show as "an exercise in harmlessness." He wrote: "Mr. Lerner's lyrics strain for freshness but don't often find it. When he has Carmelina rhyme 'Jehovah' with 'I'm starting over' and go on with 'I demand the biggest share of all the clover' it sounds like something inspired by a 3 A.M. vigil in a hotel room."

If so, it was a silent vigil. The musical's director, José Ferrer, told me that one of his directing chores was to pass notes under the locked hotel doors of lyricist-librettist Lerner and composer Burton Lane, who no longer were speaking. (". . . people not communicating. . . . It's always the same wail. . . .")

In 1983 Lerner was back with *Dance a Little Closer*, which he had adapted from Robert E. Sherwood's 1936 Pulitzer Prize–winning drama *Idiot's Delight*. (Sherwood, of course, was the playwright who had thought he could knock off a musical in six months.) Some of Charles Strouse's music recalled the lushness of Fritz Loewe's; some of Lerner's lyrics released the festering anger that lurked behind his poise. And he even got "Auld Lang Syne" onstage.

But *Dance a Little Closer* shuttered after one performance, and America's most distinguished living lyricist suffered the same ignominy that Mary Mercier had experienced her first time out. ("One-night runs suggest total ineptitude and are perforce humiliating," Walter Kerr had written.)

Three years later, on June 14, 1986, Alan Jay Lerner died of lung cancer; he was sixty-seven. Obituaries liberally reprinted lyrics from the glory-day musicals: "I Could Have Danced All Night," "On a Clear Day You Can See Forever," "I Remember It Well." Readers were reminded, yet again, of the link between *Camelot* and the lost promise of the Kennedy presidency. Alan Jay Lerner would have been pleased: For the first time in a long time, he was viewed "in the context of a lifetime" in the theater.

This time he was not dismissed.

It's amazing, the chance happenings and random coincidences that lead to larger events. "The geometry of life," John Guare called it in *Bosoms and Neglect.*

Consider Richard Wilbur, America's former poet laureate.

The route to our meeting began in the summer of 1964, during one of those college-vacation splurges in New York City, where you gorge on ten plays in eight days. Broadway was still Broadway then. In one heaping helping we saw plays starring (in alphabetical order) Elizabeth Ashley, Richard Burton, Carol Channing, Hume Cronyn, Alfred Drake, Tammy Grimes, Pat Hingle, Beatrice Lillie, Mildred Natwick, Barry Nelson, Paul Newman, Robert Redford, Kate Reid, Jason Robards, George Rose, Diana Sands, Rip Torn, Edward Woodward, and Joanne Woodward.

In that orgy of power-packed performances, maybe the most memorable of all was Alec Guinness' tortured poet in *Dylan*. Sidney Michaels' play was based in part on the memoir *Dylan Thomas in America* by John Malcolm Brinnin. Back at Illinois Wesleyan University the following September, I chanced upon a copy of Brinnin's 1955 book in the library. I read the first sentence and was hooked: "Bundled like an immigrant in a shapeless rough woolen parka, his hair as tangled as a nest from which the bird has flown, his eyes wide, scared, as if they sought the whole dreadful truth of America at once, he came into the zero cold of a frosty bright morning at Idlewild Airport."

It proved to be the most compassionate, sensitive, and gorgeously written memoir I've read. Here was an author worth meeting. I had something to do with booking speakers on campus; I immediately extended an invitation to Brinnin.

Through a scheduling snafu, the Religion Department booked a theologian for a three-day symposium that directly coincided and conflicted with Brinnin's three-day visit. Yet, by the end of the three days, I noticed that one of the religion professors was attending Brinnin's lectures rather than those sponsored by his own department. After both speakers departed, I confronted the professor with this curious observation. He replied, "Well, our man had all the answers, but your man had all the questions."

Brinnin was a hit, and we promptly invited him to return to Illinois Wesleyan University the following year. We discussed a joint poetry reading, with a second poet to be determined. "What would you think of my friend Richard Wilbur?" Brinnin asked.

Richard Wilbur! He'd been my favorite poet since before I even understood poetry. Back in 1957 (the same year he won the Pulitzer Prize), I happened upon a photoessay about Wilbur in our seventh-grade literature textbook. The essay featured photos of Wilbur on the beach at Martha's Vineyard, searching for seashells; Wilbur shopping with his wife for a lawn mower; Wilbur picnicking with his family; Wilbur striding down a white-picket-fenced lane in jeans and a long-sleeved, blue-and-white striped T-shirt, exuding all the insouciant charm of Billy Budd and all the bravado of *Carousel*'s Billy Bigelow. The seven-page layout was a shameless propaganda piece. Poets, it proclaimed, aren't freaks. They can be young, with wavy chestnut hair and ruggedly handsome features.

But the propaganda worked, and ever since then I've had a special affinity for Wilbur's poems. So, in March 1967, Wilbur and Brinnin converged on the plains of Illinois for their poetry reading. At age forty-five, Wilbur could have passed for one of the students. His resonant voice could have doubled for Gregory Peck's.

Five years later, while traveling through the Northeast, I stopped at Wesleyan University in Connecticut, where he taught, to renew our acquaintance. We met on an unseasonably warm November afternoon in Professor Wilbur's cramped English Department office. Wilbur lit his pipe, leaned back in his desk chair, and looked out the window at some falling leaves, and then we talked.

First, *Candide*. It had opened on Broadway in 1956, the same year as *My Fair Lady*. Despite its distinguished collaborators—book by Lillian Hellman, music by Leonard Bernstein, lyrics by Richard Wilbur, direction by Tyrone Guthrie—*Candide* closed after seventy-three performances. In the intervening years it had become a cult item, much talked about but little seen. (Hal Prince's successful exhumation was still three years away.)

"It seems to me there's a lot of good work in the show," Wilbur said. "Much of Lenny's music is exciting, lively. There is a certain amount of Lillian Hellman's good book still left, although it suffered terrible abuse in the original process of composition.

"It was a very contentious collaboration. I don't mean to say that there wasn't a lot of pleasure involved in the making of *Candide,* but Lillian, Lenny, and I differed with each other a great deal. In fact—and it's quite possible that my memory is wrong about this, because it's fifteen years—I think one reason why we were glad that Tyrone Guthrie joined us as our director while we were still putting the show together was because we thought he looked like General De Gaulle and that he would be decisive and would put all our quarrels to rest and tell us what to do. Actually, he did do a certain amount of that. I think certain numbers were written one way or another simply because of his insistence. Finally, I think, he got bored with superintending all our squabbles, making the decisions. But initially he did offer us a command which facilitated matters."

Hellman-Bernstein-Wilbur not only was a powerhouse collaboration, but also was a rare one. Why, I asked, do so many creative artists eventually lose interest and leave the field to lesser talents? What is it about Broadway that artists can't cope with?

"I should like to say this without bitterness," Wilbur replied, putting down his pipe, "but I don't know whether I can find mild language in which to say it. It seems to me that the Broadway scene is very much cluttered by lawyers and agents of dubious moral character, and almost anybody going seriously into musical theater is bound to find himself used and cheated and alienated.

"I think that serious artists, serious writers, serious musicians don't want to do things 'on spec' and have them fail in performance. If, indeed, they even get to performance. It's heartbreaking to write a lot of good songs and then find yourself in a position where, because of the chicanery of a few people not truly concerned in the construction of the show, these things can never be heard.

"When people call me up from New York and ask me to work on this or that musical show, at present I find it very hard to be interested, even when the proposed collaborators are splendid. I get lots of those calls, and it has to do with what you've just observed, that there aren't very many good people working on Broadway. It's a ridiculous paradox that an artistic field in which the rewards *can* be so great—both aesthetic and monetary—should have so few good practitioners in it. If you think of painting, if you think of poetry, if you think of the novel, if you think of almost any other realm of artistic life in America, there are simply more first-rate practitioners in it than we now find in the theater. And I'm afraid it has to do with the fact that the theater is, as they say, 'the entertainment industry' and is full of unpleasant people and unpleasant experiences."

Conversation turned to a more pleasant area: his Molière translations. Wilbur published *The Misanthrope* in 1955, after three years' work, *Tartuffe* in 1963, after another three years' labor. In 1971, prior to our meeting, he had completed a third, *The School for Wives.* Reportedly, the translations are so popular that their collective performance royalties paid for the college educations of the Wilburs' four children. Even as he and I spoke, Brian Bedford was repeating his Tony Award–winning performance in *The School for Wives* at a Boston matinee sixty miles away.

I mentioned a new version of *Cyrano de Bergerac* in which the translator seemed self-consciously to be avoiding the already-established Brian Hooker edition. Wilbur promptly picked up on my theme.

"It's a fascinating question, how to avoid writing around previous translations," he said. "Some translators seem to follow the old dictum—whose is it? Oscar Wilde's? T. S. Eliot's?—that little poets borrow and mature poets steal. That's incorrectly quoted. But in any case, a person like Robert Lowell going at his version of *Prometheus* will quite frankly raid other translations in the confidence that his final, full version is going to be superior to any of the material he's drawn from.

"I think probably that's the sensible way to go. If you are forever trying to avoid the solutions of other people, you're denying yourself certain potentialities. If you're doing the sort of thing I was doing—a thought-for-thought rhymed translation of Molière—there *are* only so many possible solutions for any passage.

"Actually, when I did my latest translation of *School for Wives,* I had three other translations of the play around the house, none of them in rhymed verse. When I got stuck I would feel quite free to consult these translations for suggestions. They would loosen my mind and, in some cases where they were bad, would encourage me to go ahead and say what I thought I would say. In other cases they provided me with a word which, since my mind isn't a complete thesaurus, I hadn't been able to come up with.

"The one translation I didn't look at was an already-existing rhymed translation by Donald Frame. Donald Frame is a very good French scholar, and so any translation by him would be accurate. He had, as I say, brought *The School for Wives* over into rhymed pentameter and couplets, which is what I was proposing to do. I didn't dare look at his translation, because it would continually have closed my mind to other rhyming possibilities. I suppose I should have found myself in some cases ashamed to follow his lead, ashamed to repeat it, and I would have written around his solution, to the final disadvantage of the translation.

"But then, I think I had quite a lot of self-confidence by the time I got to *The School for Wives*. I'd hung around the theater a great deal more. When I started translating Molière back in 1952, I wasn't necessarily thinking of doing a version for the stage. I think it came as a slight surprise to me how well *The Misanthrope* worked on the stage. But between 1952 and when I started the *School for Wives* translation, I had a great deal to do with the theater.

"For example, I spent a year in 1960 and 1961 on a Ford Foundation fellowship hanging around the Alley Theater in Houston. I would follow productions from the first readings through rehearsals to the full productions. I learned an awful lot about what is effective in word order, what makes for a sayable line, how a scene should build.

"I'm not suggesting that I've tampered with the structure or the scenes in Molière, or introduced words of my own arbitrarily. I haven't. But there are always, in the translation of any line or thought in Molière, many subtle little choices that you can make. Some of them, for example, are of a rhythmic character, and if you've spent some time around the theater you know which rhythm will do it best. Also, you have a little intuitive knowledge about pronounceability, which someone who is writing a closet drama is not likely to be concerned about. I have said all the lines of *School for Wives* over and over at the top of my voice, something I didn't do for the earlier translations."

Does the current success of *The School for Wives* suggest to you that it's more accessible to young audiences than, say, *The Misanthrope*?

"Your question is a hard one. Both plays are subject to contemporary misunderstanding. Young folk, and some of their teachers, are all too likely to see Alceste in *The Misanthrope* as a hero of 'tell it like it is' and a true enemy of corruption and sham, whereas he is an unconscious phony who feigns an identity through *playing* those roles. Young folk, women, and opportunistic directors are all too likely to find *School* a play about women's lib, education, or generational conflict, whereas it is none of those.

"I think that *School* is a simpler and more farcical play than *Misanthrope* and that its longer speeches are perhaps easier for the young to enjoy because they are more constantly accented by dramatic irony. But either play will do well with high-school audiences, I think, if firmly imagined in such a way as not to flatter the prejudices of the youth culture."

Are you working on another Molière?

"It's a delight to do this sort of work," Wilbur said, "but since I'm not purely a translator, but also other kinds of a writer, I'm holding off now from doing another translation. As you can imagine, when you're sitting in your study with a certain amount of free time available, it's far easier to get four lines ahead with your translation-in-progress, Mr. Molière having thought out the direction in which things are going to go, than to pick up some original poem and get somewhere with that. It's much easier to go ahead with a translation which, though it involves all kinds of responsiveness, sympathy, penetration on your part, is in some measure like the solving of a big puzzle. So one's original poetry suffers, and all of one's projects which have to be arbitrarily conceived and originally thought out also suffer."

(Eventually he would return to Molière and would translate *The Learned Ladies*. Then he tackled Racine's *Phèdre*.)

I asked Wilbur, the poet, about that seesaw relationship between content and form: When you write a poem, to what extent are you challenged by an intricate rhyme scheme?

"There still remains, even among sophisticated people, an awful lot of crude thinking about this matter," he said. "This being an age in which a very loose kind of style is the period style, there are a lot of people who think that the use of meters and rhymes must entail some kind of overprizing of mere technical effects. I suppose the people who think that way have not worked enough in such forms to realize that a considerable ease can be acquired in them, and that they can finally present no obstacle.

"One of the advantages of writing in meters, writing in any kind of a straitjacket, is that it slows you down, makes you think harder about all your word choices, also suggests thoughts to you which you might not otherwise have thought of, *frees* the mind, actually, to consider quite arbitrary directions. All of these things are known to poets of my generation. I think there are a lot of younger poets at present who have started out writing in an extremely easygoing, flat, and prosaic manner and who don't see that—provided you have enough taste and patience—the use of meters, rhymes, stanzaic patterns, can be both liberating and desirably decelerating."

The fifty-year-old poet sitting across the desk from me did not look much older than the budding Billy Bigelow who had bounded from the pages of my English textbook fourteen years earlier. How do you account for your amazing youth? I asked. You look as if you're still in your early thirties.

"Well," he replied with some embarrassment, "it's a family trait to persist in looking young for a while, and then"—a chortle crescendoed into a full laugh—"we all end old."

On a slightly more earnest note, he added, "I like to work out of doors and hike and even run in the woods. I tried to outrun my dog last week—and lost.

"I'm no doubt, like so many writers, a willing fugitive from the desk. But as you get to be fifty, your energy gets to be less. You find it harder to come home from a class, sit down, and start to write a poem. You're more likely to come home in a mood of self-pity and make yourself a martini."

Six months later, in May 1972, I received an amusing note: "As regards my youthfulness, you will be interested that I have just grown younger, by growing a beard. I went into a bar not so long ago and sat next to a man who swung round blearily and said, 'Oh, Lord, another beard. What is it that you kids are protesting about?' "

Richard Wilbur was fifty-one.

Wilbur's energy may be diminishing as he ages, but you wouldn't know it from a distance. During the past two decades, he has continued to teach and to translate and to write.

In September 1987, at age sixty-six, he was invested as poet laureate of the United States, a position he held for one year.

In 1988 he published *New and Collected Poems*, an anthology that spans four decades of work. The volume received the Pulitzer Prize.

In 1991 he published his translation of Molière's *The School for Husbands*.

Although we haven't seen each other in more than a decade, Wilbur figured in one other equation in the geometry of my life.

Back in 1964, back at college, when my route to Broadway to Brinnin to Wilbur was first being charted, we all idolized Richard Burton. We reveled in his exploits with Liz, emulated his voice, savored the memories of those who had seen him in *Camelot* four years before, wondered at his love of poetry. It was his advocacy of fellow Welshman Dylan Thomas that had led us to *Dylan* in the first place. But *Dylan* came at the end of that New York week. Our first Broadway play that summer was Burton's *Hamlet*. Watching his royal Dane from Row O of the Lunt-Fontanne Theater was as near as I'd ever imagined I'd get to this meteoric star.

Twenty years later, while a publicist at CBS, I worked on a miniseries called *Ellis Island*, a task redeemed in large measure by the casting of Richard Burton and his delightful daughter, Kate.

Burton's first scene was filmed in a greenhouse on a hot, sunny, cloudless July afternoon at Shepperton Studios, outside London. Inside the greenhouse, the temperature approached one hundred degrees. No matter. Every single member of the crew—including those ancillary workers whose presence is not required during filming—crammed into that aptly named hothouse. Simply because Richard Burton was there. Just to be around him, one felt a sense of occasion.

He was a charmer: warm, outgoing, approachable. He seemed to have memorized not only the entire Shakespeare canon, but also every poem he'd ever read, and he would recite them at length, at will. The dumbstruck listener could only ask in silence: How could one mind retain so much, so effortlessly?

He wasn't a very good interview. By 1984, he'd been asked it all too many times. So you'd ask him a question and he would talk about whatever he wanted, and if you were like me, you were just glad to be there.

"Welsh is my first language," he said. "I spoke Welsh exclusively until I was about five. Then I went to live in another Welsh village where nobody spoke Welsh. They spoke English. So I started to become bilingual by about the age of eight.

"I lived with my sister. My mother had died. One day a traveling salesman came to the door selling encyclopedias. It was called *General Knowledge for All.* And my sister bought three volumes. She felt sorry for the chap. You know, we were very poor. I don't mean barefoot poor, but we had to count the pennies. Strikes and Depression and all that. But she bought these books, and I was reading through the English-literature section, and there was this poem by George Herbert."

At this point, Burton began to recite the seventeenth-century poet's "Virtue":

> "Sweet day, so cool, so calm, so bright,
> The bridal of the earth and sky;
> The dew shall weep thy fall tonight,
> For thou must die.
>
> Sweet rose, whose hue, angry and brave,
> Bids the rash . . ."

He stopped his recitation, as if *everyone* already knew that text by heart, and continued his narrative. "I thought, 'My God, I understand it.' And that was it. I was in. I was eight and a half."

Several minutes later he said, "I'm forever being asked to write my autobiography, and I can't do it. Too many people alive, and I can't do it. There's no sense in doing it unless you can tell the truth. Nobody can tell the truth, can they? But as near the truth as you can get. But somebody asked me—it was my idea, actually—they said, 'Would you do an anthology of poetry?' So I said, 'Yes, I'll do it, but it will take some time.' But I said, 'I want to confine it entirely to snow and ice. So I've got about forty poems, like for instance Eliot's 'Journey of the Magi.'

" 'A cold coming we had of it,' " he began to recite.

At which point I asked if he was including Richard Wilbur's poem about a child's empathy for his snowman, "Boy at the Window."

"No," Burton curtly replied.

Oh, you should have that, I implored. It's a wonderful poem.

Seeing his eyes go blank, I asked, Are you familiar with Richard Wilbur's writing?

"American?" Burton asked, looking for an escape clause.

Yes. Pulitzer Prize–winning poet.

Mention of the prestigious award was like a pin pricked into Burton's balloon. The life drained from his defeated face as he conceded, "I don't know him. I missed him."

Insensitive to his vulnerability, or perhaps eager to claim my victory, I plodded on: He's a lovely poet, Richard Wilbur. He's won every major prize for poetry.

"I'm astounded," Burton said. "I thought I knew—"

Now I realized his humiliation and tried to offer a sop: He wrote the lyrics to Bernstein's music for *Candide.*

Burton leaped at the bait. "Well, those were brilliant," he said, back on a firm footing. "The lyrics are dazzling."

I offered to send him some volumes of Wilbur's poetry.

"I'll be delighted. There are American poets who are not published in this country. One of my favorite poets is Archibald MacLeish." And he was off again.

But from that moment forth, *I* was in. From that moment forth, not only was Burton friendly, we became confederates. Richard Wilbur was my entree to Richard Burton.

Several days later, on location at a country estate in Luton, I noticed him holding court far across the patio. Suddenly, in mid-story, he left the group and darted straight for me. "Quick," he said, as if I were the only soul on the set who could help him. "Who wrote *The Education of H*Y*M*A*N K*A*P*L*A*N*?"

Leo Rosten.

"That's it," and he rushed back to continue his suspended tale.

The day before he completed his role, I told him how much I'd enjoyed working with him.

"And I want to tell you, dear boy," he countered, "you're one of only two people in your profession I've ever met who's as intelligent as I am."

It's the most amusing compliment I've ever received, and among the most cherished.

Seventeen days later, Richard Burton was dead.

CHAPTER NINE

INCIDENTAL GIFTS

"I lost my audience, and I haven't been able to get it back."
—WILLIAM INGE

William Inge is the only person in this collection of interviews I didn't meet. But he was the first interview that counted for much, and in many ways he has lingered longest.

An Inge interview is not unlike an Inge play. His statements weren't profound; his sentences weren't eloquent. But beneath his words, and what mattered most, was a poignant residue of anguish, a weary hurt that Elia Kazan has defined as "a quiet terror," that bored within me and still remains.

I did not initiate the Inge interview. In 1971, I was living in Kansas City, on the fringe of Inge territory, when Clarence Olson, the book editor of the *St. Louis Post-Dispatch*, asked if I'd be willing to talk with the writer, whose second novel, *My Son Is a Splendid Driver*, had recently been published. Interview a major playwright? I relished the opportunity.

For a week I all but lived at the library, amidst the microfilm and the bound, yellowing magazines, scribbling notes on index cards, copying down remarks a younger, more confident Inge had made to others which seemed worth remembering (and which, twenty-one years later, still do):

"I hate a play that tells me what to think. I have never written a play that had any intended theme or that tried to propound any particular idea. I try to recommend my plays as I would a short trip, to be enjoyed not for the hope of its destination but for what one sees along the way."

Slowly, Inge came into shape.

He was born in 1913 in Independence, Kansas, a small, prosperous town in the southeast part of the state near the Oklahoma border, on the periphery of the Flint Hills. So many people today think of Kansas as a stark, barren wasteland. They do not know the Flint Hills.

Here, bordered by Wichita to the west, Emporia to the north, and Independence to the east, is a landscape of unparalleled beauty—the tallgrass prairie. These low, round, rippling rises roll on, one after another, beyond eye's seeing or mind's imagining. A trip today through the sea of grass in the verdant Flint Hills offers the same undulating vistas that Inge knew while growing up in the 1920s and 1930s.

These are the hills and this is the space that Inge felt he needed to escape in order to become a writer—and these are the hills and this is the space to which he repeatedly returned in his plays, films and novels.

He described this boundaryless land in *My Son Is a Splended Driver:*

> At sunset we all became quiet. The sky now dominated everything, the earth itself appearing humble and poor . . . in the sky, something important was happening. Day was being destroyed by coming night, and the burst of orange in the sky was like a final flush of blood in the body's system before a being passes away. I have seen many prairie sunsets since that time, and they have always moved me to believe that there is something going on in the sky much bigger than man himself; that man's presence upon the earth is an incidental gift that we must make the most of while it lasts, even though our strivings, our creations, our sins and our virtues are all lost in infinity.

St. Louis was one of the way stations on Inge's indirect route to New York. From 1943 to 1946 he was art, music, book, and drama critic for the now-defunct *St. Louis Star-Times.*

"I ran my tail off on that job," Inge said when he talked to me by telephone from his Los Angeles home. Throughout the conversation he spoke softly, slowly, with long pauses between sentences, between phrases even. Often I had to strain to hear his words. Even when he was reminiscing about something as innocuous as those long-ago memories, his voice was tinged with sadness.

"That job was the first time I truly considered myself a writer. I did good work for the paper and I wrote well. I still consider St. Louis the only city in the Midwest with atmosphere and color."

In 1944 he interviewed a local boy briefly home from the Chicago rehearsals of his Broadway-bound play. A year before his death, Inge said of that first meeting with Tennessee Williams: "He was very nervous. . . . I've never known such a small person to have so much energy. . . . You got nervous just to be with him." A month after his death, Williams wrote of that first meeting with William Inge, "He was embarrassingly 'impressed' by my burgeoning career. . . ."

One can only imagine these two strange, shy outcasts, both burdened by the knowledge of their "difference," each carrying the weight of secret guilts, neither yet having tasted success.

According to Williams' biographer Donald Spoto, the two young men—Inge thirty-one, Williams thirty-three—found comfort and reassurance in a brief, passionate involvement that would not be repeated through the ensuing years of their maturing friendship.

During that first meeting, reporter Inge "blurted out" his desire to be a playwright. Williams encouraged him to stop wishing and start writing. Four years later—with a man from Missouri in the White House and a general from Kansas soon to follow, and with Inge's unlikely mentor now meteorically entrenched as the American theater's most sensational writer—Inge's own timid conquest of Broadway began.

Come Back, Little Sheba, which is set in a "Midwestern city," opened in 1950 to modest success.

The Pulitzer Prize–winning *Picnic*, set in "a small Kansas town," arrived in 1953. While *Picnic* is probably Inge's most durable play, it was also, true to his depressive nature, the script with which he was least satisfied. During its tryout, director Joshua Logan persuaded the dramatist to rewrite the original unhappy ending. Said Inge on the phone: "I was content with *Picnic*. There was much about the production I loved. But I never felt fulfilled. There was still the early version I wanted seen."

Nine years after *Picnic*'s Broadway triumph, Inge published his original version under the title *Summer Brave*. It *was* seen, but not by its author. In October 1975, two years after Inge's death, on the eve of the American Bicentennial, *Summer Brave* eked out a Broadway run of less than three weeks. The cast included Jill Eikenberry as Madge; Alexis Smith as Rosemary, the spinster schoolteacher; and, as Hal, a little-known actor named Ernest Thompson, who would find success four years later as the author of *On Golden Pond.*

Bus Stop ("a small Kansas town") in 1955 was followed in 1957 by *The Dark at the Top of the Stairs* ("a small Oklahoma town," but actually Independence, Kansas). Its depiction of family life during the early 1920s was Inge's most overtly autobiographical writing to date, though on the phone he said of all his characters, "They're all me."

By 1957, Tennessee Williams, Arthur Miller, and, yes, William Inge, were Broadway's Big Three. Inge, the only one to enjoy an unbroken string of hits, was the most successful American playwright of the decade.

What were the pressures of being a serious yet commercially successful playwright in the 1950s?

"They were pretty pleasant pressures, now that I remember them," he answered. "Always being asked to be interviewed, to appear on talk shows, to attend parties. The danger is that you become a personality first and a writer second. But I'm a writer. I have to lead a solitary life to lead a creative life. I get lost in society, so I don't go out much. Then there was the terrible pressure from each production. I really don't know if I could go through the turmoil, the hellishnesss, of it all again."

Successful though he was, Inge never sought the crown that was lobbed back and forth between Williams and Miller. Inge knew his plays stayed close to home. They didn't aspire to Miller's social rages or to Williams' metaphysics. Inge did what he did best, yet he possessed precious little self-confidence in his talent, wondered if he wasn't writing on borrowed time. When eventually his time did run out, though he was stunned by the suddenness of his fall, I wonder if there wasn't also, deep within him, that perverse relief similar to what we witness when a fugitive who has assumed a new identity is finally captured: "So you've found me out at last."

In 1959 Inge encountered his first failure, *A Loss of Roses*. It too was set in Kansas. But after it failed, he abandoned the Midwest and moved the locale of his next two dramas to New York City. *Natural Affection* (1963) and *Where's Daddy?* (1965) were also Broadway failures.

"*Natural Affection* was five years ahead of its time," Inge all but whispered into the phone. "It's about the violence that's set off when society makes people feel unimportant. The times right now are frightening to me because they're so much more violent. I haven't been back to New York for three years. I'm afraid to go to New York now, to walk down the streets. That's why I think *Natural Affection* might find a new audience if it were revived."

Recalling those frustrating years of failure, Inge said: "I lost my audience and I haven't been able to get it back. I started developing, my writing changed; critics couldn't relate it to anything else I'd written. The early 1960s, when a whole new group of critics came into control in New York, was a very destructive period. Capote calls them the literary Mafia. Lots of good writers got struck down then. Brustein, Simon, and others destroyed a fine theater of the fifties. A theater which spoke for America got destroyed. Now it's pandemonium, and I don't know what they want."

Soon after Inge's death, his friend William Gibson wrote of that period, "One of our top three playwrights had simply been liquidated."

Inge turned to the source of his last success. He turned to Elia Kazan, whose understanding of outcasts reaches beyond articulation. Kazan had directed *The Dark at the Top of the Stairs*.

With Kazan at his side, Inge turned to the movies and returned to his surefire material. He wrote a novelette, *Splendor in the Grass*, set in 1929, in "Inge territory." But because Inge was unskilled at actually structuring a screenplay, Kazan not only directed the film but also wrote the script. (Inge's screen credit is an honest "Written By" rather than "Screenplay By.") Each man helped the other: Inge won an Academy Award; Kazan won the self-confidence to write full-time and to quit directing altogether.

The film's final scene is enormously moving. In his autobiography, *A Life*, Kazan writes: "It is not my favorite of my films, but the last reel is my favorite last reel, at once the saddest and the happiest. . . . What I like about this ending is its bittersweet ambivalence, full of what Bill had learned from his own life: that you have to accept limited happiness, because all happiness is limited . . . you must live with the sadness as well as the joy."

When Inge won an Oscar for *Splendor in the Grass*, it appeared that he had embarked on a successful new career. It was not to be.

"I don't get along well with film companies," he rationalized over the telephone. "In the film world the writer is always working under someone."

In 1965, Inge wrote *Bus Riley's Back in Town*, which starred Michael

Parks and Ann-Margret. "We produced a very neat little picture, original and refreshing," he said. "Ann-Margret was a very precious young talent, so her career was being highly guarded. It was a part in which she showed to good effect, which she played with humor and appeal. But her previous film, *Kitten with a Whip*, had bombed. So the studio heads at Universal-International took over and rewrote, even though my film had already completed shooting." Inge removed his name from the credits and vowed never again to write for films.

With the publication of two novels in 1970 and 1971, he entered yet another phase in his writing career. *My Son Is a Splendid Driver*, while perhaps not his most important piece of writing, is Inge's most affecting piece of reading. It was intended to be read, and it's filled out in a way that the plays, with their emotions dormant, beneath the surface, cannot be. The story traces three decades in the lives of the Hansen family, beginning in 1919, at their home in Freedom, Kansas (which is, of course, Independence).

"I started the book in the late 1950s," Inge said, "then took it up again ten years later because I felt it was too good to waste. The first half is pretty true, in fact; the second half is almost pure fiction. I know it's not the kind of book I can expect to have a best-seller with. We want sensation, the outlandish book, the dirty book. But sales are steady, and it's going into a second edition. It looks like it will have a continued life."

And Inge's life? At the time, he was teaching playwriting at the University of California at Irvine. "I enjoy teaching," he said. "I feel I have something to give my students. They tend to write very free, almost surrealistic plays. I give them no strict rules. I want to let them find themselves in their writing."

What about his own writing? How did he view that?

"It's there, and I don't know what to make of it. I'm proud of my plays, particularly *Natural Affection* and *Where's Daddy?* I've written some more plays, a lot of one-acts. They're kind of intimate and full of violence."

Any reflections on his students?

"Today's youth is totally different from my generation, with a different set of standards. They're not all trying to grow up to be bank presidents. My generation approached maturity very cautiously. This generation is taking to social responsibility at earlier ages. I see no similarities except the basic things: They're still young, they still fall in love. There's always a feeling of optimism. Essentially, I think we're an optimistic people."

A curious comment for Inge to have made, since there was no trace of optimism in his crepuscular voice. Though removed from the Broadway and Hollywood battlefields where he once fought, he was still a scarred man. You could hear the scars over the telephone. Yet, if Inge had pronounced us an optimistic people, it seemed only appropriate to ask him the question that was draped around our conversation like a shroud.

Was he at peace with himself?

"No, I don't always find myself at peace," he admitted. "I'm restless and ill at ease with myself most of the time. I use my writing as a release. I have been working more and more to be my own man. It's very hard to write, for sometimes you are dealing with your most traumatic experiences. A writer has to recognize himself and his own boundaries, has to recognize what is his right in the world, has to seek out his own depths."

During the 1950s, William Inge thought he had succeeded in recognizing himself. Then the mirror of success was shattered before his very eyes, and he was told that his talents were but incidental gifts.

He was told that he'd made the most of those gifts while they lasted, but that now they were dried out.

Now, he was told, his talent was scorched dry, seared like Kansas prairie grass under the burning sun.

No longer did he know what was his right in his world. No longer was the path clear. By the time I spoke with him, he was as blind and banished as Oedipus before Colonus.

Yet read *My Son Is a Splendid Driver*, and you sense that although his spirit was broken, his talent had not forsaken him. He had not lost his gift for writing about a time in America when the common man still merited respect. He still valued the vanished America of his youth, when vast, isolated spaces allowed men to turn their backs on the world's complexities.

Long after I hung up the telephone, one unasked question continued to echo in my mind: What happens to a man whose Muse remains anchored but whose public has set him adrift? Inside himself, what happens to that man?

A month after speaking to Inge, I attended a lecture by director-critic Harold Clurman at the University of Kansas. The irrepressible

Clurman had directed two of Inge's plays, *Bus Stop* and *Where's Daddy?*, on Broadway. There, in the heart of Inge country, I hoped he might have something to say about the playwright.

On the college circuit, Harold Clurman was a carrier of contagion, full of infectious enthusiasm. I heard him three times, and though it was often pretty much the same set speech, Clurman was always an event. He would sit on the stage through a long-winded introduction, looking less than imposing. Then he would take to the lectern, and a metamorphosis would occur.

Suddenly he was a balding bulldog with the intensity of a Jewish Winston Churchill, replete with cigar and percolating with passion.

He was a pug Cyrano de Bergerac, slashing with his walking stick at his ancient enemies: Falsehood, Compromise, Cowardice, Mediocrity.

As much a spellbinder as Harold Hill in *The Music Man,* he inspired his young audiences with direction and purpose. When his performance was over, you knew what you were about, why you wanted to be in the theater. And you continued to know for at least the next two or three days.

Clurman spoke at the University of Kansas with his usual vigor, but not about Inge. Then, during the question-and-answer session, someone disparagingly asked if it wasn't time to reevaluate Inge's position in the American theater. Wasn't it time to put him on the shelf?

Clurman stopped prowling the stage. He stood silent (that in itself was rare) for a seeming eternity.

Maybe twenty seconds.

Maybe ten.

A long time.

Finally he began his reply with a paraphrase of something I'd read in one of his reviews.

Inge, he said, "was our dramatist of the ordinary." His characters "were the common product of American society." Inge held an important place in playwriting because "the commonplace is not always the obvious." True, Clurman conceded, some of the later plays were not as effective as the early ones. But, he added, "at times Inge's writing touches the rim of poetry, and the right actors can transport it into that realm. Inge's plays always act better than one would think from reading them."

Then, as Clurman removed the ever-present cigar from his mouth, he glared at the large audience as though he were able to stare simultaneously into the eyes of every person in the huge hall, and he hurled his words like a gauntlet. "The plays of William Inge were never less than honorable!" He paused a moment to allow the audience to absorb his reply, then spat the words out again. "William Inge was never less than honorable!"

A month later I found myself in New York City, enjoying a private audience with the distinguished critic. "Audience" may seem a rather elevated word. But I hardly could call it an interview, and decidedly not a conversation. During my hour in his West Fifty-seventh Street apartment, I spoke for perhaps a total of five minutes, Clurman for fifty-five. No Inge-talk at this meeting. Halfway through the marathon I realized that I was being given free a variation of the lecture-performance for which he normally charges universities a handsome fee! (More accurately, I wasn't *having* an audience—I *was* the audience.)

Upon entering Clurman's bachelor apartment, you were immediately overwhelmed by books: books teetering precipitously on the windowsills; leaning towers of books on tabletops, stacks of books, like stalagmites, rising from the floor. Clurman was a captive of his library.

He sat me on the couch, then proceeded to pace about the small, cluttered room like a caged panther with a cigar between its fangs. As the critic paced, he continually lit and relit the cigar. At one point he ran out of matches. Clurman futilely searched all his pockets, then searched them again. Still he lectured, not missing a beat, but the agitation of his matchless state was beginning to get the best of him. Unable to bear his frustration, I interrupted the monologue to urge, "Go get a match." Gratefully he complied, leaving the room and immediately returning without having dropped a phrase of his recitation.

He spoke against the school of jaundiced criticism that lacks understanding of and appreciation for what is involved in mounting a professional production.

He spoke against critics who urge people to go to the theater merely for the sake of going. "Brazen irresponsibility," he charged. People *should* be going, Clurman emphasized, but the critic owes his reader the foremost responsibility of taste over blind enthusiasm.

He spoke of how too many theater critics today lack sufficient background in other arts—music, painting, literature—to write with perspective.

When I asked—one of my few questions—if his constant theatergoing wasn't eventually numbing, he replied, "Not really. I don't write about theater. I write about life."

As I prepared to leave Harold Clurman's apartment, he insisted on giving me a book. From a dusty windowsill he selected *Mr. George Jean Nathan Presents*, a collection of theater essays by the eminent drama critic, published and purchased in 1917. That evening, I perused my gift and discovered that Clurman had underlined only one sentence in the entire volume: "The artist is contemptuous of the crowd."

On the telephone, Inge had described his failed play *Natural Affection* as being "about the violence that's set off when society makes people feel unimportant."

Twenty months after our conversation, on June 10, 1973, he unleashed that violence on himself.

William Inge went to the garage of his California home and took his life. As the sixty-year-old writer sat in his Mercedes-Benz inhaling carbon monoxide, what Tennessee Williams once described as "Bill Inge's personal odyssey, a truly Homeric drama" finally came to an end.

Eight months after the suicide, I happened to have dinner with Joshua Logan. In addition to having directed *Picnic* on Broadway, Logan also directed the film versions of *Picnic* and *Bus Stop*. "It's hard to talk about Bill," he said when I introduced Inge's name. But as the meal progressed, Logan did reminisce, and returned to the subject time and again.

"He was a gentle person. He'd had that terrific alcoholic experience. In coming off it, he became a rather pale person, I felt. To be with him was to feel a sense of slight depression."

Several minutes later: "His writing was full of earthiness and humor and sex, which belied what you saw in person."

What did you see in person?

"He never yelled. He never showed any enthusiasm. I always felt he was the loneliest individual I ever knew in my life. He had no deep relationship, not even with a dog or cat.

"He really was a naive boy, as so many of his characters are. Once he came to our home in Stamford, Connecticut. One other guest was swimming in the pool. She swam to the side and I said, 'Bill, meet Garbo.'

"Bill, who was always rather white, turned paler still. He just sat down, speechless. He wouldn't eat lunch. When my wife called him to eat, he didn't answer. Finally he said good-bye. I went and asked him what was the matter.

" 'Meeting Garbo,' he said. 'I just had to sit and think about it.' "

Thirty minutes later, during dessert, Logan returned yet again to Inge. "He was very nice, and we were great friends. We argued about only one thing, the end of *Picnic.* He wanted it to end on a depressing note. I wanted a sense of hope. Even after the play won the Pulitzer Prize and the Drama Critics Award and became a major success, he still would rather have had Madge become the town whore."

A year later, I met Eileen Heckart at a party at the American Shakespeare Festival. *Picnic* was her first hit play. She also acted in *The Dark at the Top of the Stairs* and in the film version of *Bus Stop.* Inge dedicated *Natural Affection* to her.

"Bill was such a loner," she said, "but I adored him. There was so much heart and warmth in him. He was kind and sweet and generous. He just had his own demons."

What about that celebrated dispute between Logan and Inge during *Picnic*?

"Josh is very fast," she answered. "That would make Bill nervous, and he would leave rehearsals. We played St. Louis on the tryout tour. The play wasn't working yet, and Bill was so unhappy. He said, 'They only remember me in this town as an alcoholic.'

"I was playing Rosemary, the schoolteacher, as a virgin. But I didn't know if I was right. So I went to Bill and I said, 'You wrote this. Tell me.'

"And Bill said, 'I see her making an entrance in pink marabou.'

"And then Josh came to me and said, 'Don't you know better than to ever ask a playwright about his play? Ask the director.' "

Picnic may have undergone a metamorphosis during rehearsals, but not *The Dark at the Top of the Stairs.* "There was precious little change on the road with *Dark,*" the actress said. "I don't think you'll find better playwriting anywhere than in that script. Bill's plays exude a whole nostalgia of color and odor that is so real."

A nostalgia of color and odor . . .

Isn't that another way of saying "*not* the words"? Isn't that an actress's way of explaining what Kazan described when he wrote that Inge's plays offer actors scenes that reveal "their best gifts"? This, not because of the words Inge wrote, but because of their underlying emotions, "the ones Bill had felt when he wrote the scenes."

It's a curious thing. I've read a lot of negative criticism about Inge, but never a single critical word by anyone who ever has acted in one of his plays.

Ultimately, I think any writer can respond to William Inge as the most openly vulnerable of writers, as a temporary triumph of talent over self-destruction.

He personified that fear of being found out, of being found wanting. It's not failure we fear; failure is a given. No, it's the lure of praise, followed by the cruelty of having it all snatched away . . . and feeling inside yourself that they're right, it *should* be taken away. If they'll rob F. Scott Fitzgerald and Tennessee Williams of their self-esteem, and leave them to strangle on their own insecurity, then no writer is safe.

I'm comforted to know that, out in Independence, Kansas, the local community college sponsors an annual Inge festival, where an award is bestowed on an American playwright in recognition of a body of work. It pleases me to know they don't have to twist these writers' arms to trek out to Kansas. To the contrary, each year all the previous recipients—Robert Anderson, William Gibson, Garson Kanin, and the like—eagerly return to heap honor on the next. For a few days each year they join together to rekindle, way out there in distant Kansas, the warm glow that has been extinquished.

In memory, at least, Inge is not forgotten.

". . . our strivings, our creations, our sins and our virtues are all lost in infinity," William Inge wrote in *My Son Is a Splendid Driver*. In time they are. But for now, still, Inge's strivings and creations remain behind, available to those who wish to seek them out. The plays and novels, the colors and odors, are still as pristine as a bright orange moon or a crystal star hanging high, "like the only promises that had been kept for the world," over the lonely Flint Hills.

CHAPTER TEN

QUIET WARRIOR FROM WHARTON

"When you're a writer, you have to write these stories, even if you don't get paid."
—HORTON FOOTE

William Inge and Horton Foote might have been soulmates. Indeed, the parallels between them are obvious:

Inge was born in 1913, Foote just three years later.

Each was raised in the isolation of small-town America. Inge's Independence, Kansas, and Foote's Wharton, Texas (seven hundred miles due south), shared approximate rural populations of around three thousand.

Both boys knew that their destinies lay elsewhere, yet both men knew that their roots provided the sustenance for their writing. The 1950s found them both in New York, Inge writing to acclaim and glory, Foote writing to survive.

Now, four decades later, Inge is a memory, the victim of his own despair; Horton Foote just keeps writing, keeps striving, keeps adding to a body of work that is unprecedented in the sheer consistency and coherence of its themes.

Finally, then, it is the contrasts rather than the comparisons by which these two men are measured. In Horton Foote's resilience, and through his dogged determination, he might more aptly have ascribed to him the nickname of a two-time candidate for the presidency, Alfred E. Smith. For Horton Foote is the theater's "happy warrior." Not happy like a blithe Pollyanna, but happy in his world, and in his tunnel-vision obliviousness to the ever-changing society around him. A warrior, as in days of yore; a man whose quest has become his life.

In order to appreciate Horton Foote, you have to begin at the beginning. He was born in Wharton, Texas, in 1916. Located fifty miles southwest of Houston and forty miles north of the Gulf of Mexico, Wharton back then was on the cusp of cotton country. In spirit it was closer to Savannah, Georgia, half a continent away, than to San Antonio, 150 miles west.

"My part of Texas was all plantations," the seventy-one-year-old Foote said when we talked together in his Greenwich Village apartment in 1987. He is the only writer in this volume who was not interviewed in the 1970s. "My family had a lot of blacks around. I was raised by blacks."

Foote's slurred Texas accent added a genteel, almost whimsical quality to his statements. That accent, that voice, has probably caused a lot of people to sell Horton Foote short, to not realize that he can be as relentless as a dog with a bone when it comes to getting his work produced.

"I wasn't very good at sports," he continued, "so I spent my time listening. You could get five people, and they'd all tell you the same story, and they'd add and subtract and do riffs. So that's what influenced me as a writer. So much of my writing is just variations on a theme. I heard all these stories from the past, and I've spent my life writing them down."

Not that he knew early on that he was going to write. Far from it.

"When I was twelve," he said, "I decided I wanted to be an actor. I don't know why, because Wharton didn't even have a little theater in those days. The only live theater I ever saw was the traveling tent shows. But I got this calling, and I was just hell-bent and determined to be an actor. So then I got into every play I could get into. God only knows what kind of acting I was doing.

"I graduated from high school when I just had turned sixteen. I wanted to go to New York, but my parents thought New York was too wicked a place for a boy who had never been out of Texas. But when I was seventeen, they did let me to go California."

Foote apprenticed at the Pasadena Playhouse. "They had a strange system for teaching acting," he said. "They just put you in plays. They had no technique. The first play they put me into was a Roman comedy, and I had read maybe two Shakespeare plays in my life. But I held on, and I got invited back the second year. That's when I got cast as a Negro boy in a Paul Green play, and I had a great triumph. I suddenly felt alive on the stage for the first time. I was talking the way I'd heard people talk all my life, and it was a lesson for me."

The lesson: Stick close to what you know.

He moved to New York City, where he joined a new repertory company that eventually became known as the American Actors' Theatre. Here, he began to write. In 1940, the company mounted his one-act play *Wharton Dance.* Then they did his three-act drama *Texas Town,* in which the principal characters were modeled after Foote and his father.

For Foote, the 1940s were years of struggling fecundity:

In 1943, Sanford Meisner directed Foote's plays at the Neighborhood Playhouse.

In 1944, Martha Graham choreographed one of his plays.

In 1944, he and his good friend Vincent Donehue established a theater workshop in Washington, D.C.

In 1945, he married Lillian Vallish, from Pennsylvania. ("A lot of people who know me say that all my women are my wife.")

In 1947, television producer and director Fred Coe (Donehue's college roommate) became the founding executive producer of NBC's *Television Playhouse,* and Foote soon found himself writing for live TV.

Nothing grand, at first. His initial assignment was to polish scripts for *The Gabby Hayes Show.*

"It was the first time I really began to be able to support myself as a writer," Foote recalled. "Up till then, I supported myself with teaching jobs. I wasn't acting anymore at all. I was teaching acting. That's a hard way to make a living, and if you're trying to write too, it's exhausting.

"This was a live, half-hour show, and we always had to allow for Gabby to gabby on for three or four minutes. We did things like the fall of the Alamo inside a studio for two cents. I learned about television."

But at night, he was still working on his own scripts. By now, he had centered his writing in one locale, the one place he called home. He changed his town's name from Wharton to Harrison. From this time forward, just about everything he wrote would be set in Harrison, Texas.

Foote hoped his breakthrough would come with *The Chase,* a three-act drama about how the residents of a small Southern town (Harrison, Texas) react when an escaped murderer returns home.

"Herman Shumlin was the first producer to option it," Foote said. "I thought I'd died and gone to heaven. But it didn't get done. Then José Ferrer took an option, and he finally produced it. He cast it fairly well. Kim Stanley, who at that time was an unknown actress my wife had discovered, played the murderer's wife. But Joe and I didn't agree about the lead role, the sheriff. He cast John Hodiak, who was a lovely man. But he was a film actor, and he had no stage experience.

"Ferrer is a very nice man, and we're friends. But in retrospect, I wonder if he wasn't doing too much. These were his golden years. He had hit after hit after hit after hit. He was very supportive, but he didn't have a lot of time. He was acting in *The Shrike* across the street. The first day of rehearsal, he said to me: 'You know, you're going to have to direct this play. I'm going to have to be like a football coach and come in and give pep talks.' So he turned it over to me. My second Broadway play. My first one in the big leagues. Only Kim, and Lonny Chapman, who came from that part of the world, knew what to do with the material.

"The production wasn't what I had hoped for, because the New York theater in those days approached in a very ersatz way anything west of Hoboken."

The play closed after thirty-one performances, but Foote refused to let his story die. He "re-investigated the material" in novel form. *The Chase* was published in 1956.

"I guess I've been a minimalist before it was ever invented," Foote suggested. "Certainly in the case of *The Chase,* I errored on the side of timidity. Rather than overwrite the book, it's almost underwritten. I have too much respect for real novelists to claim I'm a novelist, and I would never want to write another one, but I'm glad I did it."

But he still wasn't through with *The Chase.*

"A director, I can't even remember his name, took it to Sam Spiegel. Sam optioned it, along with two of my short plays. He had the grand scheme of making a movie that was a microcosm of a small town. So he bought my material and fired the director. That was my first lesson. I realized that when you sell your material to a Hollywood producer, it belongs to him. It's no longer yours. They can do whatever they want to with it. I admired and liked Sam, but I didn't like the movie of *The Chase*."

Eventually Spiegel turned the story into a gory extravaganza starring Marlon Brando, Robert Redford, and Jane Fonda. He hired Lillian Hellman to write the adaptation.

"She said very openly and honestly, 'I've used *The Chase* as a departure,' " Foote recalled. "And indeed she did. She departed totally. The superstructure is there. The names are the same. But they violated the characters. They made 'em glitzy. Eventually the production got into deep, deep trouble. Sam had fired Lillian and had brought in somebody who'd worked on *Giant*. Well, my part of Texas is as far from *Giant* as it is from the Bronx. So Sam called me up and asked me to help out. I felt like the mother of Moses, who gave up her child, saw the princess take Moses, and then said, yes, she'd be the nurse.

"So I went to the location, but I couldn't do much. I mean, there it was. I asked the writer, 'Where did you learn all this—?' And he said, 'I read a book on Texas.'

"The first day of shooting, they were filming a scene in the drugstore, and there was an Indian squaw sitting on the set. And I went running back—I never ran so fast in my life—to Sam's office. I said, 'Sam, God almighty. What is an Indian doing in a drugstore in Harrison, Texas?' I never saw an Indian in my life. If an Indian had ever passed through town I don't know what would have happened. They would have let school out.

"It turned out the scene designer had read, again, some book, and had seen a photo, probably of some little town way out in West Texas, with an Indian squaw. I said, 'Sam, it cannot be.' To his credit, he tried to get it changed. But they'd already shot the scene.

"It's a strange thing about that material. The very day I optioned it to Sam Spiegel, we had another offer from a very young, passionate man named Alan Pakula. My life would have been changed if he had done it. He adored the play. He said, 'Listen, may I still meet with you and your agent? Let me tell you what I want to do with it, just in case the other deal falls through.' So we spent three and a half hours listening to this passionate fellow. He wanted José Quintero to direct it."

Still another missed opportunity might have involved Quintero. "Jason Robards understudied John Hodiak in the original production," Foote said. "Eventually he got involved with Circle in the

Square. They'd had a big success with their revival of Tennessee Williams' *Summer and Smoke,* which made a star of Geraldine Page, and now they were looking for something else to do. Robards suggested *The Chase.* He wanted to play the role he'd understudied.

"So they got in touch with me, and I met with them, and I wanted them badly to do it. But Sam wouldn't let them. So instead they did *The Iceman Cometh,* which made Jason a star. But I confess, I've sometimes wondered if José Quintero could have restored new life to my play, the way he did to *Summer and Smoke.*"

Meanwhile, Foote kept busy writing for live television. *The Trip to Bountiful,* with Lillian Gish as Carrie Watts, was broadcast on NBC in March 1953. Its enthusiastic reception led Foote to expand the script into a three-act play, which the Theatre Guild produced on Broadway later that year, again with Lillian Gish.

Indeed, throughout Foote's career, he has shown no hesitancy to rework his script from medium to medium. "Essentially," he explained, "I am so obsessed with this material that whatever form comes along, I'll push it into that form until another opportunity comes."

But where did *The Trip to Bountiful* come *from*?

"Like most of my things," Foote said, "it's a pastiche of tales I've heard and seen. I'd heard this story of a woman who had married a man who was older than she was, because the man she loved very deeply didn't want to marry her. After her husband died, she would sit on the porch every day and the other man would pass by, and they would bow to each other. That impressed me very much.

"Originally I tried to tell this woman's story early, in a scene with her father, who told her she couldn't marry the man she wanted to marry. Then I tried to set it on the day of her wedding to the man she did marry. It just wouldn't work. So, in the strange alchemy that happens, I began to think about the story from the end of her life.

"When we did it for television, it was just an hour. When I expanded it for Broadway, I added all the early part in the apartment. After the Broadway run, a very well-known director-producer liked it a lot and wanted to buy all the rights for fifteen thousand dollars. That was a lot of money to me, and I was about to sell it away when my agent said, 'I'll never handle you again if you do.' So I tightened my belt."

Two decades later, Foote's tale of Carrie Watts' escape from Houston to Bountiful (located on the bus line between Harrison and

Cotton) was resurrected when Robert Redford at the Sundance Institute asked Peter Masterson (Foote's cousin) if he wanted to direct a film.

"I had never allowed anyone to film it in all those years," Foote explained, "because for a long time I wanted Lillian to do it very badly. Producers would come to me, and they'd suggest Katharine Hepburn or somebody else, and I would say no. Years later, after Lillian was too old to do it, another producer wanted Mary Martin, and I suggested Geraldine Page. And he said, 'You just can't do it.'

"So when Pete called, I said, 'Pete, there's one thing. I cannot have an actress who is—' And he said, 'Who do you want?' And I said, 'Geraldine.' He said, 'That's who I want.'

"We had a terrible time getting her. They wanted Anne Bancroft. They wanted Jessica Tandy. Jessica's a wonderful actress, but she's a little too old. Because you have to believe this woman's son is a certain age."

After the film opened in 1985, Geraldine Page told an interviewer: "Horton has relayed a very complex idea in a very simple way—the idea of coming to see one's place in the universe. I love people who are told they cannot do something and then go ahead and do it anyway." The actress was speaking of her character, but she might have been describing Foote. Page won the Academy Award as Best Actress for her performance.

Foote allowed as how there aren't two actresses whose styles are more different that those of Lillian Gish and Geraldine Page. Then he added: "One of the great lessons for me was to realize how deeply dependent we writers are on who does our material. Both actresses were very valid. They were like two great instrumentalists playing the same piece of music. What came out was the same, yet very different. Lillian was extraordinary, and Geraldine was also extraordinary.

"I love actors, and I think it's mutual. I really adore them, I really do. They're my lifeblood."

Foote's next Broadway play after *The Trip to Bountiful*, back in 1954, back in Harrison, Texas, was *The Traveling Lady*. It made a star of Kim Stanley, but it did not run long.

The author's longtime friend Vincent J. Donehue was credited as the director. But, as Foote explained, "the tragedy was that he was replaced out of town by Harold Clurman. It was a choice of Lee Strasberg or Harold. I wanted Lee, and Kim wanted Harold. Harold was a great theoretician, but I don't feel he helped the play at all.

"Kim tends to get very nervous, so Harold thought that if we had a full runthrough with a full house on the afternoon of opening night, it would calm her down. Just the opposite happened. The runthrough was filled with actors, and they went wild about the play, screaming and bravoing and carrying on, and she gave her performance in the afternoon. The opening-night audience was very reserved. She was still wonderful, but she didn't give her performance.

"I was very hurt by the play's reception. I was very, very, very, very distressed. What saved me was there was a great critic named Stark Young, who adored the play and said he'd do anything to keep it alive. His support got me through a really rough time."

Still, there were the live television broadcasts, and Foote wrote lots of them. One of the most memorable, "Old Man," from the story by William Faulkner, was first broadcast on *Playhouse 90* in 1958.

"The story is set during a flood on the Mississippi River," Foote said, "and they were going to do it alive. I read the story and thought, 'How can I—? I can't—'

"Then I thought, 'That's not your problem. You just write it.' So I did, and they liked it. So we arrived at the big studio in Hollywood, and they had all these tanks of water. And in the middle of it, the director, John Frankenheimer, realized, 'We can't do this alive; we'll just drown the actors.' It was the first show to be successfully taped. So, in a way, as much as I love live television, I put one of the first nails in the coffin.

"But Sterling Hayden was wonderful to work with, and Geraldine Page was marvelous in it. In fact, that's really where I got to know Geraldine. You know, I'm a family man. I've always kept touch with my family, and I get very attached to people. One of the great tragedies to me about this business is that a production becomes a family and then all of a sudden it's over and everyone goes away. Geraldine and I remained friends, but we're the only ones from that production."

He adapted another Faulkner story, "Tomorrow," for television in 1961. It was directed by Robert Mulligan. The next year, Mulligan and his partner Alan Pakula asked Foote to adapt Harper Lee's novel *To Kill a Mockingbird* for the screen.

"I don't really like to do adaptations," Foote said. "So I didn't even read it. I just said I was working on something else. But my wife read the novel. She said, 'You better read it.' So I did, and I thought I could make a contribution to this.

"I never met Faulkner when I was adapting his work. He was like an icon. He got word back to me that he liked what I was doing, and that was enough. But Harper and I were of the same generation. At our very first meeting, it was like we lived next door to each other. We just fell in love with each other, so I jumped in."

Where did you jump in? How did you begin that screenplay?

"We're talking about a long time ago. Twenty-five years. But as I recall, two things got me going. First, it was Alan's idea to compress Harper's rambling structure into one year. Then I remember reading a review of the novel that compared Scout to Huckleberry Finn. That helped me to get inside the material and to find another kind of shape for it. Adaptations are very difficult. You've got to get inside somebody else's skin before you can start it. Then you always have structural problems in moving from one form to another. That condensation, that bringing it down and fitting it into another framework, is not always easy.

"I remember, for instance, the scene where the judge asks Atticus Finch to represent Tom Robinson. I put Atticus outside on the gallery and the children within hearing range in their bedroom. I did that because, as a child, when my parents would think I was asleep, I was in my bedroom, which was right on our gallery, and I would hear them tell all these things that were happening in town. So here was an opportunity to tell the story through the point of view of the children.

"And then the other child, Dill. All Harper had to do was tell me she'd based him on Truman Capote, and I just went wild. It fired my imagination."

Foote's published screenplay includes an introductory note from Harper Lee. "Horton Foote's screenplay is a work of such quiet and unobtrusive excellence that many people have commented on the fact that the film's dialogue was lifted chapter and verse from the novel," she wrote. "This is simply not so. . . . If the integrity of a film adaptation is measured by the degree to which the novelist's intent is preserved, Mr. Foote's screenplay should be studied as a classic."

Harper Lee's novel is set in the fictional town of Maycomb, Alabama, which is modeled after her hometown of Monroeville, Alabama. Foote had no interest in either Maycomb or Monroeville. In his mind, he simply moved the locale to Harrison, Texas.

In your head, you might have written, "Page One. Fade In on Harrison, Texas"? I asked.

"Absolutely," he replied.

To Kill a Mockingbird could have been set in Harrison?

"Absolutely. So much so that finally there's this terrible point where you say to yourself, 'This material now has to be mine.' You almost think of it as your work."

What are you proudest of about that screenplay?

"I think the main thing that pleases me is that it's endured. So many people seem to respond to it. It still seems to have relevance to people. I lecture from time to time at colleges, and so many kids say, 'It's my favorite movie.' It's just nice that there's still a certain validity and integrity to the piece.

"But to tell you the truth, Gregory Peck saved the film. Because Universal, the studio that made it, couldn't stand the film. But Gregory for some reason was smart enough to put in his contract that Pakula and Mulligan had the final cut. So the studio couldn't touch it. If they had gotten their hands on it, God knows what it would have turned out to be." Peck and Foote both won Academy Awards.

Foote might have parlayed his Oscar into a healthy screenwriting career. But that's not who he is. He was never much interested in writing what other people wanted him to write; his only interest has been in having other people produce what he chooses to write. Instead of reaping the harvest of post-Oscar assignments, he pursued a film version of his unsuccessful play *The Traveling Lady*. In 1965, again under the Pakula-Mulligan banner, Foote's screen adaptation of his play, now titled *Baby, the Rain Must Fall,* was released.

The 1970s found Foote, his wife, and their four children living on a farm in New Hampshire. After his mother died in 1974, he was moved to begin writing what evolved into a nine-play cycle. The nine *Orphans' Home* plays begin in 1902 and continue through 1929. They chronicle his father's experiences, mainly in Harrison, from age twelve to forty-one.

"It's kind of a small miracle that I finished them all," Foote said. His zeal in having all nine plays staged, televised, and/or filmed is equally remarkable.

Roots in a Parched Ground began as a live television script that was produced by David Susskind.

Convicts was filmed by Peter Masterson in 1988. The picture, which stars Robert Duvall, Lukas Haas, and James Earl Jones, eventually received a limited release in late 1991.

Lily Dale and *The Widow Claire* were both produced Off-Broadway in 1986.

Courtship, Valentine's Day, and *1918* were all presented on PBS under the collective title *Story of a Marriage.* The latter two had already been released as feature films. (For some unknown reason, the second film was released theatrically as *On Valentine's Day.*)

Cousins and *The Death of Papa* complete the cycle.

Foote recalled that in the early 1980s "I was working on the nine plays, and I really had just run out of money. So my agent said: 'You're so funny. They want you out there in Hollywood, and you don't like to adapt things. But if you'll just learn to bend your neck a little bit and tell them a story, they'll pay for it. They'll give you the money to do it.' They call it 'pitching an idea.' And I hate that. I'm terrible at it. I get embarrassed, and I stutter, and I blush, and the ideas sound so mundane as they're coming out.

"But I'd gotten interested in the idea of a young person starting out and trying to find a career as part of a country-western band. It seemed their experiences were kind of like my experiences starting out as an actor. The rejection was the same.

"So I went out there and pitched it, but it didn't work out. So I decided just to write it. I pulled in my belt and wrote it. When you're a writer, you have to write these stories, even if you don't get paid. There may be moments of disappointment and even despair, but you have to write. At least, I do.

"Then I called up Robert Duvall and read it to him. He said, 'I want to do it.' We tried to produce it ourselves, but we couldn't."

Eventually it did get done. *Tender Mercies* is the only original story Foote has written directly for the screen. Twenty-one years after *To Kill a Mockingbird,* Horton Foote won his second Academy Award. Again, his male star was named Best Actor.

It was during the hoopla for *Tender Mercies* that Duvall described Foote's writing as "rural Chekhov, simple but deep. . . . You can't push it. You have to just let it lay there."

"You have to watch out with my plays," Foote said. "They're like yeast. You think they're one thing; then all of a sudden the subtext gets to working."

Horton Foote has had one of the most uncompromising careers in the American theater. He has never had a Broadway success, but he has written steadily for more than half a century.

Nor is Harrison, Texas, anywhere near played out in his mind. A few years ago he returned to Wharton and purchased his family home. He makes periodic pilgrimages to stimulate his memory.

"The people of my parents' and grandparents' generation were oral historians," he said. "They would talk about the adults they remembered from when *they* were children, and those people would become almost as live as the people I knew. Then once a week my mother would take me to the town cemetery. We'd wander through the graves. I'd ask her who this one was kin to, and who was this person over here. When I was a child in Texas, the dead were almost as alive to us as the living. People weren't afraid to reminisce about them.

"But in today's world, everything's gone so fast. There's less and less time for mourning. I ride out to LaGuardia Airport, and I pass these mass graveyards. Everything's so anonymous."

Finally, then, there's no end to Horton Foote's story, only to an interview. To me, he's still the happy warrior, still writing variations on that theme, still gnawing on that bone. He is Sisyphus with a smile, ever persevering to roll that next script into production.

He is an anomaly, a fluke. But the world is a less strident, more understandable place because of him.

CHAPTER ELEVEN

HAPPY ENDING

"My plays are assembled like very good outhouses."
—JOHN PATRICK

And now for something different. The locale moves from the plains of Texas to a Caribbean sugar plantation.

During a 1979 vacation to St. Thomas, in the Virgin Islands, I learned that Pulitzer Prize–winning playwright John Patrick lives there year-round. I sought an interview, and we met at his mountaintop home.

Most writers fantasize about dropping out of the rat race and moving to a tropical island. John Patrick has done exactly that. He tasted fame, swallowed failure, said, "A plague on both your houses," and headed for the Caribbean. In one of life's more ironic and amusing anomalies, he's been able to finance his island paradise through royalties from his failures, not his hits.

The seventy-two-year-old writer greeted me in sunglasses, baggy Bermuda shorts, and a free-hanging shirt. Typical island garb. He lives on a refurbished seventeenth-century sugar plantation. The main house is a series of connected buildings (including a minitheater that seats nearly one hundred). The guesthouse is a restored windmill. Patrick's panoramic view looks out on the Atlantic Ocean to the north and the Caribbean Sea to the south, and toward Puerto Rico to the west. "It's a good life," the gentleman writer said time and again. No argument there.

Patrick's office walls are littered with mementos from the past, including his Pulitzer Prize and Tony Award for the 1953 comedy *The Teahouse of the August Moon.* "I'm glad I won them," he said. "They doubled my salary. But I wouldn't write another Broadway play or Hollywood movie for any amount of money. I don't want to listen to producers and directors and actors complain. My life is too good right here."

Patrick has traveled a circuitous route to his present idyllic life-style. Fifty years ago he happened into radio, then in 1935 gravitated to New York after writing a forgettable play titled *Hell Freezes Over.* "It was awful," he said, "but a rich woman produced it so her actor husband could play the lead. George Jean Nathan, who was the dean of American critics at that time, wrote in his review, 'Back to the ashcan with this Hollywood writer.' I didn't mind the ashcan part, but I'd never been to Hollywood in my life.

"The play only ran about a week, but Twentieth Century–Fox called and invited me to work. In other words, having a bad play on Broadway qualified you as a picture-writer. So I went up to the vice-president's office. He didn't ask me if I'd ever been to a studio, which I hadn't. He just puffed on a big cigar and said, 'How much do you want?' So I told him, which he promptly divided by three and I promptly accepted, and that's how I became a screenwriter."

Patrick was quick to admit that he had had a lot to learn.

"Audiences don't really care much about dialogue," he said. "They want to see people. They want to watch reactions. They want economy. When I did my first screenplay the producer said: 'Look, you're wasting footage. You have everybody come through a door.' That's because I didn't know the difference between writing for theater and movies."

But he learned on the job. Eventually he wrote or co-wrote thirty screenplays, including *High Society, Three Coins in the Fountain, Love Is a Many Splendored Thing, The World of Suzie Wong, Les Girls, Gigot,* and, of course, *The Teahouse of the August Moon.*

"*Teahouse* made a lot of money," Patrick said, "but I don't think it's a very good picture. Marlon Brando was not right as Sakini. When they offered it to him, he came to me and asked, 'Do you think I can play it?'

"I said, 'You're so popular they'd cast you as Little Eva just for box office. But don't ask me. Ask yourself if you can play it.'

"So he played it, and he was unhappy, and he made everyone else unhappy. There was so much hostility on that set it was like electricity. Dore Schary, who was the president of MGM then, told me that Marlon stalled so much he added a million dollars to the cost. Another actor who added a million dollars to the cost was Jackie Gleason on *Gigot* in Paris. Jackie Gleason and Marlon and Frankie Sinatra, with whom I did two pictures, are brilliantly talented, but they can be monsters to work with."

But then, Patrick didn't much enjoy working with anyone in Hollywood. "I hated that place," he said. "When you're writing a screenplay, you're the most important man in the world. Everybody at the studio is waiting to analyze your script and see how much it will cost to film. But once you finish, you're an unwanted nuisance."

Patrick's favorite films are not his more famous ones. "I think *The President's Lady*, with Susan Hayward and Charlton Heston, was a good picture," he said. "Another one, *Enchantment,* was not good, but it was the best screenplay I ever wrote. Once they finished filming it, it was the most lugubrious, dullest picture ever made. But then, almost all my scripts got changed—and usually without telling me or asking me. I never saw *Some Came Running* because of all the changes, which I would have made for free. I never saw *The Shoes of the Fisherman* for the same reason. I did two pictures with George Cukor. I think part of his genius is that he's practically the only director I know who interprets a script rather than changes it."

The more successful Patrick became, the more demands he made. "I refused to live in Hollywood," he said. "It was in my contract that I would go out for a conference, but I wouldn't stay more than ten days and I wouldn't write while I was there.

"During the conferences I wouldn't talk. I'd just sit with my arms folded and listen. Usually they got so bored with me that I rarely stayed more than five or six days. Then I'd return to my farm near West Point and work. It was self-protection. I got along fine with Ray Stark, but most of those producers were idiots."

Meanwhile, Patrick continued to write plays. *The Hasty Heart* (1945) was an admired war drama which stemmed from his World War II experiences as a captain in the American Field Service. In 1952, *The Teahouse of the August Moon,* adapted from the novel by Vern Sneider, was a critical and popular sensation that ran for 1,027 performances. But there were also the Broadway failures, plays like *The Curious Savage, Everybody Loves Opal,* and *Lo and Behold.*

Recalling those failed productions, Patrick sought an analogy from his past. "I've been a farmer," he said. "You'll see a field, and suddenly there's a storm and it's all washed away. Well, it's stupid to stand there and shake your fist at God. I've learned that you immediately go out and reseed. I always went to work within a week of a failure."

It's good that he did, because those are the plays that have made his fortune—literally. Oxymoronically, his flops have been wildly successful.

"*The Curious Savage* took a year to write," Patrick said. "We brought Peter Glenville from England to direct and we got Lillian Gish to star. It was the outstanding failure of the season. Got some of the worst notices ever written. Considering my expenses and a year's work, my net profit on that production was about ninety dollars. But the first year I released it to high schools, colleges, summer stock, and community theaters, it brought me royalties just under eighty-four thousand dollars. That outstanding flop has since brought me close to four hundred thousand dollars.

"For six years it was the most-produced play in America. It's a third-rate play, but people love it. Of course, I thought it was wonderful when I wrote it. Now I can see the flaws. I recently attended a performance in Prague. It's included in the Czechoslovakian national repertoire, along with Gorky and Shakespeare. They treated it like a classic and did it in this magnificent marble theater that has two or three balconies. The place was packed. The Czechs loved it. A third-rate play."

Another flop, *Lo and Behold*, has brought in "close to a couple hundred thousand," and *Everybody Loves Opal* was a gold mine on the dinner-theater circuit for the likes of Phyllis Diller and Martha Raye.

"There's no loyalty in the theater," Patrick said, "nor should there be. You have to give today's Broadway audiences two hours of opulence and perfection for their money. You *will* find public loyalty in England, where audiences will keep a bad play running because they're loyal to the star. That doesn't exist in this country, except for a strange kind of loyalty in community theater."

After making that discovery, Patrick quit writing for Broadway. "I stopped eight years ago when I realized that I was established enough in places like Albuquerque and Cleveland not to *have* to write for Broadway," he said. He began to send his plays directly to the Samuel French and Dramatists Play Service catalog companies. "I no longer have to bother about the headaches of raising money, the disappointment when friends lose money, problems with Actors' Equity and stagehands and critics," he said. "I can sit here for the rest of my life turning plays out like sausages, which I do. Working four hours a day, I can knock off a play in six weeks. I turn out from two to six new plays a year, they go straight into the catalogs, and they're done over and over."

But are they any good?

"It's a craft," Patrick answered. "That's all. And I'm a pretty good craftsman. If I were a carpenter I'd say the same thing. 'I can build a good outhouse.' My plays are assembled like very good outhouses."

John Patrick doesn't miss Broadway, and he especially does not miss Hollywood. "Sometimes I miss my farm," he admitted. "Look at this." As he removed a plaque from his office wall and read the inscription, Patrick once again was the gentleman farmer from West Point.

The citation, dated 1963, read:

FIRST PRIZE
INTERNATIONAL STOCK SHOW
SENIOR YEARLING BULL

"That's my proudest possession," John Patrick said. "Pulitzers and Tonys are easy. This is the toughest award. When you win this, you know you've done something."

I haven't heard about John Patrick during the last decade. But then, I haven't visited Cleveland or Albuquerque. I can only hope that—even as I write these words—he is soaking up the Caribbean sun, sipping a large, cool tumbler of Cruzán rum, and laughing at the follies he left so many miles and years behind him.

FOR FURTHER READING

I want to pay official credit here to those texts which I have quoted along the way. Citing them chapter by chapter might provide the most readable approach.

Chapter One: Man from Missouri

I have quoted briefly from two Lanford Wilson plays, *The Gingham Dog* (1969) and *Talley's Folly* (1979). Both plays were published by Hill and Wang, which has published so many of Wilson's plays, starting with his earliest Off-Off-Broadway offerings in the mid-1960s and continuing through *THE HOT L BALTIMORE*, *The Mound Builders*, and *5th of July*.

In preparing these notes, I noticed that Wilson dedicated the published text of *Talley's Folly* to Harold Clurman. How that great critic is missed by all theater-lovers!

Chapter Two: Season in the Sun

Jason Miller's play *That Championship Season* was published by Atheneum in 1972. Twenty years later, it still reads like a million bucks, still delivers the impact of a blow to the jaw.

There are numerous editions of Thomas Bulfinch's *The Age of Fable*. Mine was published by The Heritage Press in 1942.

Chapter Three: Rulebuster

I did not quote from Gilroy's novel *From Noon Till Three,* but I want to give it a plug anyway. Doubleday published it in 1973. If you locate a copy in your local library, it's well worth reading.

Gilroy himself quotes from his novel *Private,* which was published in 1970 by Harcourt Brace Jovanovich.

Chapter Four: Winners and Losers

William Goldman's *The Season,* written twenty-three years ago, is still the most entertaining, informative, unsparing, and all-round valuable book yet written about Broadway. (It's still in print. That marvelous publisher of theater books, Limelight Editions, issued a softcover edition in 1984.) If you haven't read it, do yourself a favor. Better yet, read it in tandem with his big, sad, funny, revelatory, gossipy, perception-forming book about Hollywood, *Adventures in the Screen Trade* (Warner Books, 1984).

Johnny No-Trump, alas, will not be so easy to find, although it's worth the search. You might check your library for Marilyn Stasio's *Broadway's Beautiful Losers* (Delacorte Press, 1972). Mary Mercier's comedy-drama is one of five plays included in this anthology. The acting script was published by Dramatists Play Service in 1968. *On Stage: The Making of a Broadway Play,* by Susan Jacobs (Alfred A. Knopf, 1972), does not include the text, but it does offer a cogent chronicle of the play's sad journey to oblivion. Jacobs' book was published as juvenile literature, but anyone interested in this story will find it of value.

Howard Greenberger's *The Off-Broadway Experience* (Prentice-Hall, 1971) is composed of interviews with Off-Broadway veterans and disciples. The Colleen Dewhurst interview, quoted here, offers such a forthright portrait of a young girl's maturation into an actress that it should be mandatory reading for all would-be actors and actresses.

Chapter Five: Mother and Son

Tennessee Williams' *Memoirs* was published by Doubleday in 1975.

Remember Me To Tom, by Edwina Dakin Williams as told to Lucy Freeman, was published by G. P. Putnam's Sons in 1963.

Lawrence Grobel has expanded his 1979 *Playboy* interview with Marlon Brando into a book. *Conversations with Brando* (Hyperion Press, 1991) reprints Brando's comment (in slightly modified form) about Tennessee Williams' "clean soul" on page 146.

Chapter Six: A Certain Amount of Spleen

Adrienne Kennedy's *People Who Led to My Plays* (Alfred A. Knopf, 1987) is one of the most underappreciated volumes of recent years. Back in 1988, every time I'd walk through the basement of the Strand bookstore and see stacks of this irresistible memoir on the table for remaindered books, I would be filled with sadness. It deserves to be on people's shelves, at their bedsides, not in some bargain basement.

Seascape, like nearly all of Edward Albee's plays, was published by Atheneum.

Chapter Eight: Wordsmiths

Alan Jay Lerner's graceful and witty memoir *The Street Where I Live* was published by W. W. Norton in 1978.

John Malcolm Brinnin's *Dylan Thomas in America* was first published by Little, Brown, in association with the Atlantic Monthly Press, in 1955. I don't think it's ever been out of print. The most recent edition, in softcover, was published by Paragon House in 1989.

Nothing by Richard Wilbur is quoted in this volume. Yet it's worth noting that his *New and Collected Poems* (Harcourt Brace Jovanovich, 1988) is Wilbur brought up to date . . . four decades of work between two covers.

Chapter Nine: Incidental Gifts

William Inge's novel *My Son Is a Splendid Driver* was published by Atlantic–Little, Brown in 1971. I could never go more than two or three years without rereading this lovely novel. Like so many of the books I love, it is not easy to find. But that's what libraries are for, God bless them. (In Philip Hamburger's 1986 *New Yorker* profile of Vartan Gregorian, which Hamburger included the following year in his anthology *Curious World*, (North Point), the author quotes Barbara Tuchman as saying, "Nothing sickens me more than the closed door of a library." Amen.)

Donald Spoto's biography of Tennessee Williams, *The Kindness of Strangers*, which is quoted in this chapter, was published by Little, Brown in 1985. It continues to serve as an essential study of Williams.

Reading Elia Kazan's *A Life* (Alfred A. Knopf, 1988) in galleys, before anything had been written about it, was the most memorable event in my twenty-two years as a book reviewer. This massive, mesmerizing history of American theater and film is autobiography in its purest sense, filled with the contradictory ambivalences of love, hurt, and hate.

Chapter Ten: Quiet Warrier from Wharton

Horton Foote's screenplay for *To Kill a Mockingbird,* with an introduction by Harper Lee, was published as a softcover Harvest Book by Harcourt, Brace, and World in 1964. To sit in front of a TV and follow the script while the film unreels on the screen provides a marvelous lesson in how Foote has faith in actors to bring his words to life.

INDEX

Page numbers in *italics* refer to photographs.

Aaron, Joyce, 9
Actors Studio West, 82, 91
Adventures in the Screen Trade (Goldman), 77–78
Albee, Edward, 56, 82, 84, 85, 86, *97*, 111, 121, 122–34, 138, 141–42
Albee, Edward F., 123–24
Albee, Reed and Frances, 123–24
Alley Theater, 164
All Over (Albee), 129–30
All the President's Men (film), 68, 77
Amadeus (Shaffer), 148–49
American Actors' Theatre, 185
American Dream, The (Albee), 125
American Sportsman (TV show), 33
American Theatre magazine, 122
Anderson, Maxwell, 156
Anderson, Robert, 182
Angels Fall (Wilson), 22
Annie (play), 156
Ann-Margret, 176
Anouilh, Jean, 140
Ashley, Elizabeth, 160
Attenborough, Richard, 77
Awake and Sing! (Odets), 137

Baby, the Rain Must Fall (Foote), 192
Baker's Wife, The (play), 146–47
Baldwin, James, 106, 122
Ballad of Sad Café, The (play), 125
Balm in Gilead (Wilson), 8, 10
Bancroft, Anne, 189
Barbour, John, 34
Barnes, Clive, 80, 89
Barr, Richard, 84–85, 86, 87, 88–89, 130
Beatty, Warren, 33
Bedford, Brian, 163
Behrman, S. N., 157
Belasco, David, 145
Bellamy, Peter, 81
Berlin, Irving, 157
Bernstein, Leonard, 152, 155, 156, 161–62, 169
Berrigan, Daniel, 129
Blood, Sweat and Stanley Poole (Goldman), 60
Bloom, Claire, 105, 143
Bloomgarden, Kermit, 84
Bogart, Humphrey, 19
Bosoms and Neglect (Guare), 160
Boys and Girls Together (Goldman), 61–62, 64, 76
Brady, Matthew, 52
Brando, Marlon, 108–9, 119, 121–22, 145, 187, 196–97
Breakfast at Tiffany's (play), 129, 141–42
Bridge Too Far, A (film), 77
Brigadoon (Lerner and Loewe), 152
Brinnin, John Malcolm, 160–61, 167
Broadway's Beautiful Losers (Stasio, ed.), 81, 86
Broderick, James, 79, 86
Bronson, Charles, 45, 48–49, 56
Brook, Peter, 144
Brothers (Goldman), 77
Brustein, Robert, 127, 175
Bulfinch, Thomas, 42–43
Burn This (Wilson), 22
Burrows, Abe, 128–29, 141
Burton, Kate, 167
Burton, Richard, 154, 160, 167–69
Bus Riley's Back in Town (Inge), 175–76
Bus Stop (Inge), 174, 178, 180
Butch Cassidy and the Sundance Kid (film), 64, 67–68

INDEX

Cactus Flower (play), 140
Café Cino, 9–10
Camelot (Lerner and Loewe), 152, 153–54, 160, 167
Camino Real (Williams), 103
Candide (play), 161–62, 169
Cannon, Alice M., 90
Cannon, Dyan, 82, *96*
Capote, Truman, 129, 175, 191
Carmelina (Lerner and Lane), 156, 159
Carnival (play), 140, 148
Case, Bertha, 84
Castellano, Richard, 50
Catcher in the Rye, The (Salinger), 59, 124
Catholic University, 23, 24, 30
Cat on a Hot Tin Roof (Williams), 103, 107
Chamberlain, Richard, 141
Champion, Gower, 139, 148, 149
Champion, Marge, 148, 149
Channing, Carol, 160
Chapman, Lonny, 186
Charly (film), 62–63
Chase, The (Foote), 186–88
Chekhov, Anton, 78
Child's Play (film), 145
Circle in the Square, 122, 187–88
Circle Repertory Company, 8, 12, 14, 15–16, 18–19, 21
Cleveland *Plain Dealer*, 81
Cleveland Play House, 60, 81
Cleveland Press, 81
Clurman, Harold, 127, 133, 177–80, 189–90
Clutterbuck (play), 138
Coco (Lerner), 154–55
Coe, Fred, 185
Coleman, A. D., 80
Color of Light, The (Goldman), 77
Come Back, Little Sheba (Inge), 173
Complaisant Lover, The (Greene), 85
Control (Goldman), 77
Convicts (Foote), 192
Counsellor at Law (Rice), 137
Courtship (Foote), 193
Cousins (Foote), 193
Coward, Noel, 132
Cox, Wally, 145
on critics, 14, 31–32, 34, 89, 90, 126–28, 139, 141, 143–44, 155, 175, 179
Cronyn, Hume, 85, 160
Cukor, George, 197
Curious Savage, The (Patrick), 197, 198
Cyrano de Bergerac (Rostand), 163

Dance a Little Closer (Lerner and Strouse), 159–60
Dark at the Top of the Stairs, The (Inge), 174, 175, 181
Death of a Salesman (Miller), 34, 72, 106
Death of Bessie Smith, The (Albee), 125
Death of Papa, The (Foote), 193
Delicate Balance, A (Albee), 111, 128, 131
Delon, Alain, 110
Desperate Characters (film), 53–55
Dewhurst, Colleen, 47, 90, 122
Dillman, Bradford, 82, *96*
Dinesen, Isak, 59
Donehue, Vincent, 185, 189
Doolin, Bill, 47–48
Dracula (play), 131
Drake, Alfred, 160
Dramatists Play Service, 198–99
Durning, Charles, 11
Duvall, Robert, 192, 193
Dylan (Michaels), 160, 167
Dylan Thomas in America (Brinnin), 160

Eccentricities of a Nightingale, The (Williams), 113
Eder, Richard, 159
Eikenberry, Jill, 174
Eliot, T. S., 163, 168
Ellington, Duke, 122
Ellis Island (TV mini-series), 167
Enchantment (Patrick), 197
Evans, Robert, 145–46
Everybody Loves Opal (Patrick), 197, 198
Exorcist, The (film), 24, 25, 29, 32, 33, 39, 40, 42

F. Scott Fitzgerald in Hollywood (TV movie), 36
Family Continues, The (Wilson), 12
Fanny (play), 138, 139, 146–47
Father's Day (Goldman), 73
Faulkner, William, 190, 191
Fellini, Federico, 27
Ferrer, José, 3, 159, 186
5th of July (Wilson), 16, 17–18, 20, 21
Fireside Theater Book Club, 9
Fitzgerald, F. Scott, 36–37, 41, 182
Fitzgerald, Geraldine, 24
Flanders, Ed, 57
Flint Hills (Kansas), 172, 182
"Flowers for Algernon" (Keyes), 62–64
Fonda, Jane, 82, *96*, 187
Foote, Horton, *100*, 183–94
Foote, Lillian Vallish, 185
Fornas, Irene, 9–10
Forty Carats (play), 140
42nd Street (play), 148–49
Fosse, Bob, 157
Foster, Paul, 9
Fox, Paula, 53, 54
Frame, Donald, 164
Francis, Ivor, *96*
Frankenheimer, John, 190

INDEX

Frankovich, Mike, 46–47
Friedkin, William, 29
Friel, Brian, 140, 143, 144
From Noon Till Three (Gilroy), 45, 47–49, 56
Fugitive Kind, The (film), 108–9
Fun Couple, The (play), 82, *96*

Gabby Hayes Show, The (TV show), 185
Garbo, Greta, 180–81
Garrick, David, 145
Gassner, John, 9
Gay, John, 53–54
Gazzara, Ben, 122
Genn, Leo, 51
Gershwin, George, 154
Gibson, William, 175, 182
Gielgud, John, 75
Gig, The (Gilroy), 57
Gigi (Lerner and Loewe), 152, 157, 158
Gigot (Patrick), 196, 197
Gill, Brendan, 127
Gilroy, Frank D., 45–57, 65, *95*
Gingham Dog, The (Wilson), 10, 15
Gish, Lillian, 188, 189, 198
Glass Menagerie, The (Williams), 15, 34, 103, 105, 108, 112, 115–16, 119, 121
Gleason, Jackie, 24, 197
Gleason, Linda, 23–24, 25, 33, 34, 39
Glenville, Peter, 198
Goldman, William, 59–78, 81, 82, 90, *95*, 107
Gordon, Max, 149
Grade, Lew, 54, 55
Graham, Martha, 185
Great Day in the Morning (Cannon), 90
Great Gatsby, The (film), 145–46
Great Nebula in Orion, The (Wilson), 12
Green, Paul, 185
Greenberger, Howard, 90
Greene, Graham, 85
Grimes, Tammy, 51, 160
Grizzard, George, 10
Guare, John, 160
Guinness, Alec, 160
Guthrie, Tyrone, 161, 162
Gypsy (play), 140

Haas, Lukas, 192
Hackett, Joan, 91
Hailey, Oliver, 148
Hall, Carol, 63
Hamlet (Shakespeare), 167
Happy Time, The (play), 148
Hardy, Joseph, 85, 86, 88, 147
Harper (film), 64, 65, 73
Harris, Jed, 149
Harrison, Rex, 64
Hart, Moss, 66, 69, 153, 157
Hasty Heart, The (Patrick), 197
Hayden, Sterling, 190
Haydn, Hiram, 75–76
Hayes, Helen, 24, 116
Hayward, Susan, 197
Hearst, Patty, 41
Heat (Goldman), 77
Heckart, Eileen, 181
Hell Freezes Over (Patrick), 196
Hellman, Lillian, 161, 162, 187
Hello, Dolly! (play), 140, 141, 148
Hepburn, Katharine, 189
Herbert, George, 168
Heston, Charlton, 197
High Society (Patrick), 196
Hill, George Roy, 67, 68
Hingle, Pat, 72, 79, 80, 81, 84, 160
Hirsch, Judd, 18, 19–20
Hodiak, John, 186, 187
Hoffman, Dustin, 21
Home Free! (Wilson), 10
Home of Our Own, A (TV show), 33, 38
Hooker, Brian, 163
HOT L BALTIMORE, THE (Wilson), 7–8, 11, 12–14, 15, 16, 17, 21
Houseman, John, 33
Howard, Sidney, 156
Hughes, Langston, 122
Hype & Glory (Goldman), 78

Iceman Cometh, The (O'Neill), 188
Idiot's Delight (Sherwood), 159
I Do! I Do! (play), 140
Inge, William, *99*, 138, 171–82, 183
In the Bar of a Tokyo Hotel (Williams), 116
In the Springtime the War Ended (Linakis), 65
Ireland, Jill, 45, 48–49
Irma la Douce (play), 140
Ives, Anne, 86
I Won't Dance (Hailey), 148

Jackson, Glenda, 134
Jacobs, Bernard, 148–49
Jacobs, Susan, 81
Jason and the Golden Fleece, 42–43
Johnny No-Trump (Mercier), 60, 72–73, 75, 79–91, 160
Jones, James Earl, 192
Juno and the Paycock (O'Casey), 24
Jurado, Katy, 105

Kanin, Garson, 182
Kauffmann, Stanley, 80, 143–44
Kazan, Elia, 107, 116, 157–58, 171, 175, 181–82
Kennedy, Adrienne, 121–22, 134
Kennedy, Jacqueline, 159

INDEX

Kennedy, John F., 105, 106, 159, 160
Kern, Jerome, 154
Kerr, Walter, 80–81, 127, 134, 141, 160
Keyes, Daniel, 63
King, Stephen, 78
Kitten with a Whip (film), 176
Klein, Stewart, 79, 80
Knoernschild, Thekla, 136

La Dolce Vita (film), 27
Lady from Dubuque, The (Albee), 133
Lahr, John, 16
Lane, Burton, 152, 159
Langella, Frank, 131–32
La Plume de Ma Tante (play), 140–41
Last Licks (Gilroy), 57
Learned Ladies, The (Molière), 165
Lee, Harper, 190–92
Lehmann-Haupt, Christopher, 107
Lemon Sky (Wilson), 8, 11, 17
Lerner, Alan Jay, *98*, 151–60
Les Girls (Patrick), 196
Life, A (Kazan), 175
Life magazine, 145
Light of Day (film), 42
Lillie, Beatrice, 160
Lily Dale (Foote), 193
Linakis, Stephen, 65
Lithgow, John, 134
Lo and Behold (Patrick), 197, 198
Loewe, Frederick, 151–53, 154, 159
Logan, Joshua, 138, 139, 173, 180–81
Lolita (play), 133
Long Day's Journey into Night (O'Neill), 24, 30
Loss of Roses, A (Inge), 174
Love Is a Many Splendored Thing (Patrick), 196
Love Life (Lerner and Weill), 157
Lowell, Robert, 163
Luce, Henry, 144
Lupica, Mike, 78
LuPone, Patti, 147

McCullers, Carson, 125
MacDonald, Ross, 64
MacGraw, Ali, 145–46
McGuire, Michael, 24, 25
MacLaine, Shirley, 53, 54–55
MacLeish, Archibald, 169
McNally, Terrence, 9
McQ (film), 47
McQueen, Steve, 145
Madness of Lady Bright, The (Wilson), 10
Magic (Goldman), 59–60, 76, 77
Magnani, Anna, 108–9
Mann, Theodore, 90
Man Who Had Three Arms, The (Albee), 133
Marathon Man (Goldman), 69–70, 73, 76, 77
Marat/Sade (play), 140, 143–44
Margulis, Al, 136, 137
Margulis, Sadie and Sam J., 136
Margulois, Celia and Samuel, 136, 137
Mars, Ken, 53
Martin, Mary, 189
Mason, Marshall, 12, 18, 19
Masquerade (film), 64
Masterson, Peter, 189, 192
Mastroianni, Tony, 81
Meisner, Sanford, 185
Memoirs (Williams), 101–4, 106–8, 109, 110, 117
Mercier, Mary, 59, 60, 72–73, 75, 79–91, *96*, 160
Meredith, Don, 41
Merrick, David, *98*, 103–4, 105, 129, 135–49
Merrick, Leonore Beck, 137
Michaels, Sidney, 160
Migrants, The (TV movie), 11
Miller, Arthur, 34, 56, 72, 81, 106, 174
Miller, Jason, 23–43, *94*
Misanthrope, The (Molière), 163, 164–65
Misery (film), 78
Miss Liberty (Sherwood and Berlin), 157
Mohr, Irwin, 137, 140
Molière, J. B. P., 85–86, 163–65, 167
Monroe, Marilyn, 40, 116
Moon for the Misbegotten, A (O'Neill), 47
Moore, Mary Tyler, 141
Morrison, Hobe, 80
Mound Builders, The (Wilson), 8, 16–17
Moving Target, The (MacDonald), 64
Mulligan, Robert, 33, 190, 192
My Fair Lady (Lerner and Loewe), 66, 152, 156
My Son Is a Splendid Driver (Inge), 171, 172, 176, 177, 182

Nabokov, Vladimir, 133
Namath, Joe, 28
Nathan, George Jean, 180, 196
Natural Affection (Inge), 174–75, 176, 180, 181
Natwick, Mildred, 160
Nelson, Barry, 51, 160
Newman, Edwin, 80
Newman, Paul, 53, 160
Newmark, Melvin, 137
Newsday, 79
Newsweek magazine, 125, 137
New York Times, 8, 50, 57, 77, 80–81, 88, 89, 90, 101, 107, 129–30, 143, 159
Nickel Ride, The (film), 33, 39, 40

INDEX

Night of the Iguana, The (Williams), 15, 103, 116
1918 (Foote), 193
Nobody Hears a Broken Drum (Miller), 24, 36
Norton, Elliot, 127
No Way to Treat a Lady (Goldman), 62, 76

O'Casey, Sean, 24
Odd Couple, The, 24
Odets, Clifford, 137
Off-Broadway Experience, The (Greenberger), 90
"Old Man" (Faulkner), 190
Oliver! (play), 140
Olivier, Laurence, 70
O'Loughlin, Gerald, 53
Olson, Clarence, 171
On a Clear Day You Can See Forever (Lerner), 154
Once in Paris . . . (Gilroy), 56–57
O'Neill, Eugene, 24, 47, 188
On Golden Pond (Thompson), 174
Only Game in Town, The (Gilroy), 51, 53
On Stage: The Making of a Broadway Play (Jacobs), 81
Oppenheimer, George, 79
Orphans' Home (Foote), 192–93
Orpheus Descending (Williams), 103, 108–9
Osborne, John, 140
Out of Africa (Dinesen), 59
Owens, Rochelle, 9

Page, Geraldine, 110, 188, 189, 190
Pagnol, Marcel, 146
Paint Your Wagon (Lerner and Loewe), 152, 158
Pakula, Alan, 187, 190–92
Papas, Irene, 50
Paper Chase (film), 33
Paramount Pictures, 145–46
Parks, Michael, 175–76
Pasadena Playhouse, 184–85
Patric, Jason, 42
Patrick, John, *100*, 195–99
Patton (film), 65
Peck, Gregory, 192
People Who Led to My Plays (Kennedy), 121–22
Period of Adjustment (Williams), 103, 104
Perry, Antoinette, 125
Peterpat (Rudd), 91
Peters, Bernadette, 79, 86
Phèdre (Racine), 165
Philadelphia, Here I Come! (Friel), 143, 144
Piazza, Ben, *96*
Picnic (Inge), 138–39, 173–74, 180, 181
Pinter, Harold, 72
Playboy magazine, 119
Playhouse 90 (TV series), 190
Playwrights Company, 156–57
Polanski, Roman, 33
Porter, Cole, 154
Preminger, Otto, 67
President's Lady, The (Patrick), 197
Previn, André, 152
Price, The (Miller), 81
Prince, Hal, 162
Princess Bride, The (Goldman), 73, 75, 76, 78
Private (Gilroy), 51–53
Professionals, The (film), 64
Promises, Promises (play), 140

Quinn, Anthony, 105, 143
Quintero, José, 90, 110, 187–88

Racine, Jean, 165
Randall, Tony, 33
Rattigan, Terence, 140
Red Devil Battery Sign, The (Williams), 105, 106, 142–43
Redford, Robert, 160, 187, 189
Reid, Kate, 160
Reiner, Rob, 78
Rice, Elmer, 137, 156
Rimers of Eldritch, The (Wilson), 10, 17
Robards, Jason, 75, 160, 187–88
Robertson, Cliff, 62–64
Rodgers, Richard, 152
Rogers, Wayne, 57
Roots in a Parched Ground (Foote), 192
Rose, George, 160
Rosencrantz and Guildenstern Are Dead (Stoppard), 140
Rose Tattoo, The (Williams), 103
Ross, Katherine, 67
Rostand, Edmond, 163
Rosten, Leo, 169
Roundabout Theatre Company, 57
Royal Shakespeare Company, 144
Rudd, Enid, 91
Russian Tea Room, 104
Ryan, Cornelius, 77

Salinger, J. D., 59, 124
Samuel French catalog, 198–99
Sandbox, The (Albee), 125
Sands, Diana, 160
Scardino, Don, 79, 81, 86
Schary, Dore, 197
Schlesinger, John, 69, 70
School for Husbands, The (Molière), 167
School for Wives, The (Molière), 163–65
Scott, George C., 90

INDEX

Seascape (Albee), 130–32
Season, The (Goldman), 59, 60, 70–72, 78, 81
Serenading Louie (Wilson), 11, 12
Shaffer, Peter, 148–49
Shakespeare, William, 167
Shawn, Dick, 91
Shelton, Reid, 156
Shepard, Sam, 9
Sherin, Edwin, 105
Sherwood, Robert, 156–57, 159
Shoes of the Fisherman, The (Patrick), 197
Shootist, The (film), 47
Shore, Dinah, 41
Shrike, The (play), 186
Shumlin, Herbert, 186
Silliphant, Stirling, 63
Simon, John, 32, 127, 175
Simon, Neil, 65
"Simple Pleasures of the Rich, The" (Goldman), 74
Sinatra, Frank, 197
1600 Pennsylvania Avenue (Lerner and Bernstein), 155–56
Smith, Alexis, 174
Smith, Alfred E., 183
Smith, Delos V., Jr., *96*
Smith, Michael, 9
Sneider, Vern, 197
Soldier in the Rain (Goldman), 76
Some Came Running (Patrick), 197
Sometimes a Great Notion (film), 53
Sondheim, Stephen, 149, 157
Sorvino, Paul, 147
Spiegel, Sam, 186–87, 188
Splendor in the Grass (Inge), 175
Spoto, Donald, 173
St. Louis Globe-Democrat, 136
St. Louis Post-Dispatch, 60, 171
St. Louis Star-Times, 172–73
Stanley, Kim, 186, 189–90
Stark, Ray, 197
Stasio, Marilyn, 81
Stepford Wives, The (film), 70
Stevens, George, 53
Stitt, Milan, 19
Stix, John, 84
Stoppard, Tom, 140
Story of a Marriage (Foote), 193
Strasberg, Lee, 189
Streetcar Named Desire, A (Williams), 33, 103, 106, 119, 126
Street Where I Live, The (Lerner), 152, 158
Strouse, Charles, 159
Subject Was Roses, The (Gilroy), 49–50, 51, 57
Sugar (play), 148
Summer and Smoke (Williams), 103, 109–10, 113, 188
Summer Brave (Inge), 173–74
Sundance Institute, 189
Sunday in New York (play), 140
Susann, Jacqueline, 104
Susskind, David, 192
Sweet Bird of Youth (Williams), 103, 111–12

Take Me Along (play), 140
Tale Told, A (Wilson), 21–22
Talley's Folly (Wilson), 7, 16, 17, 18–20, 21
Tandy, Jessica, 85, 189
Tartuffe (Molière), 85–86, 163
Taylor, Elizabeth, 53, 167
Taylor, Laurette, 116
Teahouse of the August Moon, The (Patrick), 196–97
Television Playhouse (TV series), 185
Temple of Gold, The (Goldman), 74
Tender Mercies (Foote), 193
Terry, Megan, 9
Texas Town (Foote), 185
That Championship Season (Miller), 24, 25–29, 32–34, 37, 38, 39, 40, 41
That Summer—That Fall (Gilroy), 50–51
Theatre Arts magazine, 9
Thing of It Is, The . . . (Goldman), 73
Thomas, Dylan, 160, 167
Thomas, Mary, 42
Thomas, Richard, 86
Thompson, Ernest, 174
Thompson, Sada, 53, 72, 79, 81, 85–86
Three Coins in the Fountain (Patrick), 196
Tillich, Paul, 103
Time magazine, 136, 144–45
Tinsel (Goldman), 77
Tiny Alice (Albee), 125–26, 128, 134
To Kill a Mockingbird (film), 190–92, 193
"Tomorrow" (Faulkner), 190
Topol, 147
Torn, Rip, 160
Traveling Lady, The (Foote), 189–90, 192
Trial of the Catonsville Nine, The (Berrigan), 129
Trip to Bountiful, The (Foote), 188–89
Tucker, Forrest, 38
Twain, Norman, 84
Twentieth-Century Fox, 196

Updike, John, 70
Utall, Ivan, 84

Valentine's Day (Foote), 193
Vanderbilt, Gloria, 116

INDEX

Variety, 80
Village Voice, The, 80
Voight, Jon, 50

Wait Till Next Year (Goldman and Lupica), 78
Walken, Christopher, 11, 111–12
Washington Theater Club, 11
Watts, Richard, 127
Wayne, John, 46–47, 57
Webber, Andrew Lloyd, 149
Weill, Kurt, 157
Weiss, Peter, 140
Wharton Dance (Foote), 185
Where's Daddy? (Inge), 174, 176, 178
Who'll Save the Plowboy? (Gilroy), 49
Who's Afraid of Virginia Woolf? (Albee), 122, 124, 125, 128, 130, 133–34
Widow Claire, The (Foote), 193
Wigger (Goldman), 75
Wilbur, Richard, *99*, 151, 160, 161–67, 168–69
Wilde, Oscar, 163
Wilder, Clinton, 85
Wilder, Gene, 82
Williams, Dakin, 112, 114–15, 116–17, 118, 119
Williams, Edwina Dakin, *97*, 101, 107, 112–19
Williams, Rose, 114, 115
Williams, Tennessee, 11, 15, 33, 34, *96*, 101–12, 113, 114, 115–19, 121, 122, 126, 132, 135, 142–43, 173, 174, 180, 182, 188
Wilson, Lanford, 7–22, 23, *94*
Windham, Donald, 110
WNBC-TV, 80
WNEW-TV, 79
Woodard, Alfre, 42
Woodward, Charles, 87
Woodward, Edward, 160
Woodward, Joanne, 108, 160
World of Suzie Wong, The (Patrick), 196
Worth, Irene, 111
Wright, Richard, 122

Yablans, Frank, 146
Young, Stark, 190

Zeffirelli, Franco, 87
Ziegfeld, Florenz, 149
Zoo Story, The (Albee), 125

MORE GUIDES TO THE PERFORMING ARTS FROM NEWMARKET PRESS

sourcebook for buying and listening to classical music from Baroque to New Age covers 60 composers and 150 recording artists performing classical music today. "An excellent guide." *(ALA Booklist)* 336 pages. Glossary. Index. 6" x 9".

DISCOVERING GREAT SINGERS OF CLASSIC POP: *A New Listener's Guide to the Sounds and Lives of the Top Performers and Their Recordings, Movies, and Videos.* Roy Hemming & David Hajdu.

The lives, sounds, and styles of 52 top crooners and canaries from the 1920s to the present who have influenced the development of pop music and American cultural history are "written about with loving expertise by two writers who can make singers and and their songs live on paper." (Clive Barnes) 320 pages. 38 photographs. Discography. Videography. Bibliography. Index. 6" x 9".

THE MELODY LINGERS ON: *The Great Songwriters and Their Movie Musicals.* Roy Hemming.

Lavishly illustrated with 162 evocative photos and movie stills, the 16 songwriters covered include: Arlen, Berlin, Gershwin, Kern, Porter, Rodgers, Whiting, Nacio Brown, Carmichael, Loesser, Schwartz, Styne, and Van Heusen. 400 pages. 162 photographs. Filmography. Discography. Bibliography. Index. 8 1/4" x 10 3/4".

SHOPTALK: *Conversations about Theater and Film with Twelve Writers, One Producer—and Tennessee Williams' Mother.* Dennis Brown. Foreword by Kevin Kline.

Fourteen influential figures of stage and screen, collectively winners of 11 Pulitzer Prizes and 8 Academy Awards, discuss their successes and failures, and the pain behind behind both in these unusual, perceptive interviews. 224 pages. 14 photographs. Index. 5 5/16" x 8".

NEWMARKET PICTORIAL MOVIEBOOKS: See next page for listing.